CREATIVE
HOMEOWNER®

Northeastern
Inspired Home Designs

CREATIVE HOMEOWNER®, Upper Saddle River, New Jersey

COPYRIGHT © 2005

CREATIVE
HOMEOWNER®

A Division of Federal Marketing Corp.
Upper Saddle River, NJ

VP/Business Development: Brian H. Toolan
VP/Editorial Director: Timothy O. Bakke
Production Manager: Rose Sullivan

Home Plans Publishing Consultant: James D. McNair III
Editorial Assistant: Nicole Porto

Design and Layout: Arrowhead Direct (David Kroha,
    Cindy DiPierdomenico, Judith Kroha)
Cover Design: 3r1

Current Printing (last digit)
10 9 8 7 6 5 4 3 2 1

Northeastern Inspired Home Designs
Library of Congress Control Number: 2004113797
ISBN: 1-58011-237-4

CREATIVE HOMEOWNER®
A Division of Federal Marketing Corp.
24 Park Way
Upper Saddle River, NJ 07458
www.creativehomeowner.com

Printed in China

Note: The homes as shown in the photographs and renderings in this book may differ from the actual blueprints. When studying the house of your choice, please check the floor plans carefully.

PHOTO CREDITS

Front cover: *top* plan 211075, page 8; *bottom row left to right* plan 111004, page 28; plan 121090, page 12; plan 111004, page 28 **back cover:** *top* plan 321041, page 21; *center* 221022, page 248; *bottom left* plan 131030, page 112; *bottom right* plan 161029, page 194 **page 1:** plan 151014, page 229 **page 3:** *top* plan 121084, page 59; *center* plan 161029, page 194; *bottom* plan 111021, page 271 **page 4:** plan 161033, page 172 **page 5:** plan 271089, page 83 **page 6:** *top* plan 121064, page 20; *bottom* plan 121037, page 54 **page 7:** plan 121031, page 263 **pages 30–31:** *both* courtesy of Kraftmaid Cabinetry, Inc. **page 32:** *both* courtesy of Wellborn Cabinet **page 33:** courtesy of Kraftmaid Cabinetry, Inc. **page 34:** courtesy of Wellborn Cabinet **page 35:** *top left* courtesy of Merillat Industries; *top right* courtesy of Wellborn Cabinet; *bottom left* courtesy of Merillat Industries **page 70:** George Ross/CH **page 71:** courtesy of Kohler Co. **page 72:** George Ross/CH, designer: Lyn Peterson **page 73:** courtesy of Motif Designs, designer: Lyn Peterson **page 74:** courtesy of Kohler Co. **page 75:** *top* courtesy of American Standard; *bottom* courtesy of Motif Designs, designer: Lyn Peterson **page 76:** *both* courtesy of Motif Designs, designer: Lyn Peterson **page 77:** George Ross/CH, designer: Lyn Peterson **pages 114–129:** illustrations by Warren Cutler, Tony Davis (site plans), Elizabeth Eaton, Biruta Hansen, Paul Mirocha, Gordon Morrison, Michael Rothman, Michael Wanke **pages 164–165:** George Ross/CH **page 166:** *all* Christine Elasigue/CH **page 167:** *top right* George Ross/CH; *bottom all* Christine Elasigue/CH **page 168:** *left* George Ross/CH; *right top to bottom* Christine Elasigue/CH **pages 169–171:** *all* Christine Elasigue/CH **page 212:** courtesy of Mannington Floors **page 213:** courtesy of Congoleum **page 214:** *top* courtesy of Congoleum; *bottom* courtesy of Mannington Floors **page 215:** courtesy of Dal-Tile **page 216:** *left* courtesy of Mannington Floors; *right* courtesy of Congoleum **page 217:** *left* courtesy of Mannington Floors; *right* courtesy of Dal-Tile **page 239:** courtesy of Central Fireplaces **pages 240–242:** courtesy of Aladdin Steel Products **page 244:** George Ross/CH **page 245:** Randall Perry **page 246:** courtesy of Heatilator **pages 264–268:** *all* courtesy of Kraftmaid Cabinetry, Inc. **page 269:** courtesy of IKEA **page 280:** plan 131027, page 225

Photographers & Manufacturers: American Standard, Piscataway, NJ; 800-442-1902. Dal-Tile, Dallas TX; 214-398-1411. George Ross, Montclair, NJ; 973-744-5171. Kohler Co., Kohler, WI; 800-456-6422. Kraftmaid Cabinetry, Middlefield, OH; 440-632-5333. Merillat Industries, Adrian, MI; 517-263-0771. Motif Designs, New Rochelle, NY; 914-633-1170. Wellborn Cabinet, Ashland, AL; 800-336-8040.

Contents

Getting Started

Maybe you can't wait to bang the first nail. Or you may be just as happy leaving town until the windows are cleaned. The extent of your involvement with the construction phase is up to you. Your time, interests, and abilities can help you decide how to get the project from lines on paper to reality. But building a house requires more than putting pieces together. Whoever is in charge of the process must competently manage people as well as supplies, materials, and construction. He or she will have to

- Make a project schedule to plan the orderly progress of the work. This can be a bar chart that shows the time period of activity by each trade.
- Establish a budget for each category of work, such as foundation, framing, and finish carpentry.
- Arrange for a source of construction financing.
- Get a building permit and post it conspicuously at the construction site.
- Line up supply sources and order materials.
- Find subcontractors and negotiate their contracts.
- Coordinate the work so that it progresses smoothly with the fewest conflicts.
- Notify inspectors at the appropriate milestones.
- Make payments to suppliers and subcontractors.

You as the Builder

You'll have to take care of every logistical detail yourself if you decide to act as your own builder or general contractor. But along with the responsibilities of managing the project, you gain the flexibility to do as much of your own work as you want and subcontract out the rest. Before taking this path, however, be sure you have the time and capabilities. Do you also have the

time and ability to schedule the work, hire and coordinate subs, order materials, and keep ahead of the accounting required to manage the project successfully? If you do, you stand to save the amount that a general contractor would charge to take on these responsibilities, normally 15 to 30 percent of the construction cost. If you take this responsibility on but mismanage the project, the potential savings will erode and may even cost you more than if you had hired a builder in the first place. A subcontractor might charge extra for hav-

Acting as the builder, above, requires the ability to hire and manage subcontractors.

Building a home, opposite, includes the need to schedule building inspections at the appropriate milestones.

ing to return to the site to complete work that was originally scheduled for an earlier date. Or perhaps because you didn't order the windows at the beginning, you now have to pay for a recent cost increase. (If you had hired a builder in the first place he or she would absorb the increase.)

order direct: 1-800-523-6789

Hiring a Builder to Handle Construction

A builder or general contractor will manage every aspect of the construction process. Your role after signing the construction contract will be to make regular progress payments and ensure that the work for which you are paying has been completed. You will also consult with the builder and agree to any changes that may have to be made along the way.

Leads for finding builders might come from friends or neighbors who have had contractors build, remodel, or add to their homes. Real-estate agents and bankers may have some names handy but are more likely familiar with the builder's ability to complete projects on time and budget than the quality of the work itself.

The next step is to narrow your list of candidates to three or four who you think can do a quality job and work harmoniously with you. Phone each builder to see whether he or she is interested in being considered for your project. If so, invite the builder to an interview at your home. The meeting will serve two purposes. You'll be able to ask the candidate about his or her experience, and you'll be able to see whether or not your personalities are compatible. Go over the plans with the builder to make certain that he or she understands the scope of the project. Ask if they have constructed similar houses. Get references, and check the builder's standing with the Better Business Bureau. Develop a short list of builders, say three, and ask them to submit bids for the project.

When submitting bids, all of the builders should base their estimates on the same specifications.

Contracts

Lump-Sum Contracts

A lump-sum, or fixed-fee, contract lets you know from the beginning just what the project will cost, barring any changes made because of your requests or unforeseen conditions. This form works well for projects that promise few surprises and are well defined from the outset by a complete set of contract documents. You can enter into a fixed-price contract by negotiating with a single builder on your short list or by obtaining bids from three or four builders. If you go the latter route, give each bidder a set of documents and allow at least two weeks for them to submit their bids. When you get the bids, decide who you want and

call the others to thank them for their efforts. You don't have to accept the lowest bid, but it probably makes sense to do so since you have already honed the list to builders you trust. Inform this builder of your intentions to finalize a contract.

Cost-Plus-Fee Contracts

Under a cost-plus-fee contract, you agree to pay the builder for the costs of labor and materials, as verified by receipts, plus a fee that represents the builder's overhead and profit. This arrangement is sometimes referred to as "time and materials." The fee can range between 15 and 30 percent of the incurred costs. Because you ultimately pick up the tab—whatever the costs—the contractor is never at risk, as he is with a

lump-sum contract. You won't know the final total cost of a cost-plus-fee contract until the project is built and paid for. If you can live with that uncertainty, there are offsetting advantages. First, this form allows you to accommodate unknown conditions much more easily than does a lump-sum contract. And rather than being tied down by the project documents, you will be free to make changes at any point along the way. This can be a trap, though. Watching the project take shape will spark the desire to add something or do something differently. Each change costs more, and the accumulation can easily exceed your budget. Because of the uncertainty of the final tab and the built-in advantage to the contractor, you should think twice before entering into this form of contract.

Contract Content

The conditions of your agreement should be spelled out thoroughly in writing and signed by both parties, whatever contractual arrangement you make with your builder. Your contract should include provisions for the following:

- The names and addresses of the owner and builder.
- A description of the work to be included ("As described in the plans and specifications dated . . .").
- The date that the work will be completed if time is of the essence.
- The contract price for lump-sum contracts and the builder's allowed profit and overhead costs for changes.
- The builder's fee for cost-plus-fee contracts and the method of accounting and requesting payment.
- The criteria for progress payments (monthly, by project milestones) and the conditions of final payment.
- A list of each drawing and specification section that is to be included as part of the contract.

Once the work begins, communicate with your builder to keep the work proceeding smoothly.

- Requirements for guarantees. (One year is the standard period for which contractors guarantee the entire project, but you may require specific guarantees on certain parts of the project, such as a 20-year guarantee on the roofing.)
- Provisions for insurance.
- A description of how changes in the work orders will be handled.

The builder may have a standard contract that you can tailor to the specifics of your project. These contain complete specific conditions with blanks that you can fill in to fit your project and a set of "general conditions" that cover a host of issues from insurance to termination provisions. It's always a good idea to have an attorney review the draft of your completed contract before signing it.

Working with Your Builder

The construction phase officially begins when you have a signed copy of the contract and copies of any insurance required from the builder. It's not unheard of for a builder to request an initial payment of 10 to 20 percent of the total cost to cover mobilization costs, those costs associated with obtaining permits and getting set up to begin the actual construction. If you agree to this, keep a careful eye on the progress of the work to ensure that the total paid out at any one time doesn't get too far out of sync with the actual work completed.

What about changes? From here on, it's up to you and your builder to proceed in good faith and to keep the channels of communication open. Even so, changes of one sort or another beset every project, and they usually add to its cost.

Light at the End of the Tunnel.

The builder's request for a final inspection marks the end of the construction phase—almost. At the final inspection meeting, you and the builder will inspect the work, noting any defects or incomplete items on a "punch list." When the builder tidies up the punch list items, you should reinspect. Sometimes, builders go on to another job and take forever to clean up the last few details, so only after all items on the list have been completed satisfactorily should you release the final payment, which often accounts for the builder's profit.

Some Final Words

Having a positive attitude is important when undertaking a project as large as building a home. A positive attitude can help you ride out the rigors and stress of the construction process.

Stay Flexible. Expect problems, because they certainly will occur. Weather can upset the schedule you have established for subcontractors. A supplier may get behind on

Inspect your newly built home, if possible, before the builder closes it up and finishes it.

deliveries, which also affects the schedule. An unexpected pipe may surprise you during excavation. Just as certain, every problem that comes along has a solution if you are open to it.

Be Patient. The extra days it may take to resolve a construction problem will be forgotten once the project is completed.

Express Yourself. If what you see isn't exactly what you thought you were getting, don't be afraid to look into changing it. Or you may spot an unforeseen opportunity for an improvement. Changes usually cost more money, though, so don't make frivolous decisions.

Finally, watching your home go up is exciting, so stay upbeat. Get away from your project from time to time. Dine out. Take time to relax. A positive attitude will make for smoother relations with your builder. An optimistic outlook will yield better-quality work if you are doing your own construction. And though the project might seem endless while it is under way, keep in mind that all the planning and construction will fade to a faint memory at some time in the future, and you will be getting a lifetime of pleasure from a home that is just right for you.

Plan #211075

Dimensions: 80' W x 84' D
Levels: 2
Square Footage: 3,568
Main Level Sq. Ft.: 2,330
Upper Level Sq. Ft.: 1,238
Bedrooms: 4
Bathrooms: 3½
Foundation: Crawl space
Materials List Available: Yes
Price Category: H

Images provided by designer/architect.

The porte-cochere—or covered passage over a driveway—announces the quality and beauty of this spacious country home.

Features:

- Front Porch: Spot groups of potted plants on this 779-sq.-ft. porch, and add a glider and some rocking chairs to take advantage of its comfort.

- Family Room: Let this family room become the heart of the home. With a fireplace to make it cozy and a wet bar for easy serving, it's a natural for entertaining.

- Game Room: Expect a crowd in this room, no matter what the weather.

- Kitchen: A cooktop island and a pantry are just two features of this fully appointed kitchen.

- Master Suite: The bedroom is as luxurious as you'd expect, but the quarter-circle raised tub in the master bath might surprise you. Two walk-in closets and two vanities add a practical touch.

Main Level Floor Plan

Copyright by designer/architect.

Upper Level Floor Plan

Plan #181080

Dimensions: 44'8" W x 36' D

Levels: 2

Square Footage: 2,042

Main Level Sq. Ft.: 934

Upper Level Sq. Ft.: 1,108

Bedrooms: 3

Bathrooms: 2½

Foundation: Full basement

Materials List Available: Yes

Price Category: D

Images provided by designer/architect.

The second-floor balcony and angled tower are only two of the many design elements you'll love in this beautiful home.

Features:

- Family Room: Corner windows and sliding glass doors to the backyard let natural light pour into this spacious, open area.

- Living Room: Decorate around the deep bay to separate it from the adjacent dining area.

- Dining Room: Large windows and French doors to the kitchen are highlights here.

- Kitchen: The U-shaped counter aids efficiency, as does the handy lunch counter.

- Master Suite: From the sitting area in the bay to the walk-in closet and bath with tub and shower, this suite will pamper you.

- Balcony: Set a row of potted plants and a table and chairs on this perch above the street.

Main Level Floor Plan

Copyright by designer/architect.

Upper Level Floor Plan

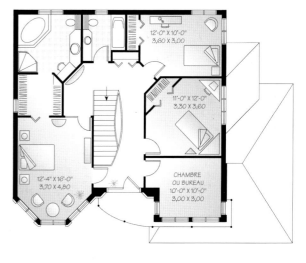

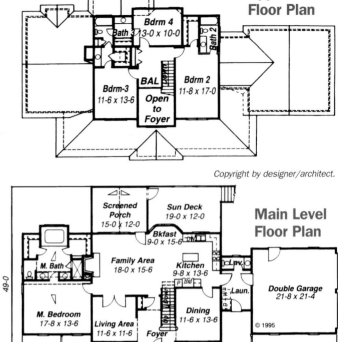

Upper Level Floor Plan

Bath 3 | Bdrm 4 13-0 x 10-0 | Bath 2

Bdrm-3 11-6 x 13-6 | BAL Open to Foyer | Bdrm 2 11-8 x 17-0

Copyright by designer/architect.

Main Level Floor Plan

Screened Porch 15-0 x 12-0 | Sun Deck 19-0 x 12-0

Bkfast 9-0 x 15-6

M. Bath | Family Area 18-0 x 15-6 | Kitchen 9-8 x 13-6 | Laun. | Double Garage 21-8 x 21-4

M. Bedroom 17-8 x 13-6 | Living Area 11-6 x 11-6 | Foyer | Dining 11-6 x 13-6

© 1995

Front Porch

49-0

82-0

Plan #141017

Dimensions: 82' W x 49' D
Levels: 2
Square Footage: 2,480
Main Level Sq. Ft.: 1,581
Upper Level Sq. Ft.: 899
Bedrooms: 4
Bathrooms: 3½
Foundation: Basement, crawl space, or slab
Materials List Available: No
Price Category: E

Images provided by designer/architect.

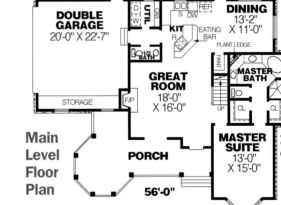

Main Level Floor Plan

DOUBLE GARAGE 20'-0" X 22'-7"

UTIL | DINING 13'-2" X 11'-0"

KIT | EATING BAR | PLANT LEDGE

STORAGE | F/P | GREAT ROOM 18'-0" X 16'-0"

MASTER BATH

PORCH | MASTER SUITE 13'-0" X 15'-0"

56'-0"

44'-5"

Plan #241010

Dimensions: 56' W x 44'5" D
Levels: 2
Square Footage: 2,044
Main Level Sq. Ft.: 1,203
Upper Level Sq. Ft.: 841
Bedrooms: 3
Bathrooms: 2½
Foundation: Slab
Materials List Available: No
Price Category: D

Images provided by designer/architect.

Upper Level Floor Plan

Copyright by designer/architect.

CL | BEDR'M-2 11'-9" X 10'-9" | BATH

BEDR'M-3 12'-0" X 12'-7" | HALL | DN

PLAYROOM 18'-0" X 14'-0"

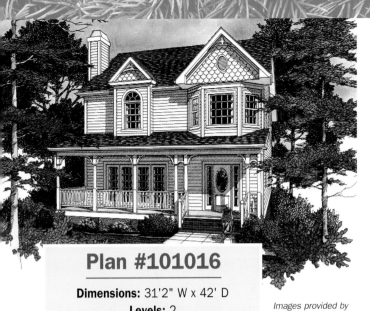

Plan #101016

Dimensions: 31'2" W x 42' D

Levels: 2

Square Footage: 1,985

Main Level Sq. Ft.: 1,009

Upper Level Sq. Ft.: 976

Bedrooms: 3

Bathrooms: 2½

Foundation: Slab, crawl space, or basement

Materials List Available: No

Price Category: D

Main Level Floor Plan

Images provided by designer/architect.

Upper Level Floor Plan

Copyright by designer/architect.

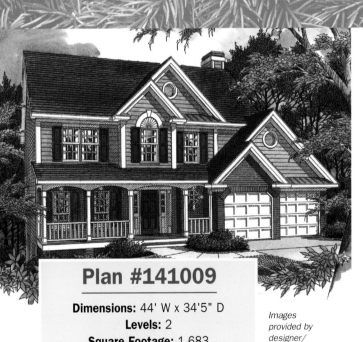

Plan #141009

Dimensions: 44' W x 34'5" D

Levels: 2

Square Footage: 1,683

Main Level Sq. Ft.: 797

Upper Level Sq. Ft.: 886

Bedrooms: 3

Bathrooms: 2½

Foundation: Basement, crawl space or slab

Materials List Available: No

Price Category: C

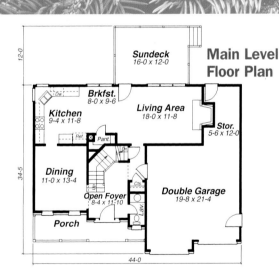

Main Level Floor Plan

Images provided by designer/architect.

Upper Level Floor Plan

Copyright by designer/architect.

Plan #121090

Dimensions: 60' W x 58' D

Levels: 2

Square Footage: 2,645

Main Level Sq. Ft.: 1,972

Upper Level Sq. Ft.: 673

Bedrooms: 4

Bathrooms: 2½

Foundation: Basement

Materials List Available: Yes

Price Category: F

Images provided by designer/architect.

You'll be amazed at the amenities that have been designed into this lovely home.

Features:

• Den: French doors just off the entry lead to this lovely room, with its bowed window and spider-beamed ceiling.

• Great Room: A trio of graceful arched windows highlights the volume ceiling in this room. You might want to curl up to read next to the see-through fireplace into the hearth room.

• Kitchen: Enjoy the good design in this room.

• Hearth Room: The shared fireplace with the great room makes this a cozy spot in cool weather.

• Master Suite: French doors lead to this well-lit area, with its roomy walk-in closet, sunlit whirlpool tub, separate shower, and two vanities.

Main Level Floor Plan

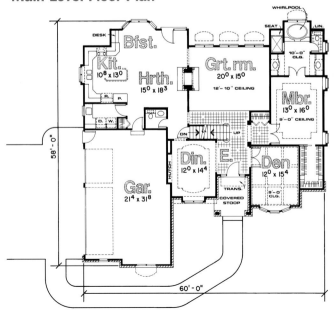

Upper Level Floor Plan

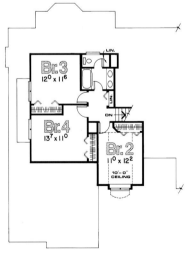

Copyright by designer/architect.

Plan #181085

Dimensions: 56'4" W x 44' D
Levels: 2
Square Footage: 2,183
Main Level Sq. Ft.: 1,232
Second Level Sq. Ft.: 951
Bedrooms: 3
Bathrooms: 2½
Foundation: Basement
Materials List Available: Yes
Price Category: D

Images provided by designer/architect.

This country home features an inviting front porch and a layout designed for modern living.

Features:

- Ceiling Height: 8 ft.
- Solarium: Sunlight streams through the windows of this solarium at the front of the house.
- Living Room: Walk through French doors, and you will enter this inviting living room. Family and friends will be drawn to the corner fireplace.
- Formal Dining Room: Usher your guests directly from the living room into this formal dining room. The kitchen is located on the other side of the dining room for convenient service.
- Kitchen: This generously sized kitchen is a delight, it offers a center island, separate eat-in area, and access to the back deck.
- Bonus Room: This room just off the entry hall can become a family room, a bedroom, or an office.
- Master Suite: Curl up by the corner fireplace in this master retreat, with its walk-in closet and lavish bath with separate shower and tub.

Main Level Floor Plan

Upper Level Floor Plan

Copyright by designer/architect.

Copyright by designer/architect.

Plan #321007

Dimensions: 76' W x 55'2" D
Levels: 1
Square Footage: 2,695
Bedrooms: 3
Bathrooms: 2½
Foundation: Basement
Materials List Available: Yes
Price Category: F

Images provided by designer/architect.

SMARTtip

Decorative Poles

Drapery poles are supported by the brackets fastened to the window frame or wall. The brackets that are provided with the poles generally coordinate and blend in with the pole finish. Brackets can be simple but also decorative. If you opt for a spectacular, attention-grabbing bracket, consider choosing less showy finials for the ends of the pole.

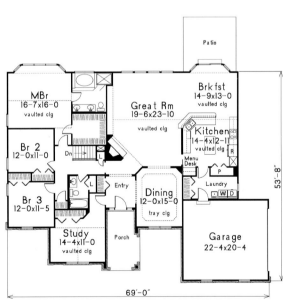

Copyright by designer/architect.

Plan #321005

Dimensions: 69' W x 53'8" D
Levels: 1
Square Footage: 2,483
Bedrooms: 4
Bathrooms: 2
Foundation: Basement
Materials List Available: Yes
Price Category: E

Images provided by designer/architect.

SMARTtip

Art in Pools

The tiled walls and floor of a pool make great canvases for art, so incorporate a serious or whimsical design. Also, make the stairs wide and shallow to form a wading area for kids.

Plan #121052

Dimensions: 56' W x 70' D

Levels: 1

Square Footage: 2,093

Bedrooms: 4

Bathrooms: 2

Foundation: Basement

Materials List Available: Yes

Price Category: D

Images provided by designer/architect.

You'll love this one story home with all the amenities that usually go with a larger home with more levels.

Features:

- **Entry:** As you enter this home, you'll have a long view into the great room, letting you feel welcome right away.

- **Great Room:** Enjoy the fireplace in this large room during cool evenings, and during the day, bask in the sunlight streaming through the arched windows that flank the fireplace.

- **Den:** French doors from the great room open into this room that features a spider-beamed ceiling.

- **Kitchen:** An island, pantry, and built-in desk make this kitchen a versatile work space. It includes a lovely breakfast area, too, that opens into the backyard.

- **Master Suite:** This secluded suite features an angled ceiling in the private bathroom.

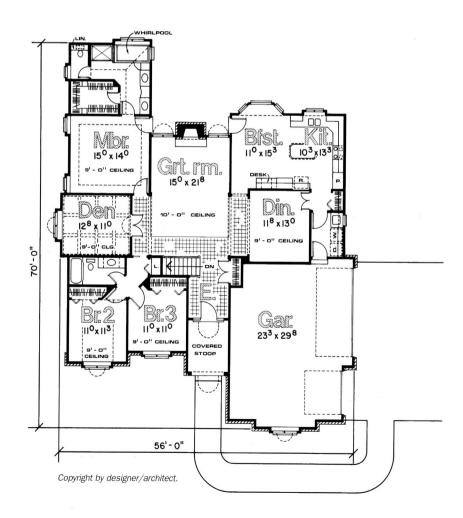

Copyright by designer/architect.

Plan #161016

Dimensions: 59'4" W x 58'8" D
Levels: 2
Square Footage: 2,101
Main Level Sq. Ft.: 1,626
Upper Level Sq. Ft.: 475
Bedrooms: 3
Bathrooms: 2½
Foundation: Basement
Materials List Available: Yes
Price Category: D

Images provided by designer/architect.

You'll love the exciting roofline that sets this elegant home apart from its neighbors as well as the embellished, solid look that declares how well-designed it is—from the inside to the exterior.

Features:

- **Great Room:** Made for relaxing and entertaining, the great room is sunken to set it off from the rest of the house. A balcony from the second floor looks down into this spacious area, making it easy to keep track of the kids while they are playing.

- **Kitchen:** Convenience marks this well laid-out kitchen where you'll love to cook for guests and for family.

- **Master Bedroom:** A vaulted ceiling complements the unusual octagonal shape of the master bedroom. Located on the first floor, this room allows some privacy from the second floor bedrooms. It is also ideal for anyone who no longer wishes to climb stairs to reach a bedroom.

Rear Elevation

Main Level Floor Plan

Deck
Breakfast 9-2 x 16
Sunken Great Room 16-10 x 21
Kitchen 8 x 13-4
Bath
Walk-in closet
Dining Room 16 x 11-8
Foyer
Master Bedroom 14 x 17-4
Bath
Slope ceiling   Slope ceiling
Hall
Laundry
Two-car Garage 21 x 20-8
58'-8"
59'-4"

Copyright by designer/architect.

Upper Level Floor Plan

Bedroom 15x 10-8
Great Room Below
Bath
Bedroom 14x 10-6
Foyer Below

Plan #211062

Dimensions: 74'6" W x 75' D

Levels: 1

Square Footage: 2,682

Bedrooms: 4

Bathrooms: 3½

Foundation: Slab, optional crawl space

Materials List Available: Yes

Price Category: F

Images provided by designer/architect.

If you're looking for a beautiful home that combines luxurious amenities with a separate, professional office space, this could be the one.

Features:

- **Living Room:** Enjoy an 11-ft. ceiling, brick fireplace, and built-in shelving in this room.

- **Dining Room:** A 2-story ceiling gives presence to this room.

- **Kitchen:** A breakfast bar here is open to the breakfast room beyond for ease of serving.

- **Breakfast Room:** A built-in corner china closet adds to the practicality you'll find here.

- **Office:** A separate entrance makes it possible to run a professional business from this home.

- **Master Suite:** Separated for privacy, this suite includes two vanities and a walk-in closet.

- **Porch:** The rear screened porch opens to a courtyard where you'll love to entertain.

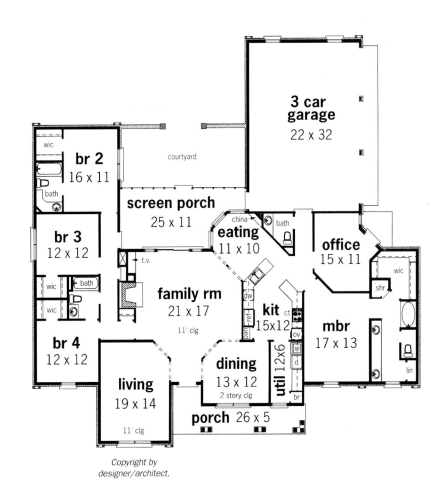

Copyright by designer/architect.

Plan #151100

Dimensions: 69'6" W x 31' D
Levels: 2
Square Footage: 2,247
Main Level Sq. Ft.: 1,154
Upper Level Sq. Ft.: 1,093
Bedrooms: 3
Bathrooms: 2½
Foundation: Crawl space, slab, or basement
Materials List Available: Yes
Price Category: E

Images provided by designer/architect.

This home suits a busy family life as easily as it makes a perfect backdrop for lavish entertaining.

Features:

• Porches: Take advantage of these generous porches to create some lovely sitting areas.

• Great Room: Furnish this room to create a cozy sitting area by the fireplace, a game table near the rear windows, and a media spot in the front.

• Dining Room: You can entertain a crowd in this well-positioned room.

• Kitchen: The family cook will love the center island, ample pantry, and convenient snack bar.

• Master Suite: You'll love the boxed ceiling, huge walk-in closet, and bath with a whirlpool tub, separate shower, a linen closet and two vanities.

• Bedrooms 2 & 3: Both rooms have plenty of closet space and a door to the bath where they each have a private vanity.

Main Level Floor Plan

Upper Level Floor Plan

Copyright by designer/architect.

Plan #131003

Dimensions: 60' W x 39'10" D
Levels: 1
Square Footage: 1,466
Bedrooms: 3
Bathrooms: 2
Foundation: Basement, crawl space, or slab
Materials List Available: Yes
Price Category: B

Victorian styling adds elegance to this compact and easy-to-maintain ranch design.

Features:

• Ceiling Height: 8 ft.

• Foyer: Bridging between the front door and the great room, this foyer is a surprise feature.

• Great Room: A 10-ft. ceiling adds to the spacious feeling of this room, while the corner fireplace gives it an intimate feeling. Sliding glass doors at the rear of the room open to the backyard.

• Dining Room: This formal room adjoins the great room, allowing guests and family to flow between the rooms.

• Breakfast Room: Turrets add a Victorian feeling to this room that's just off the kitchen and overlooks the front porch.

• Master Suite: Privacy is assured in this suite, which is separated from the main part of the house. A compartmented bath and large walk-in closet add convenience to its beauty.

Images provided by designer/architect.

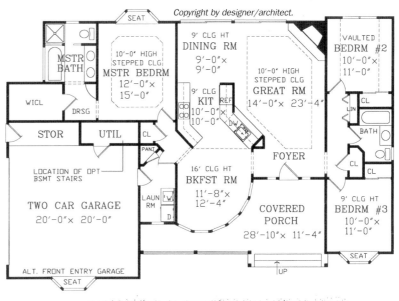

Copyright by designer/architect.

Breakfast Room

Plan #121064

Dimensions: 44' W x 40' D
Levels: 2
Square Footage: 1,846
Main Level Sq. Ft.: 919
Upper Level Sq. Ft.: 927
Bedrooms: 4
Bathrooms: 2½
Foundation: Basement
Materials List Available: Yes
Price Category: D

Images provided by designer/architect.

You'll love the features and design in this compact but amenity-filled home.

Features:

- Entry: A balcony overlooks this two-story entry, where a plant shelf tops the coat closet.

- Great Room: A trio of tall windows points up the large dimensions of this room, which is sure to be the hub of your home. Arrange the

furniture to create a cozy space around the fireplace, or leave it open to the room.

- Kitchen: You'll love to work in this well-designed kitchen area.

- Master Suite: On the second floor, this master suite features a tiered ceiling and two walk-in closets. In the bath, you'll find a double vanity, whirlpool tub, and separate shower.

Main Level Floor Plan

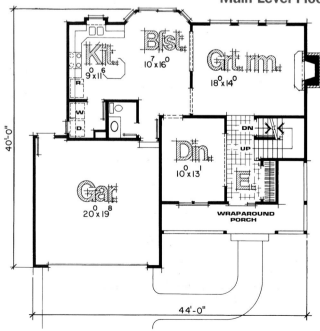

Upper Level Floor Plan

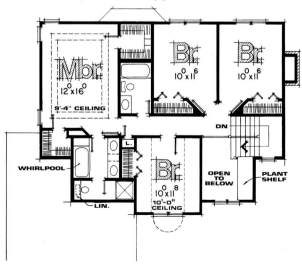

Copyright by designer/architect.

Plan #161020

Dimensions: 60' W" x 50'4" D

Levels: 2

Square Footage: 2,082;
2,349 with bonus space

Main Level Sq. Ft.: 1,524

Upper Level Sq. Ft.: 558

Bedrooms: 3

Bathrooms: 2½

Foundation: Basement

Materials List Available: Yes

Price Category: D

Images provided by designer/architect.

Upper Level Floor Plan

Main Level Floor Plan

Copyright by designer/architect.

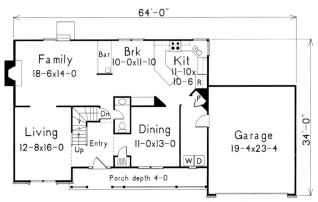

Main Level Floor Plan

Upper Level Floor Plan

Copyright by designer/architect.

Plan #321041

Dimensions: 64' W x 34' D

Levels: 2

Square Footage: 2,286

Main Level Sq. Ft.: 1,283

Upper Level Sq. Ft.: 1,003

Bedrooms: 4

Bathrooms: 2½

Foundation: Basement, crawl space, or slab

Materials List Available: No

Price Category: E

Images provided by designer/architect.

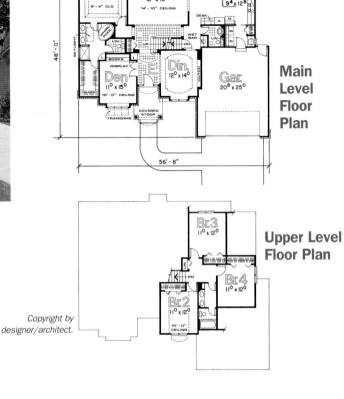

Main Level Floor Plan

Upper Level Floor Plan

Images provided by designer/architect.

Copyright by designer/architect.

Plan #121088

Dimensions: 56'8" W x 48' D

Levels: 2

Square Footage: 2,340

Main Level Sq. Ft.: 1,701

Upper Level Sq. Ft.: 639

Bedrooms: 4

Bathrooms: 2½

Foundation: Basement

Materials List Available: Yes

Price Category: E

Main Level Floor Plan

Upper Level Floor Plan

Images provided by designer/architect.

Copyright by designer/architect.

Plan #121086

Dimensions: 55'4" W x 37'8" D

Levels: 2

Square Footage: 1,998

Main Level Sq. Ft.: 1,093

Upper Level Sq. Ft.: 905

Bedrooms: 3

Bathrooms: 2½

Foundation: Basement

Materials List Available: Yes

Price Category: D

Plan #151002

Dimensions: 67' W x 66' D

Levels: 1

Square Footage: 2,444

Bedrooms: 3

Bathrooms: 2½

Foundation: Basement, crawl space, or slab

Materials List Available: Yes

Price Category: E

Images provided by designer/architect.

Copyright by designer/architect.

Plan #121092

Dimensions: 65'4" W x 52'8" D

Levels: 1

Square Footage: 1,887

Bedrooms: 3

Bathrooms: 2½

Foundation: Basement

Materials List Available: Yes

Price Category: D

Images provided by designer/architect.

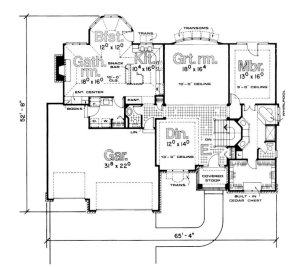

Copyright by designer/architect.

Optional Basement Floor Plan

Plan #151118

Dimensions: 54'2" W x 73'6" D
Levels: 2
Square Footage: 2,784
Main Level Sq. Ft.: 1,895
Upper Level Sq. Ft.: 889
Bedrooms: 4
Bathrooms: 2½
Foundation: Crawl space, slab, or basement
Materials List Available: Yes
Price Category: F

The classic good looks of the exterior of this lovely home are matched inside by clean lines and contemporary comforts.

Features:

- Great Room: Opening from the foyer, this room contains a fireplace and media center, and it leads to the rear grilling porch.

- Living Room: A high ceiling sets an elegant tone in this spacious, formal room.

- Dining Room: Equally formal, this room is nicely adjacent to the kitchen for serving ease.

- Kitchen: Built for a gourmet cook, the kitchen has plenty of counter and cabinet space.

- Breakfast Area: Sharing a snack bar with the kitchen, this area also leads to the grilling porch.

- Master Suite: The bedroom features a bay window, and the bath has a walk-in closet, whirlpool tub, glass shower, and double vanity.

Main Level Floor Plan

Upper Level Floor Plan

Plan #151117

Dimensions: 66' W x 55' D

Levels: 1

Square Footage: 1,957

Bedrooms: 3

Bathrooms: 3

Foundation: Crawl space, slab, or basement

Materials List Available: Yes

Price Category: D

You'll love this home if you have a family-centered lifestyle and enjoy an active social life.

Features:

- Foyer: A 10-ft. ceiling sets the tone for this home.

- Great Room: A 10-ft. boxed ceiling and fireplace are the highlights of this room, which also has a door leading to the rear covered porch.

- Dining Room: Columns mark the entry from the foyer to this lovely formal dining room.

- Study: Add the French doors from the foyer to transform bedroom 3, with its vaulted ceiling, into a quiet study.

- Kitchen: This large kitchen includes a pantry and shares an eating bar with the adjoining, bayed breakfast room.

- Master Suite: You'll love the access to the rear porch, as well as the bath with every amenity, in this suite.

Images provided by designer/architect.

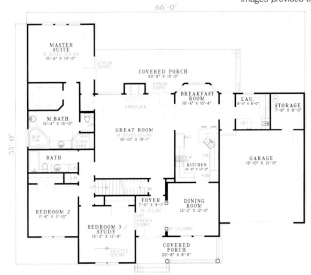

Copyright by designer/architect.

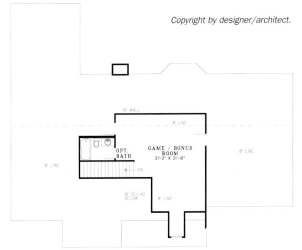

Bonus Area

Plan #121051

Dimensions: 64' W x 44' D
Levels: 1
Square Footage: 1,808
Bedrooms: 3
Bathrooms: 2½
Foundation: Basement
Materials List Available: Yes
Price Category: D

You'll love the way that natural light pours into this home from the gorgeous windows you'll find in room after room.

Features:

• Great Room: You'll notice the bayed, transom-topped window in the great room as soon as you step into this lovely home. A wet-bar makes this great room a natural place for entertaining, and the see-through fireplace makes it cozy on chilly days and winter evenings.

• Kitchen: This well-designed kitchen will be a delight for everyone who cooks here, not only because of the ample counter and cabinet space but also because of its location in the home.

• Master Suite: Angled ceilings in both the bedroom and the bathroom of this suite make it feel luxurious, and the picturesque window in the bedroom gives it character. The bath includes a corner whirlpool tub where you'll love to relax at the end of the day.

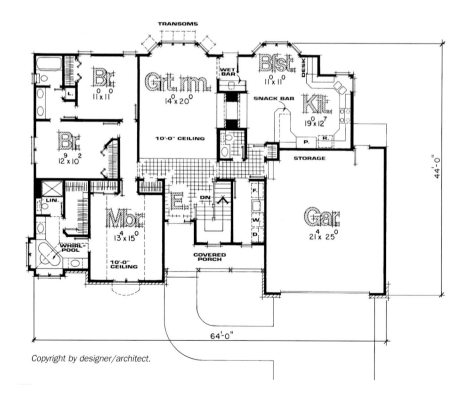

Copyright by designer/architect.

Plan #121050

Dimensions: 64' W x 50' D

Levels: 1

Square Footage: 1,996

Bedrooms: 2

Bathrooms: 2

Foundation: Basement

Materials List Available: Yes

Price Category: D

Images provided by designer/architect.

This compact design includes features usually reserved for larger homes and has styling that is typical of more-exclusive home designs.

Features:

- **Entry:** As you enter this home, you'll see the formal living and dining rooms—both with special ceiling detailing—on either side.

- **Great Room:** Located in the rear of the home for convenience, this great room is likely to be your favorite spot. The fireplace is framed by transom-topped windows, so you'll love curling up here, no matter what the weather or time of day.

- **Kitchen:** Ample counter and cabinet space make this kitchen a dream in which to work.

- **Master Suite:** A tray ceiling and lovely corner windows create an elegant feeling in the bedroom, and two walk-in closets make it easy to keep this space tidy and organized. The private bath has a skylight, corner whirlpool tub, and two separate vanities.

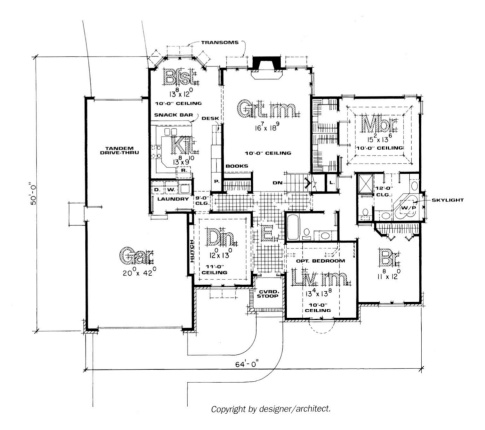

Copyright by designer/architect.

Living Room

Plan #111004

Dimensions: 76' W x 85' D
Levels: 1
Square Footage: 2,698
Bedrooms: 4
Full Bathrooms: 3½
Foundation: Slab
Materials List Available: No
Price Category: F

If you've been looking for a home that includes a special master suite, this one could be the answer to your dreams.

Features:

- **Living Room:** Make a sitting area around the fireplace here so that the whole family can enjoy the warmth on chilly days and winter evenings. A door from this room leads to the rear covered porch, making this room the heart of your home.

- **Kitchen:** An island with a cooktop makes cooking a pleasure in this well-designed kitchen, and the breakfast bar invites visitors at all times of day.

- **Utility Room:** A sink and a built-in ironing board make this room totally practical.

- **Master Suite:** A private fireplace in the corner sets a romantic tone for this bedroom, and the door to the covered porch allows you to sit outside on warm summer nights. The bath has two vanities, a divided walk-in closet, a standing shower, and a deluxe corner bathtub.

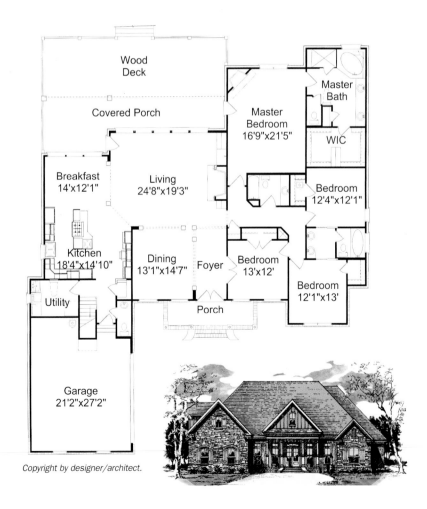

Kitchen

Dining Room

Master Bath

Master Bath

SMARTtip

How to Quit Smoking — Lighting Your Fireplace

Before attempting to light a wood fire, make certain that the damper is open all the way. This allows a good draft (flow of air up the chimney) to prevent smoke from blowing back into the room. To ensure a good draft—particularly if your home is well insulated—open a window a bit when lighting a fire.

The opposite of draft is downdraft, which occurs when cold air flows down the chimney and into the room. If the fireplace is properly designed and maintained, the smoke shelf will prevent backpuffing from downdraft most of the time by redirecting cold air currents back up the chimney. The open damper also helps prevent backpuffing.

Also, build a fire slowly to let the chimney liner heat up, which will create a good draft and minimize the chances of downdraft.

Don't wait until fall to inspect the chimney. Do this job, or call a chimney sweep, when the weather is mild. Because some repairs take a while to make, it's best to have them done when the fireplace is not normally in use. If you do the inspection yourself, wear old clothes, eye goggles, and a mask.

Kitchens for Families

From every standpoint, the importance of the kitchen and its design cannot be underestimated. The heart of the home beats in the kitchen. There's the hum of the refrigerator, the whir of the food processor, the crunch of the waste-disposal unit, and the bubbling of dinner simmering on the stove. These are the reassuring sounds of a home in action. The kitchen is also a warehouse, a communications center, a place to socialize, and the hub of family life. According to industry studies, 90 percent of American families eat some or all of their meals in the kitchen. It is also the command center where household bills are paid and vacations are planned. The kitchen is even a playroom at times. Emotions, as well as tasks, reside here. When you were little, this is where you could find mom whenever you needed her. It's where the cookies were kept. When other rooms were cold and empty, the kitchen was a place of warmth and companionship. It is from the kitchen that the family sets off into the day. And it is to the kitchen that they return at nightfall.

The Great Room Concept

Today, the family life that was once contained by the kitchen is spilling into an adjoining great room. Usually a large, open room, great rooms and kitchens are often considered part of the same space. It is here where the family gathers to watch TV, share meals, and do homework. In short, great rooms/kitchens are the new heart of the home and the places where families do most of their living. In most designs, a kitchen and great room are separated by a snack counter, an island, or a large pass-through.

Kitchen Layouts That Work

The basic layout of your kitchen will depend on the home design you choose. Look for aisles that have at least 39 inches between the front of the cabinets and appliances or an opposite-facing island. If it's possible, a clearance of 42 inches is better. And given more available space, a clear-

Large kitchen/great rooms, below, are now considered the true heart of the family home.

In large kitchens, opposite, look for plenty of counter and storage space, but insist on compact, efficient work areas.

ance of 48 to 49 inches is ideal. It means that you can open the dishwasher to load or unload it, and someone will still be able to walk behind you without doing a side-to-side shuffle or a crab walk. It also means that two people can work together in the same area. Any more than 49 inches, and the space is too much and involves a lot of walking back and forth. Fifty-four inches, for example, is too big a stretch. In large kitchens, look for balance; the work areas should have generous proportions, but to be truly efficient they should be compact and well designed.

Food Prep Areas and Surfaces. In many families, much of the food preparation takes place between the sink and the refrigerator. When you think of the work triangle, think of how much and how often you use an appliance. For example, sinks are generally used the most, followed by the refrigerator. The use of the cooktop is a matter of personal habit. Some families use it everyday, others use it sporadically. How close does it really need to be in relation to

the sink and refrigerator? Make your primary work zone the link between the sink and the refrigerator; then make the cooktop a secondary zone that's linked to them.

Cabinets Set the Style

Cabinets are the real furniture of a kitchen, making their selection both an aesthetic and functional choice. They are also likely to account for the largest portion of the budget.

Laminate. There are different brands and grades of plastic laminate, but cabinets made from this material generally are the least expensive you can buy. For the most part, they are devoid of detail and frameless, so don't look for raised panels, moldings, or inlaid beads on plastic laminate cabinets.

Although the surface is somewhat vulnerable (depending on the quality) to scratches and chips, plastic laminate cabinets can be refaced relatively inexpensively. Laminates come in a formidable range of

colors and patterns. Some of the newer speckled and patterned designs, which now even include denim and canvas, not only look great but won't show minor scratches and scars.

Wood. Wood cabinets offer the greatest variety of type, style, and finish. Framed cabinets (the full frame across the face of the cabinets may show between the doors) are popular for achieving a traditional look, but they are slightly less roomy inside. That's because you lose the width of the frame, which can be as much as an inch on each side. Frameless cabinets have full overlay doors and drawer fronts. With frameless cabinets, you gain about 2 inches of interior space per cabinet unit. Multiply that by the number of cabinet doors or drawer units you have, and add it up. It's easy to see that if space is at a premium, choose the frameless or full-overlay type. Besides, most cabinet companies now offer enough frameless styles to give you a traditional look in cabinetry, if that's your style.

Be creative with storage, above. Here a tall cabinet tops a drawer unit that holds dish towels and tablecloths.

A great room, below, works best when a well-defined kitchen area flows effortlessly into the living area.

The Decorative Aspect of Cabinets

While the trend in overall kitchen style is toward more decorative moldings and carvings, the trend in cabinet doors is toward simpler designs. Plain panels, for instance, are now more popular than raised panels. They allow you to have more decoration elsewhere. Ornamentation is effective when it is used to provide a focal point over a hood, fridge, or sink. Instead of installing a single crown profile, you might create a three- or four-piece crown treatment, or add a carving of grapevines, acanthus leaves, or another decorative motif. In the traditional kitchen, add them, but sparingly.

Finishes. Of all of the choices you will need to make regarding wood cabinets, the selection of the finish may be the hardest. Wood can be stained, pickled, painted, or oiled. Your selection will be determined in part by whether you order stock or custom cabinets. Finishing options on stock cabinets are usually limited, and variations are offered as an upgrade. Translation: more money. Try working with the manufacturer's stock cabinets. It not only costs less but also speeds up the process. There is usually a reason why manufacturers offer certain

woods in certain choices: it's because those choices work best with other elements in the room.

Wood Stains. Today, stains that are close to natural wood tones are popular, particularly natural wood finishes. Cherry is quickly becoming the number-one wood in the country. Pickled finishes, very popular in the early 1990s, are now looking dated. Some woods, particularly oak, have more grain than others. Some, such as maple, are smoother. And others, such as birch, dent more easily. The quality and inherent characteristics of the wood you choose will help determine whether it is better to stain, pickle, or paint. For staining, you need a good-quality clear wood. Pickling, because it has pigment in the stain, masks more of the grain but is still translucent. Because paint completely covers the grain, painted wood cabinets are usually made of lesser-quality paint-grade wood.

Painted Wood. Paint gives wood a smooth, clean finish. You can paint when you want a change or if the finish starts to show wear. This comes at no small expense, though, because the painter will have to sand the surfaces well before applying several coats of paint. If you choose painted cabinets, be sure to obtain a small can of the exact same paint from your kitchen vendor. There is usually a charge for this, but it allows you to do small touch-ups yourself, ridding your cabinets of particularly hideous scars without a complete repainting. While in theory the color choice for painted cabinets is infinite, manufacturers generally offer four shades of white and a few other standard color options from which to choose.

Pickled Wood. Pickled cabinets fall midway between full-grain natural cabinets and painted ones. Pickling is a combination of stain and paint, allowing some of the grain to show. It subdues the strongest patterns, while it covers over the lesser ones. The degree depends on your choice and on the options available from the manufacturer.

Hardware. Handles are easier to maneuver than knobs. Advocates of universal design, which takes into consideration the capabilities of all people—young and old, with and without physical limitations— recommend them. Knobs do not work easily for children or elderly people with arthritis. A handle with a backplate will keep fingerprints off the cabinet door.

Fitting Cabinets into Your Layout

This calls for attention to the kitchen layout. In specifying cabinets, first let common sense and budget be your guide. Kitchen geography can help you determine how much storage you need and where it should be. Mentally divide your kitchen into zones: food preparation, food consumption, and so on. And don't forget about the nonfood areas. Do you see yourself repotting plants or working on a hobby in the kitchen? You'll need work space and cabinet space for those extra activities.

A kitchen workhorse, the island, is not new to kitchen design. It's as old as the solid, slightly elevated, central table of medieval kitchens in England. But where that table was a work surface, today's island

can hold cabinets, a sink, a cooktop, a beverage refrigerator, and it can serve to divide areas of the kitchen.

How Tall Is Too Tall?

Upper cabinets are typically 12 inches deep; base, or lower, cabinets are 24 inches deep. With the exception of a desk unit, standard base cabinets are always the same height, 36 inches. Although most people prefer clean lines and planes as much as possible, some circumstances call for variations in the height of lower cabinets. There may be an often-used area where you want a countertop at which you can work while seated, for example.

Upper cabinets come in two or three standard heights: 30, 36, and 42 inches. The 30-inch ones look short; 36-inch cabinets look standard, and 42-inch ones can look too tall if your ceiling is not unusually high. In general, there is a slight up-charge for 30-inch cabinets and a big jump in price for 42-inch units. Order another size and you will pay double-custom prices. But you don't need to. For greater variation, install upper cabinets at varying heights. The old standard was to install 30-inch upper cabinets under a soffit—the often,

but not always, boxed-in area just under the ceiling and above the wall cabinets. Now, unless you have very tall ceilings, soffits are practically obsolete. Provided you have standard-height, 8-foot ceilings, the way to go now seems to be 36-inch cabinets with the remaining space of 6 inches or so filled with decorative trim up to the ceiling. It is a nicer, more refined look than cabinets that extend all the way to the ceiling, unless you prefer something contemporary and totally sleek and without ornament.

Size and Space. You don't want a massive bank of cabinets, either. Add up the dimensions wherever you're considering wall units. The counter is 36 inches high; backsplashes typically range from 15 to 17 inches. So with 36-inch-high upper cabinets, we're talking 7½ feet in all, 8 feet if you chose 42-inch-high wall units. Your own size can help determine which ones to choose. Determine what's comfortable by measuring your reach. A petite person will lose access to the top third of a cabinet. An inch or two can make a very big difference.

Also, be sure that the small appliances you keep on the countertop fit under the wall cabinets. Having them sit at the front edge of a countertop is an accident waiting to happen. A lot of people who have "appliance garages" discovered this. Whenever they pulled out the appliance, which places it nearer the counter's edge, they watched their mixer or coffeemaker tumble to the floor.

Often people need extra storage, so they extend the cabinets up to the ceiling. This provides the added extra storage space, but it can only be reached by a step stool. An open soffit above the upper cabinets provides just as much space for oversize, infrequently used objects, and it is equally accessible by stepladder. Plus it can be both a display area and perfect home for hard-to-store items: pitchers, trays, salad bowls, vases, collectibles, platters, covered servers, and so forth.

Light, natural wood finishes, left, are a popular cabinet choice.

Kitchen offices, left, are becoming increasingly popular. This desk and office storage matches the kitchen cabinets.

Just remember to allow plenty of room for air to circulate around the TV.

Kitchen Storage Solutions

There are many storage options that are extremely useful. At the top of the list is a spice drawer or rack attached to an upper cabinet or door. Both drawer and door spice racks are offered as factory options when you order cabinets, or you can retrofit them into existing cabinets. They provide visible access to all spices, so you don't end up with three tins of cinnamon, nine jars of garlic salt, four tiny bottles of vanilla, and no red pepper.

Lazy Susans. These rotating trays make items in the back of corner cabinets accessible. Consider adding inexpensive, plastic lazy Susans in a small upper cabinet. They will make the seasonings and cooking items you use everyday easily accessible.

Pie-cut door attachments can provide the same accessibility as a lazy Susan. Your choice depends on how much and what kind of storage you need. If a corner cabinet is home to sodas, chips, and cooking materials, install a pie-cut. A lazy Susan is more stable, best for pots, bowls, and larger, heavier objects.

The Kitchen Desk

Consider whether you will actually sit at a kitchen desk. Many people don't. Instead, they use it as the family message center and generally stand or perch on a stool. An additional, taller counter simply introduces more clutter to a room that is already overburdened with paraphernalia. And forget a desk-high cabinet, too. Instead use a standard counter-height cabinet to streamline whenever and wherever you can in the room.

Think about outfitting the desk area with a phone and answering machine and a corkboard for notes, your family's social schedule, invitations, and reminders. If you have room, a file drawer makes sense for storing school and business papers that need to be easy to retrieve. Also, if you don't have a separate study, and there's room, the kitchen may be a place to keep the family computer. Not only will you likely be using it more in the future for household record-keeping, but you can also help the kids with their homework and monitor their Internet use. In those cases, it makes sense to add a desk for comfort.

A Niche for the TV. Many people also want a TV in the kitchen. Plan for it. Who wants to see the back of the set or look at cords stretching across work areas, atop the refrigerator or the stove? Space and an outlet can be built into the lower portion of a well-placed wall cabinet or an open unit.

Pullouts, Rollouts, and Dividers.

Pullout fittings maximize the use of very narrow spaces. There are just two options for these areas: vertical tray-storage units or pullout pantries. You can find a 12-inch-wide base cabinet that is a pullout pantry with storage for canned goods and boxed items.

Pullout racks for cabinets and lid-rack dividers for drawers are also available from some cabinet suppliers. They are handy, but if you have enough cabinet storage space, the best thing is to store pots and pans with the lids on them in a couple of large cabinets.

Rollout cabinets are great and offer a lot of flexibility. They are adjustable to accommodate bulky countertop appliances and

Pullout cutting boards, above left, increase usable counter space.

Accessories for tall, narrow cabinets, left, come in handy for storing cookie sheets and trays.

Decorative molding, above, can enhance any cabinet. Most manufacturers offer a variety of molding options.

Knife, Towel, and Bread Storage. If you want a place to store knives, use slotted storage on a countertop. Frequently, islands have false backs because they are deeper than base cabinets. Slots for knives can be cut into the area of the countertop that covers the void behind the base cabinet.

You can obtain all these storage options at the time you buy your cabinets. But you don't have to and may not even want to until you see how you really end up using your kitchen. A carpenter or handyman can often make them or install off-the-shelf units. Think outside of the box. We get in a rut; it is hard to be objective. Ask friends where they keep their kitchen stuff, and analyze every aspect of how you use your kitchen. Store things at point of use, such as leftover containers and sandwich bags near the refrigerator; mixing bowls and carving knives near the sink.

stock pots, and they can save a lot of steps and banging around.

You can also divide a base cabinet vertically into separate parts. Some of the vertical spaces are further subdivided horizontally—good places for storing cutting boards, cookie trays, baking tins, and big glass baking dishes.

Other Organizers

Buy cutlery drawers carefully. They are often too big and too clumsy, and they fail to take advantage of the full interior of the drawer. They are as bad as bookshelves spread too far apart. Consider cutlery dividers that are almost no wider than a spoon, with separate sections for teaspoons, cereal spoons, breakfast and dinner knives, lunch forks, dinner forks, and serving pieces. Add to this a section for miscellaneous utensils such as spoons for iced tea, chopsticks, and so on. Drawer dividers should be adjustable in case your needs, or your cutlery, change.

Plan #211047

Dimensions: 74'6" W x 50' D

Levels: 1

Square Footage: 2,009

Bedrooms: 3

Bathrooms: 2

Foundation: Slab

Materials List Available: Yes

Price Category: D

You'll love the contemporary mix of open areas and individual rooms in this well-planned home.

Features:

- **Porches:** The front porch is accented by a planter for its entire length, and the back porch makes a lovely place to relax alone or entertain a crowd.

- **Family Room:** Exposed beams, a fireplace with a raised hearth, bookshelves, and a door to the porch make this the natural heart of your home.

- **Living Room:** This room and the dining room opposite it can be used for formal occasions or casual family times.

- **Kitchen & Eating Nook:** The efficient kitchen layout includes a pantry and island sink area. You'll find a built-in china closet in the adjoining eating nook that's lit by a large bay window.

- **Master Suite:** Enjoy the light from the sliding glass doors and the luxury of the walk-in closet, dressing area, and bath with tub and shower.

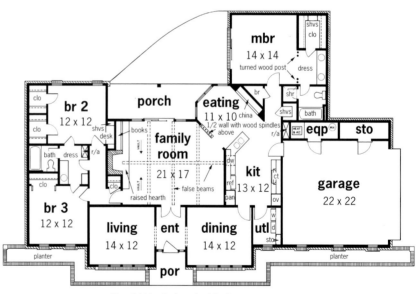

Plan #211030

Dimensions: 75' W x 37' D
Levels: 1
Square Footage: 1,600
Bedrooms: 3
Bathrooms: 2
Foundation: Slab
Materials List Available: Yes
Price Category: C

Images provided by designer/architect.

You'll love the way your family can make use of the well-designed living space in this home.

Features:

• Living Room: The exposed beams in the 16-ft. tall vaulted ceiling, stone hearth for the fireplace, and 6-in. sunken floor add up to pure luxury.

• Dining Room: A divider sets off this room, but even so, it feels open to the other areas.

• Kitchen: A built-in snack bar separates this room from the dining room. A large pantry closet and amply counter area make it a cook's delight.

• Sewing Room: Set between the kitchen and the laundry room, this area is ideal for the sewer.

• Master Suite: A sunken floor and sitting room are luxurious amenities to add to the walk-in closet and bath with separate tub and shower.

• Storage Room: Just off the garage, this large room has open space and built-in shelves.

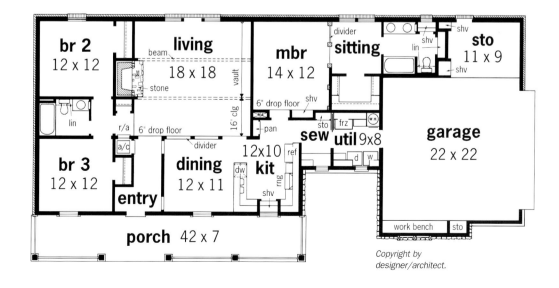

Copyright by designer/architect.

Plan #161038

Dimensions: 58'6" W x 49' D

Levels: 2

Square Footage: 2,209

Main Level Sq. Ft.: 1,542

Upper Level Sq. Ft.: 667

Bedrooms: 3

Bathrooms: 2½

Foundation: Basement

Materials List Available: No

Price Category: E

Brick trim, sidelights, and a transom window at the entry are a few of the many features that convey the elegance and style of this exciting home.

Images provided by designer/architect.

Features:

- Great Room: This great room is truly the centerpiece of this elegant home. The ceiling at the rear wall is 14 ft. and slopes forward to a second floor study loft that overlooks the magnificent fireplace and entertainment alcove. The high ceiling continues through the foyer, showcasing a deluxe staircase.

- Kitchen: This modern kitchen is designed for efficient work patterns and serves both the formal dining room and breakfast area.

- Master Suite: The highlight of this master suite is a wonderful whirlpool tub. Also included are two matching vanities and a large walk-in closet.

- Bonus Room: A bonus room above the garage completes this exciting home.

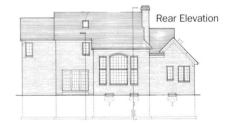

Rear Elevation

Main Level Floor Plan

Copyright by designer/architect.

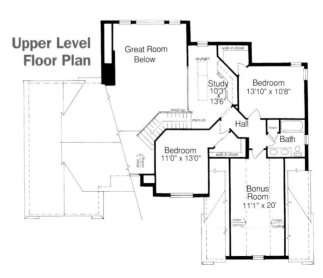

Upper Level Floor Plan

Plan #161039

Dimensions: 61' W x 41'8" D
Levels: 2
Square Footage: 2,320
Main Level Sq. Ft.: 1,595
Upper Level Sq. Ft.: 725
Bedrooms: 4
Bathrooms: 2½
Foundation: Basement
Materials List Available: Yes
Price Category: E

Images provided by designer/architect.

A touch of old-world charm combines with the comfort and convenience of modern amenities to create a delightful home.

Features:

- Great Room: This great room is the focal point of this lovely home. The wonderful room has a two-story ceiling, fireplace, and French doors to the rear yard. Split stairs lead to a second floor balcony.

- Dining Room: Adjacent to the foyer, this formal dining room has a boxed window, furniture alcove, and butler's pantry.

- Kitchen: This kitchen is a wonderful food-preparation area, consisting of a walk-in pantry, oven cabinet, and center island.

- Master Suite: This master bedroom has a sloped ceiling and relaxing garden bath that showcases a whirlpool tub, shower, double-bowl vanity, and large walk-in closet.

Rear Elevation

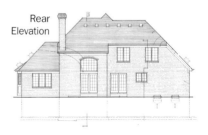

Main Level Floor Plan

Upper Level Floor Plan

Copyright by designer/architect.

Plan #131051

Dimensions: 64'4" W x 53'4" D
Levels: 2
Square Footage: 2,431
Main Level Sq. Ft.: 1,293
Upper Level Sq. Ft.: 1,138
Bedrooms: 4
Bathrooms: 2½
Foundation: Basement, crawl space, or slab
Materials List Available: Yes
Price Category: F

Gracious and charming with a wraparound front porch and a backyard terrace, this home also has a ready-to-finish third floor all-purpose room and a full bath.

Features:

• Main Level Ceiling Height: 8 ft.

• Family Room: A comfortable space for the entire family to gather, this delightful room can be warmed by a heat-circulating fireplace.

• Dining Room: A cozy dinette boasts a sliding glass door with access to a gorgeous backyard terrace with an optional calm reflecting pool.

• Kitchen: Adjoining the dining area, the kitchen offers plenty of storage and counter space. The laundry room and half-bath are nearby for convenience.

• Garage: The garage is tucked way back to keep it from intruding into the traditional facade.

Main Level Floor Plan

Images provided by designer/architect.

Rear Elevation

Upper Level Floor Plan

Optional 3rd Level Floor Plan

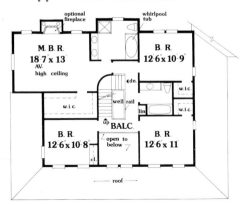

Copyright by designer/architect.

Plan #121083

Dimensions: 72' W x 45'4" D
Levels: 2
Square Footage: 2,695
Main Level Sq. Ft.: 1,881
Upper Level Sq. Ft.: 814
Bedrooms: 4
Bathrooms: 3½
Foundation: Basement
Materials List Available: Yes
Price Category: F

Images provided by designer/architect.

You'll love this home for its soaring entryway ceiling and well-designed layout.

Features:

- **Entry:** A balcony from the upper level looks down into this two-story entry, which features a decorative plant shelf.
- **Great Room:** Comfort is guaranteed in this large room, with its built-in bookcases framing a lovely fireplace and trio of transom-topped windows along one wall.
- **Living Room:** Save both this formal room and the formal dining room, both of which flank the entry, for guests and special occasions.
- **Kitchen:** This convenient work space includes a gazebo-shaped breakfast area where friends and family will gather at any time of day.

Main Level Floor Plan

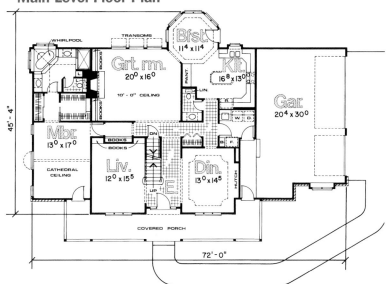

Upper Level Floor Plan

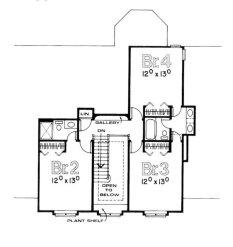

Copyright by designer/architect.

Plan #131013

Dimensions: 50' W x 41'8" D
Levels: 1
Square Footage: 1,489
Bedrooms: 3
Bathrooms: 2
Foundation: Basement, crawl space, or slab
Materials List Available: Yes
Price Category: C

Images provided by designer/architect.

You'll love the Victorian details on the exterior of this charming ranch-style home.

Features:

- **Front Porch:** This porch is large enough so that you can sit out on warm summer nights to catch a breeze or create a garden of potted ornamentals.

- **Great Room:** Running from the front of the house to the rear, this great room is bathed in natural light from both directions. The volume ceiling adds a luxurious feeling to it, and the fireplace creates a cozy place on chilly afternoons.

- **Kitchen:** Cooking will be a pleasure in this kitchen, thanks to the thoughtful layout and well-designed work areas.

- **Master Suite:** Enjoy the quiet in this room, where it will be easy to relax and unwind, no matter what the time of day. The walk-in closet gives you plenty of storage space, and you're sure to appreciate both the privacy and large size of the master bath.

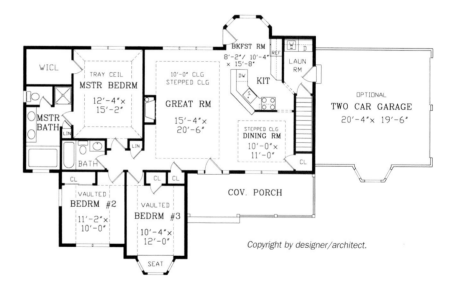

Copyright by designer/architect.

Rear Elevation

Plan #201062

Dimensions: 70'10" W x 59'5" D

Levels: 1

Square Footage: 2,551

Bedrooms: 4

Bathrooms: 2½

Foundation: Crawl space, slab

Materials List Available: Yes

Price Category: E

Images provided by designer/architect.

This home offers sophisticated Louisiana styling, plus all the space and amenities you need.

Features:

- Ceiling Height: 9 ft. unless otherwise noted.

- Great Room: Family and friends will be drawn to this great room, with its raised ceiling.

- Kitchen: This large, well-designed kitchen will bring out the gourmet cook in you. It has plenty of storage and counter space.

- Formal Living Room: This room is perfectly suited to entertaining guests.

- Formal Dining Room: Host elegant dinner parties in this lovely room.

- Master Bedroom: This private retreat features a raised ceiling.

- Master Bath: Enjoy the large walk-in closet, deluxe tub, walk-in shower, his and her vanities, and skylight in this truly plush master bathroom.

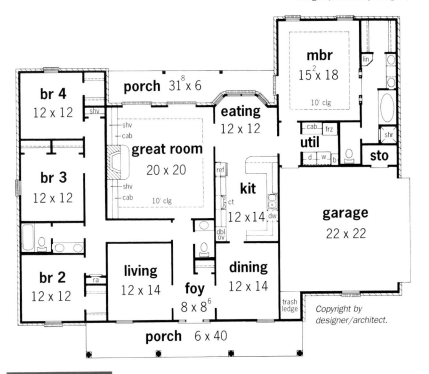

Copyright by designer/architect.

SMARTtip

Practical Role of a Window

Always consider the way a window opens and closes before choosing a window treatment. Double-hung windows pose the fewest problems. However, casement windows and French doors that swing into a room require a design that will not obstruct their paths of operation.

Plan #161024

Dimensions: 54'4" W x 26'8" D
Levels: 2
Square Footage: 1,698
Main Level Sq. Ft.: 868
Upper Level Sq. Ft.: 830
Bonus Space Sq. Ft.: 269
Bedrooms: 3
Bathrooms: 2½
Foundation: Basement
Materials List Available: No
Price Category: C

The covered porch, dormers, and center gable that grace the exterior let you know how comfortable your family will be in this home.

Features:

- Great Room: Walk from windows overlooking the front porch to a door into the rear yard in this spacious room, which runs the width of the house.

- Dining Room: Adjacent to the great room, the dining area gives your family space to spread out and makes it easy to entertain a large group.

- Kitchen: Designed for efficiency, the kitchen area includes a large pantry.

- Master Suite: Tucked away on the second floor, the master suite features a walk-in closet in the bedroom and a luxurious attached bathroom.

- Bonus Room: Finish the 269-sq.-ft. area over the 2-bay garage as a guest room, study, or getaway for the kids.

Images provided by designer/architect.

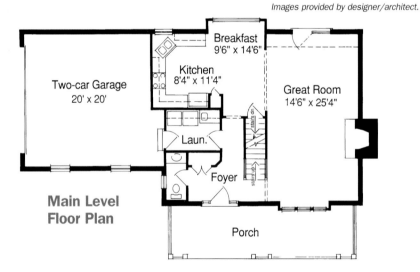

Main Level Floor Plan

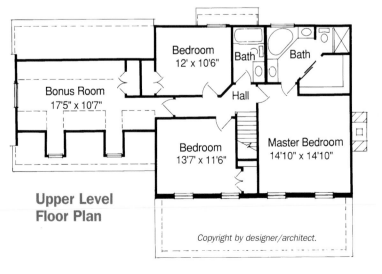

Upper Level Floor Plan

Copyright by designer/architect.

Plan #121068

Dimensions: 54' W x 49'10" D
Levels: 2
Square Footage: 2,391
Main Level Sq. Ft.: 1,697
Upper Level Sq. Ft.: 694
Bedrooms: 4
Bathrooms: 2½
Foundation: Basement
Materials List Available: Yes
Price Category: E

Images provided by designer/architect.

This home allows you a great deal of latitude in the way you choose to finish it, so you can truly make it "your own."

Features:

• Living Room: Located just off the entryway, this living room is easy to convert to a stylish den. Add French doors for privacy, and relish the style that the 12-ft. angled ceiling and picturesque arched window provide.

• Great Room: The highlight of this room is the two-sided fireplace that easily adds as much design interest as warmth to this area. The three transom-topped windows here fill the room with light.

• Kitchen: A center island, walk-in pantry, and built-in desk combine to create this wonderful kitchen, and the attached gazebo breakfast area adds the finishing touch.

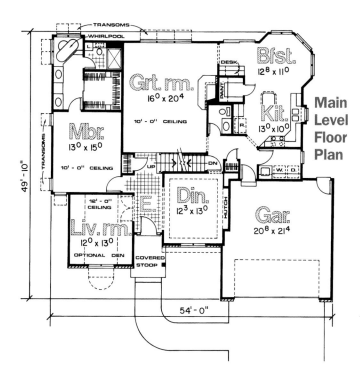

Main Level Floor Plan

Upper Level Floor Plan

Copyright by designer/architect.

Plan #121067

Dimensions: 56' W x 59'4" D
Levels: 2
Square Footage: 2,708
Main Level Sq. Ft.: 1,860
Upper Level Sq. Ft.: 848
Bedrooms: 4
Bathrooms: 3½
Foundation: Basement
Materials List Available: Yes
Price Category: F

Images provided by designer/architect.

You'll love this home because it is such a perfect setting for a family and still has room for guests.

Features:

- Family Room: Expect everyone to gather in this room, near the built-in entertainment centers that flank the lovely fireplace.
- Living Room: The other side of the see-through fireplace looks out into this living room, making it an equally welcoming spot in chilly weather.
- Kitchen: This room has a large center island, a corner pantry, and a built-in desk. It also features a breakfast area where friends and family will congregate all day long.
- Master Suite: Enjoy the oversized walk-in closet and bath with a bayed whirlpool tub, double vanity, and separate shower.

Main Level Floor Plan

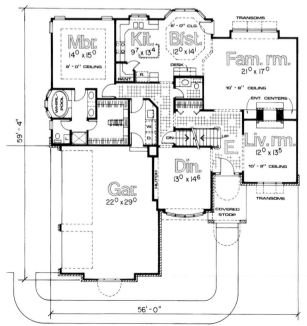

Upper Level Floor Plan

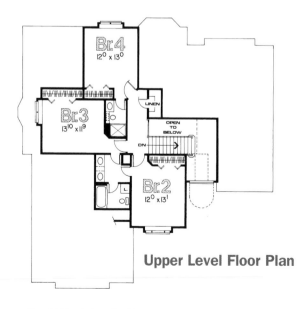

Copyright by designer/architect.

Plan #121074

Dimensions: 68'8" W x 47'8" D
Levels: 2
Square Footage: 2,486
Main Level Sq. Ft.: 1,829
Upper Level Sq. Ft.: 657
Bedrooms: 4
Bathrooms: 2½
Foundation: Basement
Materials List Available: Yes
Price Category: E

Images provided by designer/architect.

Enjoy the natural light that streams through the many lovely windows in this well-designed home.

Features:

- Living Room: This room is sure to be your family's headquarters, thanks to the lovely 15-ft. ceiling, stacked windows, central location, and cozy fireplace.

- Dining Room: A boxed ceiling adds formality to this well-positioned room.

- Kitchen: The island cooktop in this kitchen is so large that it includes a snack bar area. A pantry gives ample storage space, and a built-in desk—where you can set up a computer station or a record-keeping area—adds efficiency.

- Master Suite: For the sake of privacy, this master suite is located on the opposite side of the home from the other living areas. You'll love the roomy bedroom and luxuriate in the private bath with its many amenities.

Main Level Floor Plan

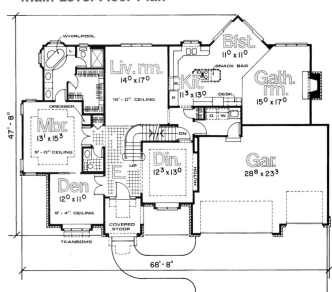

Upper Level Floor Plan

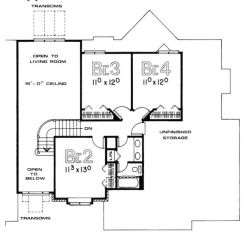

Copyright by designer/architect.

Plan #241008

Dimensions: 65' W x 56'8" D
Levels: 1
Square Footage: 2,526
Bedrooms: 4
Bathrooms: 3
Foundation: Slab
Materials List Available: No
Price Category: E

A covered back porch—with access from the master suite and the breakfast area—makes this traditional home ideal for siting near a golf course or with a backyard pool.

Features:

- Great Room: From the foyer, guests enter this spacious and comfortable great room, which features a handsome fireplace.

- Kitchen: This kitchen—the hub of this family-oriented home—is a joy in which to work, thanks to abundant counter space, a pantry, a convenient eating bar, and an adjoining breakfast area and sunroom.

- Master Suite: Enjoy the quiet comfort of this coffered-ceiling master suite, which features dual vanities and separate walk-in closets.

- Additional Bedrooms: Two secondary bedrooms, which share a full bath, are located at the opposite end of the house from the master suite. Bedroom 4—in front of the house—can be converted into a study.

Images provided by designer/architect.

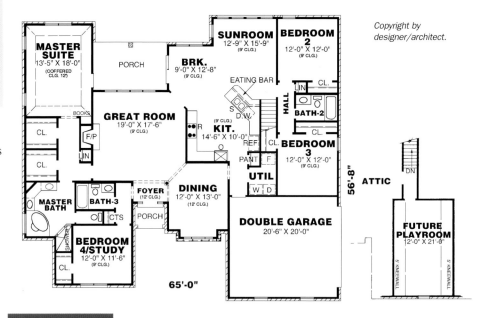

Copyright by
designer/architect.

Plan #241001

Dimensions: 65' W x 56'3" D
Levels: 1
Square Footage: 2,350
Bedrooms: 3
Bathrooms: 2½
Foundation: Slab
Materials List Available: No
Price Category: E

Classic, traditional rooflines combine with arched windows to draw immediate attention to this lovely three-bedroom home.

Features:

- Great Room: The foyer introduces you to this impressive great room, with its grand 10-ft. ceiling and handsome fireplace.

- Kitchen: Certain to become the hub of such a family-oriented home, this spacious kitchen, which adjoins the breakfast area and a delightful sunroom, features an abundance of counter space, a pantry, and a convenient eating bar.

- Master Suite: You will enjoy the privacy and comfort of this master suite, which features a whirlpool tub, split vanities, and a separate shower.

- Study: Adjourn to the front of the house, and enjoy the quiet confines of this private study with built-in bookshelves to work, read, or just relax.

Images provided by designer/architect.

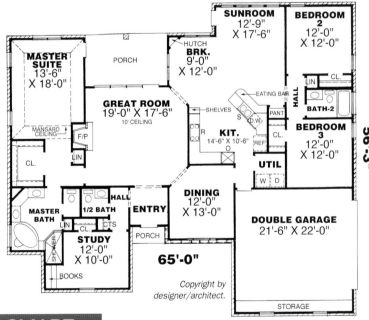

Copyright by designer/architect.

SMARTtip

Kitchen Counters

Make use of counter inserts to help with the cooking chores. For example, ceramic tiles inlaid in a laminate counter create a heat-proof landing zone near the range. A marble or granite insert is tailor-made for pastry chefs. And a butcher-block inlay is a great addition to the food prep area.

Plan #151037

Dimensions: 50' W x 56' D

Levels: 1

Square Footage: 1,538

Bedrooms: 3

Bathrooms: 2

Foundation: Crawl space, slab, or basement

Materials List Available: Yes

Price Category: C

Images provided by designer/architect.

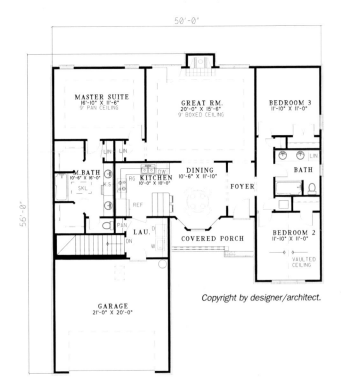

Copyright by designer/architect.

Plan #321003

Dimensions: 67'4" W x 48' D

Levels: 1

Square Footage: 1,791

Bedrooms: 4

Bathrooms: 2

Foundation: Basement

Materials List Available: Yes

Price Category: C

Images provided by designer/architect.

Copyright by designer/architect.

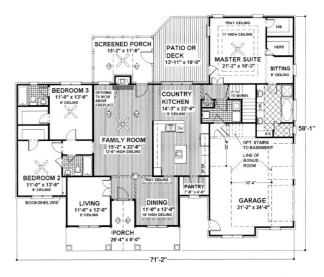

Images provided by designer/architect.

Copyright by designer/architect.

Plan #101011

Dimensions: 71'2" W x 58'1" D

Levels: 1

Square Footage: 2,184

Bedrooms: 3

Bathrooms: 3

Foundation: Slab, crawl space, or basement

Materials List Available: No

Price Category: D

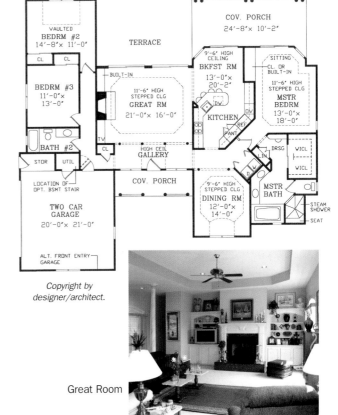

Images provided by designer/architect.

Copyright by designer/architect.

Great Room

Plan #131009

Dimensions: 64'10" W x 57'8" D

Levels: 1

Square Footage: 2,018

Bedrooms: 3

Bathrooms: 2

Foundation: Basement, crawl space, or slab

Materials List Available: Yes

Price Category: D

Plan #241009

Dimensions: 62'9" W x 38'6" D

Levels: 2

Square Footage: 1,974

Main Level Sq. Ft.: 1,480

Upper Level Sq. Ft.: 494

Bedrooms: 3

Bathrooms: 2½

Foundation: Slab

Materials List Available: No

Price Category: D

Images provided by designer/architect.

You'll love the comfort your friends and family will find inside this impressive-looking home.

Features:

- Great Room: A massive fireplace flanked by windows anchors this spacious room.

- Dining Room: The tall windows give an elegant feeling in this well-positioned room.

- Kitchen: The eating bar and angled sink add convenience to this step-saving design.

- Master Suite: You'll love the vaulted ceiling and bath, which has a huge closet, tub, shower, and dual vanity.

Main Level Floor Plan

Upper Level Floor Plan

Copyright by designer/architect.

Plan #101014

Dimensions: 52' W x 28' D

Levels: 2

Square Footage: 1,598

Main Level Sq. Ft.: 812

Upper Level Sq. Ft.: 786

Bedrooms: 3

Bathrooms: 2½

Foundation: Slab, crawl space

Materials List Available: No

Price Category: C

This lovely Victorian home has a perfect balance of ornamental features and modern amenities.

Features:

- Ceiling Height: 8 ft. unless otherwise noted.

- Foyer: An impressive beveled glass-front door invites you into this roomy foyer.

- Kitchen: This bright and open kitchen offers an abundance of counter space to make cooking a pleasure.

- Breakfast Room: You'll enjoy plenty of informal family meals in this sunny and open spot next to the kitchen.

- Family Room: The whole family will be attracted to this handsome room. A full-width bay window adds to the Victorian charm.

- Master Suite: This dramatic suite features a multi-faceted vaulted ceiling and his and her closets and vanities. A separate shower and 6-ft. garden tub complete the lavish appointments.

Main Level Floor Plan

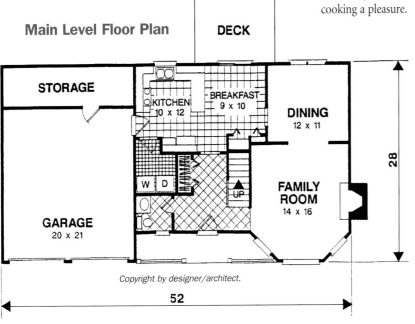

Copyright by designer/architect.

Upper Level Floor Plan

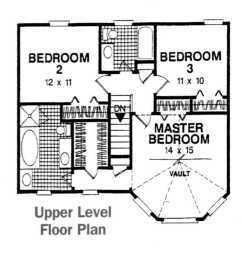

Plan #121037

Dimensions: 46' W x 47'10" D
Levels: 2
Square Footage: 2,292
Main Level Sq. Ft.: 1,158
Upper Level Sq. Ft.: 1,134
Bedrooms: 4
Bathrooms: 2½
Foundation: Basement
Materials List Available: Yes
Price Category: E

This convenient and comfortable home is filled with architectural features that set it apart.

Features:

• Ceiling Height: 8 ft. unless otherwise noted.

• Foyer: You'll know you have arrived when you enter this two-story area highlighted by a decorative plant shelf and a balcony.

• Great Room: Just beyond the entry is the great room where the warmth of the two-sided fireplace will attract family and friends to gather. A bay window offers a more intimate place to sit and converse.

• Hearth Room: At the other side of the fireplace, the hearth offers a cozy spot for smaller gatherings or a place to sit alone and enjoy a book by the fire.

• Breakfast Area: With sunlight streaming into its bay window, the breakfast area offers the perfect spot for informal family meals.

• Master Suite: This private retreat is made more convenient by a walk-in closet. It features its own tub and shower.

Main Level Floor Plan

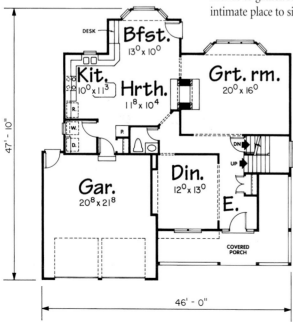

Upper Level Floor Plan

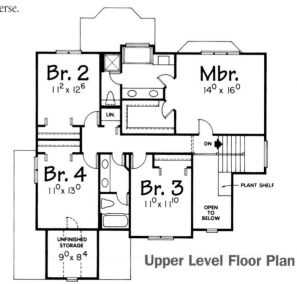

Plan #121020

Dimensions: 64' W x 46' D
Levels: 2
Square Footage: 2,480
Main Level Sq. Ft.: 1,369
Upper Level Sq. Ft.: 1,111
Bedrooms: 4
Bathrooms: 3
Foundation: Basement
Materials List Available: Yes
Price Category: E

Images provided by designer/architect.

Tapered columns and an angled stairway give this home a classical style.

Features:

- Ceiling Height: 8 ft.

- Living Room: Just off the dramatic two-story entry is this distinctive living room, with its tapered columns, transom-topped windows, and boxed ceiling.

- Formal Dining Room: The tapered columns, transom-topped windows, and boxed ceiling found in the living room continue into this gracious dining space.

- Family Room: Located on the opposite side of the house from the living room and dining room, the family room features a beamed ceiling and fireplace framed by windows.

- Kitchen: An island is the centerpiece of this convenient kitchen.

- Master Suite: Upstairs, a tiered ceiling and corner windows enhance the master bedroom, which is served by a pampering bath.

Main Level Floor Plan

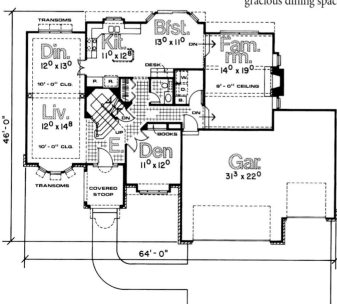

Upper Level Floor Plan

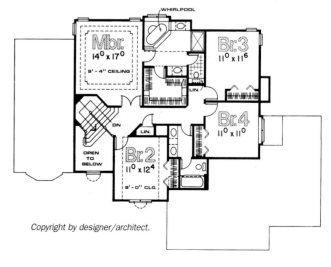

Copyright by designer/architect.

Images provided by designer/architect.

Plan #141015

Dimensions: 46' W x 36'8" D
Levels: 2
Square Footage: 2,350
Main Level Sq. Ft.: 1,155
Upper Level Sq. Ft.: 1,195
Bedrooms: 4
Bathrooms: 2½
Foundation: Basement
Materials List Available: Yes
Price Category: E

This home offers classic Victorian details combined with modern amenities.

Features:

- Ceiling Height: 9 ft. unless otherwise noted.
- Porch: Enjoy summer breezes on this large wraparound porch, with its classic turret corner.
- Family Room: This room has a fireplace and two sets of French doors. One set of doors leads to the porch; the other leads to a rear sun deck.
- Living Room: This large room at the front of the house is designed for formal entertaining.
- Kitchen: This convenient kitchen features an island and a writing desk.
- Master Bedroom: Enjoy the cozy sitting area in the turret corner. The bedroom offers access to a second story balcony.
- Laundry: The second-floor laundry means you won't have to haul clothing up and down stairs.

Main Level Floor Plan

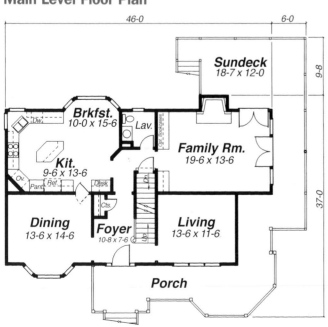

Upper Level Floor Plan

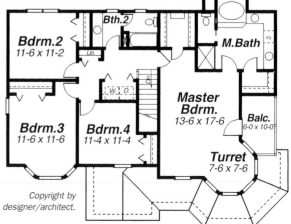

Copyright by designer/architect.

Plan #141013

Dimensions: 64' W x 38'4" D
Levels: 2
Square Footage: 1,936
Main Level Square Footage: 1,312
Second Level Square Footage: 624
Bedrooms: 3
Bathrooms: 2½
Foundation: Basement
Materials List Available: No
Price Category: D

Images provided by designer/architect.

This story-and-a-half design features a welcoming front porch that exudes country style.

Features:

- Ceiling Height: 9 ft. unless otherwise noted.

- Formal Dining Room: Columns add an elegant feel to your formal dining experience. The dining room is open to the foyer and great room for a more spacious feel.

- Master Bedroom: This bedroom is located on first floor separated from other bedrooms for privacy.

- Great Room: This room has a fireplace along with French doors that open to rear sundeck.

- Balcony: This small balcony overlooks the open foyer.

Main Level Floor Plan

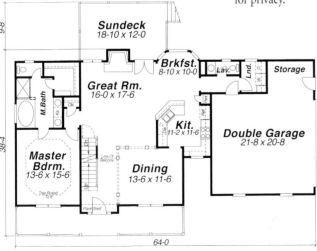

Upper Level Floor Plan

Copyright by designer/architect.

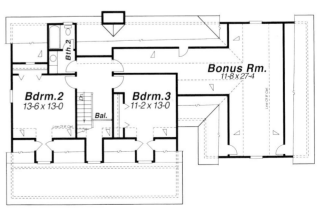

Plan #121009

Dimensions: 50' W x 58' D
Levels: 1
Square Footage: 1,422
Bedrooms: 3
Bathrooms: 2
Foundation: Basement
Materials List Available: Yes
Price Category: B

Images provided by designer/architect.

This amenity-filled home is perfect for the growing family or as a retirement retreat.

Features:

- Ceiling Height: 8 ft. unless otherwise noted.

- Great Room: This inviting space is the perfect place for gatherings of all sizes. It shares 12-ft. ceilings with the dining room and kitchen.

- Dining Room: In addition to the 12-ft. ceiling, arched openings, and built-in book cases make this an elegant place to dine.

- Private Porch: After dinner, step through a door in the dining room to enjoy a summer breeze in this inviting porch.

- Master Suite: The boxed ceiling lends drama to this suite and a walk-in closet adds convenience. Luxury comes from the whirlpool bath.

- Garage: You won't be short of parking and storage space in this two-bay garage. As a bonus there is space for a workbench.

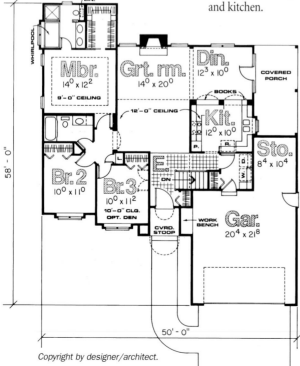

Copyright by designer/architect.

SMARTtip

Window Cornices

You can transform plain rooms by making jogs in cornice molding that will hold shades, blinds, and other window treatments. You can create individual pockets over each window or continue the molding past narrow wall sections between windows to form a more expansive detail. Housings below the cornice can be painted or papered.

Plan #121084

Dimensions: 40' W x 42' D
Levels: 2
Square Footage: 1,728
Main Level Sq. Ft.: 845
Upper Level Sq. Ft.: 883
Bedrooms: 4
Bathrooms: 2½
Foundation: Basement
Materials List Available: Yes
Price Category: C

Images provided by designer/architect.

If you're looking for a home where the whole family will be comfortable, you'll love this design.

Features:

- Great Room: The heart of the home, this great room has a fireplace with a raised hearth, a sloped ceiling, and transom-topped windows.
- Dining Room: A cased opening lets you flow from the great room into this formal dining room. A built-in display hutch is the highlight here.
- Kitchen: What could be nicer than this wraparound kitchen with peninsula snack bar? The sunny, attached breakfast area has a pantry and built-in desk.
- Master Suite: A double vanity, whirlpool tub, shower, and walk-in closet exude luxury in this upper-floor master suite.

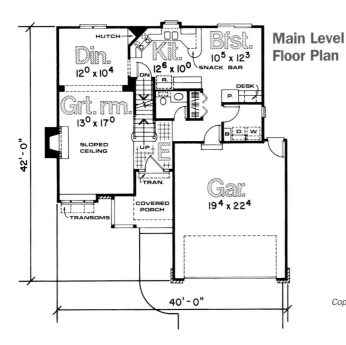

Main Level Floor Plan

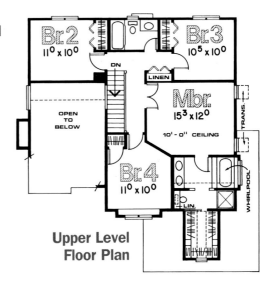

Upper Level Floor Plan

Copyright by designer/architect.

Plan #241005

Dimensions: 53' W x 55'9" D
Levels: 1
Square Footage: 1,670
Bedrooms: 3
Bathrooms: 2
Foundation: Slab
Materials List Available: No
Price Category: C

This charming starter home, in split-bedroom format, combines big-house features in a compact design.

Features:

- Great Room: With easy access to the formal dining room, kitchen, and breakfast area, this great room features a cozy fireplace.

- Kitchen: This big kitchen, with easy access to a walk-in pantry, features an island for added work space and a lovely plant shelf that separates it from the great room.

- Master Suite: Separated for privacy, this master suite offers a roomy bath with whirlpool tub, dual vanities, a separate shower, and a large walk-in closet.

- Additional Rooms: Additional rooms include a laundry/utility room—with space for a washer, dryer, and freezer—a large area above the garage, well-suited for a media or game room, and two secondary bedrooms.

Images provided by designer/architect.

Copyright by designer/architect.

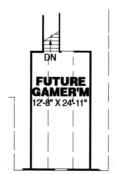

SMARTtip

Window Scarf

The best way to wrap a window scarf around a pole is as follows:

- Lay out the material on a large, clean surface. Gather the fabric at the top of each jabot, and use elastic to hold it together.

- Swing one jabot into place over the pole and, starting from there, wind the swag portion as many times as you need around the pole until you reach the elastic at the second jabot, which should have landed at the opposite pole end.

- Readjust wraps along the pole. Generally, wrapped swags just touch or slightly overlap.

- For a dramatic effect, stuff the wrapped swags with tissue paper or thin foam, depending on the translucence and weight of fabric.

- Release elastics at tops of jabots.

Plan #161052

Dimensions: 57'8" W x 58' D
Levels: 2
Square Footage: 2,484
Main Level Sq. Ft.: 1,710
Upper Level Sq. Ft.: 774
Bedrooms: 4
Bathrooms: 3½
Foundation: Basement
Materials List Available: Yes
Price Category: E

Images provided by designer/architect.

You'll love the airy feeling of the open floor plan in this spacious, comfortable home.

Features:

- Foyer: This elegant two-story space sets the gracious tone you'll find throughout this home.

- Great Room: A fireplace and decorative window highlight this room with a two-story ceiling.

- Dining Room: You'll find expansive windows in this formal dining room.

- Kitchen: This kitchen has an L-shaped work area for efficiency and access to the laundry room.

- Breakfast Room: A window area makes a perfect frame for table and chairs, and a door leads to the porch.

- Master Suite: A walk-in closet and bath with a double vanity impart luxury to this suite.

Main Level Floor Plan

Upper Level Floor Plan

Copyright by designer/architect.

Images provided by designer/architect.

Plan #271022

Dimensions: 37'8" W x 38'8" D

Levels: 2

Square Footage: 1,317

Main Level Sq. Ft.: 894

Upper Level Sq. Ft.: 423

Bedrooms: 3

Bathrooms: 2

Foundation: Basement

Materials List Available: Yes

Price Category: B

You'll love the floor plan, which makes this compact home feel open and spacious.

Features:

• Living Room: The 17-ft. vaulted ceiling and natural light from the clerestory make this room feel airy, and the fireplace makes it cozy.

• Dining Room: Large glass sliding doors open onto the deck for versatility in this large room.

• Kitchen: A central island adds work space to this step-saving kitchen.

• Master Bedroom: You'll love the walk-in closet, as well as the large corner window area.

• Garage: The two-car garage can easily give some extra storage space for tools and out-of-season clothes.

• Upper Floor: Each of the rooms has a walk-in closet, and the bath is conveniently situated for each room.

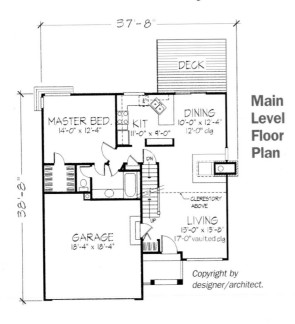

Main Level Floor Plan

Copyright by designer/architect.

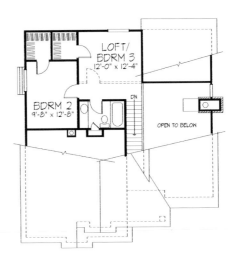

Upper Level Floor Plan

Plan #321057

Dimensions: 38' W x 39'4" D
Levels: 2
Square Footage: 1,524
Main Level Sq. Ft.: 951
Upper Level Sq. Ft.: 573
Bedrooms: 3
Bathrooms: 2½
Foundation: Basement
Materials List Available: Yes
Price Category: C

Images provided by designer/architect.

You'll love the comfort you'll find in this compact home, which also sports a practical design.

Features:

- **Entry:** This two-story entry is lit by a lovely oval window on the second-floor level.
- **Living Room:** A masonry fireplace sets a gracious tone, and the large windows and sliding door leading to the patio give natural lighting.
- **Dining Room:** The bay window here makes a perfect spot to place a table in this room.
- **Kitchen:** Situated between the living and dining rooms for convenience, the kitchen is designed as an efficient work area.
- **Master Suite:** A large walk-in closet and sliding doors to the patio are highlights of the bedroom, and the private bath features a double vanity.
- **Upper Level:** You'll find two walk-in closets in one bedroom and one in the other.

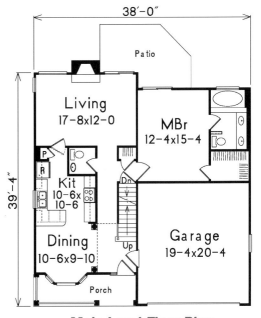

Main Level Floor Plan

38'-0"

Patio

Living 17-8x12-0

MBr 12-4x15-4

Kit 10-6x 10-6

Dn

Dining 10-6x9-10

Up

Garage 19-4x20-4

Porch

39'-4"

Upper Level Floor Plan

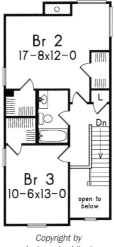

Br 2 17-8x12-0

L

Dn

Br 3 10-6x13-0

open to below

Copyright by designer/architect.

Plan #161009

Dimensions: 60'9" W x 49' D

Levels: 1

Square Footage: 1,651

Bedrooms: 3

Bathrooms: 2

Foundation: Slab

Materials List Available: Yes

Price Category: C

The warm, textured exterior combines with the elegance of double-entry doors to preview both the casual lifestyle and formal entertaining capabilities of this versatile home.

Features:

- Great Room: Experience the openness provided by the sloped ceiling topping both this great room and the formal dining area. Enjoy the warmth and light supplied by the gas fireplace and dual sliding doors.

- Kitchen: This kitchen, convenient to the living space, is designed for easy work patterns and features an open bar that separates the work area from the more richly decorated gathering rooms.

- Master Bedroom: Separated for privacy, this master bedroom includes a tray ceiling and lavishly equipped bath.

- Basement: This full basement allows you to expand your living space to meet your needs.

Images provided by designer/architect.

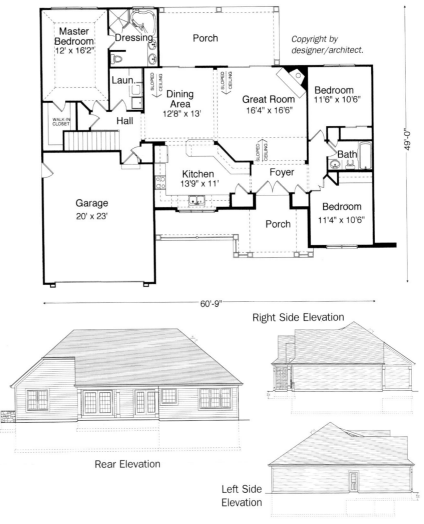

Copyright by designer/architect.

Plan #161003

Dimensions: 60' W x 47' D
Levels: 1
Square Footage: 1,508
Bedrooms: 3
Bathrooms: 2
Foundation: Basement
Materials List Available: Yes
Price Category: C

Multiple gables and a cozy front porch invite you to this enchanting one-story home.

Features:

• Great Room: This bright and cheery room features a sloped ceiling and fireplace. The great room is designed for convenience, with easy access to the foyer and dining area, creating the look and feel of a home much larger than its actual size.

• Dining Area: Adjacent to the great room, this dining area has multiple windows and angles that add light and dimension.

• Kitchen: This spacious kitchen is designed for easy work patterns with an abundance of counter and cabinet space. It also features a snack bar.

• Master Bedroom: Designed for step-saving convenience, this master bedroom includes a compartmented bath, double-bowl vanity, and large walk-in closet.

Images provided by designer/architect.

Copyright by designer/architect.

Rear Elevation

Copyright by designer/architect.

Plan #101008

Dimensions: 67'8" W x 52'6" D

Levels: 1

Square Footage: 2,088

Bedrooms: 3

Bathrooms: 2½

Foundation: Slab, crawl space, or basement

Materials List Available: Yes

Price Category: D

Images provided by designer/architect.

Accentuating Your Bathroom with Details

No matter how big or small the room, details will pull the style together. Some of the best details that you can include are the smallest—drawer pulls from an antique store or shells in a glass jar or just left on the countertop. Add period flavor with crown molding, or dress up contemporary fixtures with polished stone fittings.

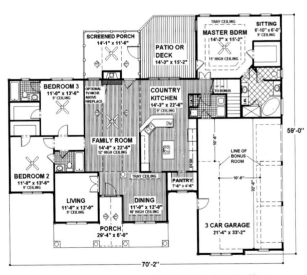

Copyright by designer/architect.

Plan #101009

Dimensions: 70'2" W x 59' D

Levels: 1

Square Footage: 2,097

Bedrooms: 3

Bathrooms: 3

Foundation: Slab

Materials List Available: No

Price Category: D

Images provided by designer/architect.

Single-Level Decks

A single-level deck can use a strong vertical element, such as a pergola or a gazebo, to make it interesting. A simple and less-expensive option is a potted conical shrub or a clematis growing on a trellis.

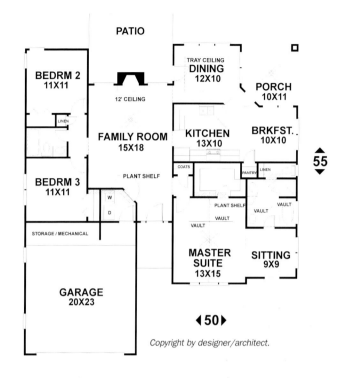

Plan #101003

Dimensions: 50' W x 55' D

Levels: 1

Square Footage: 1,593

Bedrooms: 3

Bathrooms: 2

Foundation: Slab, crawl space, or basement

Materials List Available: Yes

Price Category: C

Images provided by designer/architect.

PATIO

BEDRM 2
11X11

DINING
12X10
TRAY CEILING

PORCH
10X11

12' CEILING

LINEN

FAMILY ROOM
15X18

KITCHEN
13X10

BRKFST.
10X10

55

BEDRM 3
11X11

PLANT SHELF

COATS

PANTRY

LINEN

W D

PLANT SHELF

VAULT

VAULT

STORAGE / MECHANICAL

VAULT

VAULT

MASTER SUITE
13X15

SITTING
9X9

GARAGE
20X23

◀50▶

Copyright by designer/architect.

Plan #161007

Dimensions: 66'4" W x 43'10" D

Levels: 1

Square Footage: 1,611

Bedrooms: 3

Bathrooms: 2

Foundation: Basement

Materials List Available: Yes

Price Category: C

Images provided by designer/architect.

Dining
13' x 11'6"

Screened Porch
19' x 12'

Great Room
16' x 17'2"

Master Bedroom
11'9" x 15'

walk-in closet

10' center ceiling height

Two-Car Garage
20'8" x 21'

Kitchen
11' x 15'6"

Dressing

Foyer
10' ceiling height

Bath

Bedroom
10'8" x 11'6"

Laun.

43'-10"

Porch

Bedroom
10'6" x 10'6"

66'-4"

Copyright by designer/architect.

Rear Elevation

Plan #131007

Dimensions: 59'10" W x 47'8" D
Levels: 1
Square Footage: 1,595
Bedrooms: 3
Bathrooms: 2
Foundation: Crawl space, slab, basement, or walkout
Materials List Available: Yes
Price Category: D

Imagine living in this home, with its traditional country comfort and individual brand of charm.

Features:

- **Exterior elements:** The mixture of a front porch with a cameo front door, decorative posts, bay windows, and dormers will delight you.

- **Great Room:** A tray ceiling gives distinction to this large room, and a wet bar eases entertaining.

- **Screened Porch:** At dusk and dawn, this porch is sure to be your favorite outdoor spot.

- **Kitchen:** Eat any meal in this large kitchen for a touch of homey charm.

- **Dining Room:** Perfect for hosting a formal dinner, this bayed dining room can increase your enjoyment of simple family meals.

- **Master Bedroom:** For the sake of privacy, this room is somewhat secluded. Decorate to emphasize the elegant tray ceiling.

Images provided by designer/architect.

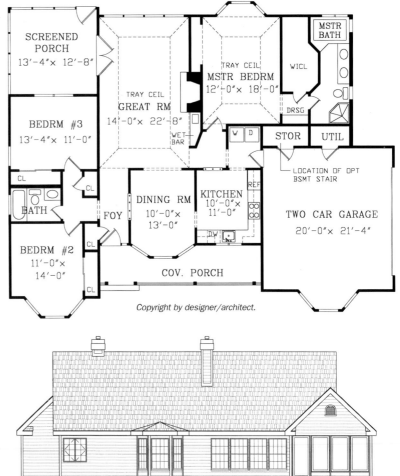

Copyright by designer/architect.

Rear Elevation

Alternate Front View

Foyer / Dining Room

Add the Extras

Simple or plain, it's the little conveniences and miscellaneous touches that push the dining experience to perfection. Here are some extra things to think about.

- You can never have too many serving trays when you entertain outside. For carrying food or drinks from the kitchen or the grill, trays are indispensable.

- A serving cart on wheels makes a perfect movable outdoor bar and provides an additional serving surface. Look for one at yard sales or buy one new.

- Chances are you won't have a sideboard, but a few small tables to hold excess items are great substitutes for one. They're also easier to position in the different places where you need them.

- For cooler weather or even a summer's evening with a bit of nip in the air, nothing beats an outdoor fireplace for comfort. You could build one into the house, but various types of stand-alone units are sold in home centers. To add a Southwest ambiance, consider a chiminea, a clay fireplace. Try burning some piñon pine, and you'll feel as if you're in Santa Fe. Be sure to follow manufacturers' instructions when using these fireplaces. You might also have to store them during the winter.

- Pots of fragrant plants—lavender, scented geraniums, flowering tobacco, or jasmine—provide a sensual aroma. Flowers such as roses climbing up an arbor or trellis are beautiful, evoke a romantic feeling, and lend a delicate scent to the atmosphere as well.

Nothing adds romance and intrigue to an evening soiree as candlelight does. Include just a few candles for an intimate dinner. Use more for a larger gathering, placing one or more on each table. Scatter luminaries around the yard. As the beautiful evening dusk begins, light candles, a few at a time, so your eyes can adjust to the dimming light. Not only do the candles illuminate the night in a magical way but they can also keep bugs at bay.

Great Room

Country-Style Bathrooms

Call it pure Americana, English, Swedish, Italian, or French. The style is basic, casual, and warm—and every country has its own version. "Country" often implies a deeper connection with the outdoors and the simple life than other styles and uses an abundance of natural elements. For a Country bath, start with plain wood cabinetry stained a light maple, or add a distressed, crackled, or pickled finish. Door styles are usually framed, sometimes with a raised panel. Install a laminate countertop, and coordinate it with the tile you select for the room. Hand-painted tiles with a simple theme lend a custom touch.

For added Country charm, stencil a wall border or select a wallpaper pattern with a folk-art motif or floral prints. Checks and ticking stripes are also popular in a country-style room—on the wall, as a tile pattern, or on the shower-curtain fabric. If you feel creative, apply a painted finish to the wall. Otherwise, check out the many wallpaper designs on the market that emulate the look of sponging, ragging, combing, and other special painted effects.

Install a double-hung window in the room. (Casement windows look too contemporary in this setting.) Some window-treatment ideas include a balloon topper over miniblinds or shutters, for privacy, combined with a matching or contrasting lace café curtain. If you have a casement window in the bathroom that you do not want to change, install pop-in muntins to give the unit more of a traditional or old-fashioned look.

A skirted pedestal sink or pine chest-turned-vanity, along with reproduction faucets, will add a nostalgic charm to a Country bathroom. Bring a playful note to this informal design with whimsical hardware fabricated in wrought iron, brushed pewter, or porcelain. Hardware and fittings that are polished look too refined for this style.

Popular Country colors include red gingham and denim blue. Choose a checkerboard floor or a mosaic of broken tiles if hardwood is not available. Or consider laminate flooring that gives you the look of real wood without the maintenance. Some styles even come with a painted-floor design.

The Country bath is the type of room that begs for baskets, old bottles, and ceramic vases filled with wildflowers. Accessorize with these items or a collection of favorite things, and you've created a very personal space.

A yellow-and-white floor, below, adds a dollop of sunshine underfoot.

A pedestal sink, opposite, is a hallmark of Country style.

A Country Bath with Efficient Style

Although the ancient Greeks and Romans, along with other prosperous early civilizations, maintained luxurious public bathhouses, it was a long road to the private, plumbed-in tub with the toilet alongside that we know today. A relatively modern convenience, the bathroom typically packs lots of essential equipment into a small space, so it's in special need of old-fashioned details to become part of a welcoming country house.

In the 1790s the French produced shoe-shaped bathtubs; Benjamin Franklin brought one back to the United States so he could enjoy soaking, reading, and relaxing for hours.

But before the late nineteenth century, for most North Americans, bathing was utilitarian. Periodically, someone filled a portable tub with hand-pumped and stove-heated water from buckets, and each family member had a turn.

By the 1870s the houses of well-to-do North Americans had flush toilets, but only the wealthiest owned a plumbed-in tub in the same room. Most folks endured the inconvenience of chamber pots, water pitchers, and washbowls in their bedrooms. Finally, nearing the twentieth century, plumbing became increasingly common, and average homeowners carved out bathroom space from a bedroom. The old-fashioned claw-foot tub not only resembled formal furniture pieces but kept the often unreliable plumbing more accessible. Into the 1920s and '30s, closed-in tubs and crisp white tile became fashionable, celebrating thoroughly modern convenience.

Today's Typical Bathroom

Though the recent trend has been toward larger bathrooms, the standard is still focused on efficient use of space. This offers the decorator an unexpected side benefit, because even minor flourishes and ornamentation go a long way toward making the Country bathroom attractive and full of character. Follow the advice below to make this sometimes sterile room charming in a Country-style way.

Design It to Suit Its Use
Not only are we spoiled with indoor plumbing, we have come to expect more than one bathroom. With bathrooms in such abundance, each may be slanted toward a different role, with different decorating demands and possibilities.

The master bath is a private retreat,

Beadboard and Shaker-style pegs, opposite, provide a Country ambiance.

This Country-style bathroom, above, features a traditional floral wall treatment and light-colored cabinetry.

deserving some luxurious amenities, such as a makeup table, television and sound system, exercise equipment, or spa features. Space permitting, the bathroom can hold a piece or two of country furniture, such as a painted bench, an armoire,

a wicker chair, or an added cabinet.

A family bathroom, on the other hand, may be where everyone showers or bathes—even the dog. It requires ample storage for toys, towels, and toiletries for kids and grownups. So keep an eye out for big baskets, quaint containers, shelves, and a capacious hamper for laundry. Because space is often at a premium, seek out useful shelves, towel bars, magazine racks, storage containers, and robe hooks styled with a bit of panache, whether in ceramic, brass,

hand-painted finishes, or unusual materials. Everything should be water resistant and easy to clean, too.

Powder rooms are half-baths often located in the house's social or "public" areas. Because they're not subject to long, steamy showers or much of the morning get-up-and-go routine, durability and storage are less of an issue. Here you can indulge your decorating with delicate, eye-catching finishes, pretty collections, or displays that enhance the space.

Apply General Decorating Principles

Even if it's a small space, assess the room's strengths and weaknesses. A room's odd angles and small size can seem picturesque in lively, high-contrast finishes. Think about harmonies of scale, proportion, line, and color spiced with subtle differences. Because a bathroom tends toward slick modern surfaces, rough baskets and earthenware pots of ferns might be refreshing. Light finishes visually enlarge a small space, but wall-to-wall pastels can seem dull without a few bright notes.

Borrow Ideas from Other Rooms

Bathrooms can be too utilitarian, so have fun with unexpected elements, such as elaborate window treatments, handsome moldings, a slipper-chair, potted plants, and artwork, as long as the materials can hold up to dampness.

Fixtures

As in the kitchen, even bathrooms designed in the most authentic Country spirit can accommodate modern accoutrements. Consider a reproduction of a high-tank Victorian-style toilet, claw-foot tub, and classic gooseneck faucet with porcelain crosshandles.

Antique fixtures may be an attractive addition to your bathroom, but the inconvenience of future repairs may be a drawback.

Toilets

Many Country decorators choose standard, unobtrusive wares, often in versatile white or neutral, and concentrate their decorating efforts on elements and accessories that are easy to change, such as paint, wallpaper, linens, and rugs.

Basic two-piece toilets in white vitre-

"Brick" style ceramic tile is right at home in a Country scheme, opposite.

Use traditional fixtures, such as this crosshandle faucet set, above right, in a Country bathroom.

Period-furniture-style pieces, right, provide a distinct Country flavor.

ous china are unassuming features in a Country scheme, though more expensive, contemporary one-piece models may be your preference. New toilets feature a variety of internal mechanisms designed to meet a low-flush standard of using 1.6 gallons or less per flush. In addition to standard gravity-fed mechanisms, pressure-assisted systems use internal water pressure to compress air, which creates a more forceful flush.

Tubs and Showers

The tub and shower areas have the greatest visual weight in the room's design. Though they're most economical when combined (and a tub makes the most assuredly leakproof shower pan), the trend, especially in the master bath, is to separate the functions by creating separate fixtures for them. Tubs and shower enclosures can be found in a wide range of materials and styles. Cast-iron tubs are an attractive addition to any bathroom. However, the easier installation and lighter weight of modern plastics and ceramics make them more practical.

To keep the water contained, a clear glass shower door will do the job. A shower curtain, particularly if it consists of a waterproof liner combined with a frivolous fabric drapery, can add a soft, colorful, and easy-to-change touch amid all the hard surfaces. You can also pull it almost completely out of the way to show off any decorative tilework or handsome fittings within in the tub alcove.

Sinks and Fittings

Bathroom sinks, which designers refer to as lavatories, can be made of vitreous china, cast iron, enameled steel, fiberglass, solid-surfacing material, stone, faux stone, or metal. Pedestal sinks, or wall-mounted lavatories with metal or carved-wood legs, encompass a variety of handsome vintage styles. Remember, today a beautiful fixture can stand alone as a piece of sculpture in the room.

Faucets. Faucets span a wide price range. In appearance, they can be considered as "jewelry" for the bathroom when fabricated in rich vintage styles, perhaps with china or bright crosshandles and a gooseneck spout. Brass is the traditional finish, but chrome can look at home fashioned after nostalgic styles. Single-lever controls, though undeniably modern, are convenient and easy to use.

Vanities

The vanity is often the keynote of a bathroom's country style because cabinetmaking is a venerable craft. An old but not valuable cabinet, small chest of drawers, or table can be converted into a charming vanity, though it must be carefully sealed against water. You'll also find vanities with evocative Country details made of rustic pine, smooth maple, or pickled oak, with planked or raised panel doors. Stock cabinetry often works well in standardized bathroom spaces. Custom cabinetry opens up more options and may offer accessories such as matching display shelves, moldings, or a bracket for a vase or candle.

Finishing Touches

Country bathrooms use many of the same practical finishing materials as Country kitchens. Wood instantly adds warmth and character and a "furnished" feeling. In the bath, consider softwoods such as fir, redwood, and pine or dense hardwoods like teak and maple for tongue-and-groove wainscoting, moldings, or furniture pieces.

Mirrors enhance a sense of space, albeit with a harder modern look. Downplay this by extending the mirror into a corner or framing it with molding.

Ceramic tile is a classic Country bathroom material, and it can be the decorative standout. There are some options to lend interest to a low-key background—for example, a play of different shapes, such as triangles, squares, and rectangles interlocked on a white wall. Or turn the square grid diagonally for an energetic diamond design. Try a stamped high-relief pattern or a heavy rope-molding trim to give a plain color more tactile appeal. Clay-colored tones and faux stone add a natural spirit to bare white walls and floors.

Lighting

In a room where people shave, put on makeup, remove splinters, and the like, good lighting, both natural and artificial, is essential.

Modern bathroom faucets, below left, can look like antique fixtures.

This bathroom, with its floral wallcovering and traditional faucet, below right, says "Country."

Use of a whirligig, opposite, reinforces the Country decor.

Just as in any room, windows add light and charm to a bath. Those with divided-light sash or projected bays add particular elegance. Skylights and clerestory windows can fetch sunlight with no worries about privacy.

All bathroom lighting fixtures should be suitable for damp areas. A ceiling-mounted fixture, perhaps a bowl-type pendant or a smaller chandelier, can cast a good general glow. Paired wall sconces alongside the mirror eliminate the shadows that can be cast by an overhead source.

Accessories

In limited space, every added object should be carefully chosen. Some fanciful touches with a Country sensibility might include a vintage sugar and creamer set to hold toothbrushes and cottonballs. An old teapot can be a charming planter or a place to store combs and brushes.

And don't forget the old model-home trick of displaying big fluffy towels to instantly make the room feel cozy and welcoming.

Plan #311025

Dimensions: 76'8" W x 62' D

Levels: 1

Square Footage: 2,561

Main Level Sq. Ft.: 2,561

Opt. Bonus Sq. Ft. 1,494

Bedrooms: 3

Bathrooms: 2½

Foundation: Basement, crawl space, or slab

Materials List Available: Yes

Price Category: E

Images provided by designer/architect.

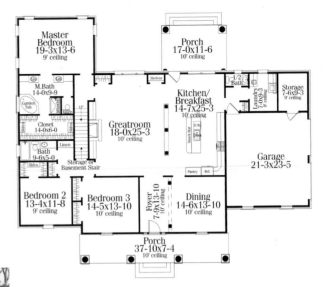

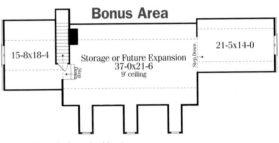

Rear View

Bonus Area

Copyright by designer/architect.

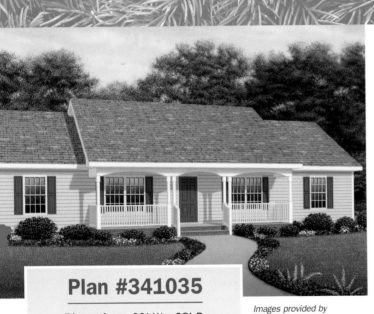

Plan #341035

Dimensions: 60' W x 28' D

Levels: 1

Square Footage: 1,680

Bedrooms: 4

Bathrooms: 2

Foundation: Crawl space, slab (basement option for fee)

Materials List Available: Yes

Price Category: C

Images provided by designer/architect.

Copyright by designer/architect.

Plan #341036

Dimensions: 51'6" W x 34' D

Levels: 1

Square Footage: 1,134

Bedrooms: 3

Bathrooms: 2

Foundation: Crawl space, slab (basement option for fee)

Materials List Available: Yes

Price Category: B

Images provided by designer/architect.

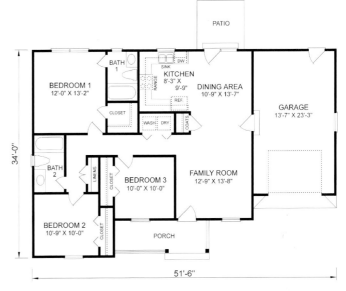

Copyright by designer/architect.

Plan #341037

Dimensions: 48' W x 62'4" D

Levels: 1

Square Footage: 1,784

Bedrooms: 3

Bathrooms: 2

Foundation: Crawl space, slab (basement option for fee)

Materials List Available: Yes

Price Category: C

Images provided by designer/architect.

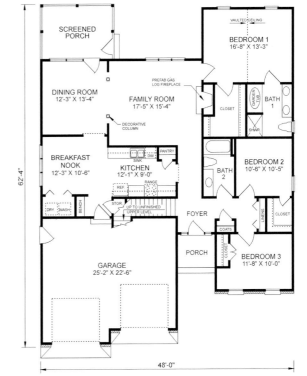

Copyright by designer/architect.

Plan #161040

Dimensions: 63'4" W x 48' D

Levels: 2

Square Footage: 2,403

Main Level Sq. Ft.: 1,710

Upper Level Sq. Ft.: 695

Bedrooms: 4

Bathrooms: 3½

Foundation: Basement

Materials List Available: Yes

Price Category: E

Designed with attention to detail, this elegant home will please the most discriminating taste.

Images provided by designer/architect.

Features:

- **Great Room:** The high ceiling in this room accentuates the fireplace and the rear wall of windows. A fashionable balcony overlooks the great room.

- **Dining Room:** This lovely formal dining room is introduced by columns and accented by a boxed window.

- **Kitchen:** This wonderful kitchen includes a snack bar, island, and large pantry positioned to serve the breakfast and dining rooms with equal ease.

- **Master Suite:** This master suite features a dressing room, private sitting area with 11-ft.

ceiling, whirlpool tub, double-bowl vanity, and large walk-in closet.

- **Additional Bedrooms:** Three additional bedrooms complete this spectacular home.

Rear Elevation

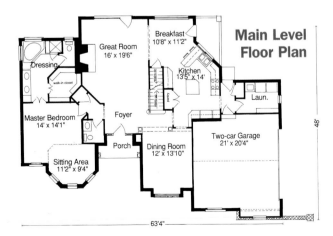

Main Level Floor Plan

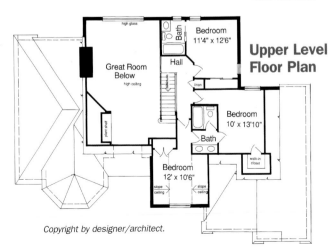

Upper Level Floor Plan

Copyright by designer/architect.

Plan #131036

Dimensions: 72' W x 69'10" D
Levels: 1
Square Footage: 2,585
Bedrooms: 4
Bathrooms: 3
Foundation: Crawl space, slab, or basement
Materials List Available: Yes
Price Category: F

Images provided by designer/architect.

This sprawling brick home features living spaces for everyone in the family and makes a lovely setting for any sort of entertaining.

Features:

- Foyer: Pass through this foyer, which leads into either the living room or dining room.

- Living Room: An elegant 11-ft. stepped ceiling here and in the dining room helps to create the formality their lines suggest.

- Great Room: This room, with its 10-ft.-7-in.-high stepped ceiling, fireplace, and many built-ins, leads to the rear covered porch.

- Kitchen: This kitchen features an island, a pantry closet, and a wraparound snack bar that serves the breakfast room and gives a panoramic view of the great room.

- Master Suite: Enjoy a bayed sitting area, walk-in closet, and private bath with garden tub.

- Office: A private entrance and access to a full bath give versatility to this room.

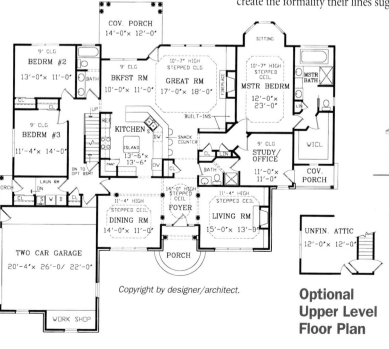

Copyright by designer/architect.

Optional Upper Level Floor Plan

Rear Elevation

Great Room

Plan #321051

Dimensions: 69'8" W x 46' D

Levels: 2

Square Footage: 2,624

Main Level Sq. Ft.: 1,774

Upper Level Sq. Ft.: 850

Bedrooms: 4

Bathrooms: 2½

Foundation: Basement

Materials List Available: Yes

Price Category: F

Images provided by designer/architect.

The dramatic exterior design allows natural light to flow into the spacious living area of this home.

Features:

- Entry: This two-story area opens into the dining room through a classic colonnade.

- Dining Room: A large bay window, stately columns, and doorway to the kitchen make this room both beautiful and convenient.

- Great Room: Enjoy light from the fireplace or the three Palladian windows in the 18-ft. ceiling.

- Kitchen: The step-saving design features a walk-in pantry as well as good counter space.

- Breakfast Room: You'll love the light that flows through the windows flanking the back door.

- Master Suite: The vaulted ceiling and bayed areas in both the bed and bath add elegance. You'll love the two walk-in closets and bath with a sunken tub, two vanities, and separate shower.

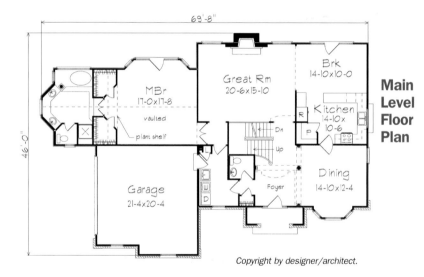

Main Level Floor Plan

Copyright by designer/architect.

Master Bath

Upper Level Floor Plan

Plan #271089

Dimensions: 66' W x 51' D
Levels: 2
Square Footage: 2,476
Main Level Sq. Ft.: 1,266
Upper Level Sq. Ft.: 1,210
Bedrooms: 3
Bathrooms: 2½
Foundation: Daylight basement
Materials List Available: No
Price Category: E

This traditional-looking home is filled with modern amenities that will charm any family.

Features:

• Great Room: A handsome fireplace flanked with windows creates the focal point in this room, where the whole family will relax and entertain.

• Dining Room: A huge bay window makes an ideal frame for a table, and the door to the backyard makes outdoor entertaining easy.

• Study: Separated from the great room by the office, this study can be a quiet retreat.

• Kitchen: Here, you'll find a walk-in pantry, ample counter space, and a central island.

• Owner's Suite: The large bedroom is complemented by the bath with a tub in the bay, two vanities, and a walk-in closet.

• Additional Bedrooms: Both rooms have a walk-in closet and a large window area for natural light.

Main Level Floor Plan

Copyright by designer/architect.

Upper Level Floor Plan

Plan #311004

Dimensions: 68'2" W x 57'4" D

Levels: 1

Square Footage: 2,046

Bedrooms: 3

Bathrooms: 2½

Foundation: Basement, crawl space, or slab

Materials List Available: Yes

Price Category: D

The open design of the public spaces in this home makes it ideal for an active family life or frequent entertaining.

Features:

• Great Room: Open to the foyer, this spacious room has a fireplace flanked by built-ins and a bank of windows at the rear.

• Dining Room: This large front room is convenient to the kitchen but isolated enough to be just right for a formal dinner party or a casual family meal.

• Kitchen: The angled work space creates efficient traffic patterns, and the snack bar makes it easy for small visitors to share the news of their day.

• Breakfast Room: The expansive window area lights this room, and the door to the rear porch makes outside entertaining easy.

• Master Suite: You'll feel coddled by the large window area, two walk-in closets, and bath with two vanities, tub, and shower.

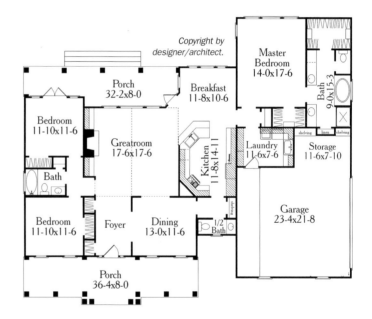

Copyright by designer/architect.

Porch 32-2x8-0

Bedroom 11-10x11-6

Greatroom 17-6x17-6

Breakfast 11-8x10-6

Master Bedroom 14-0x17-6

Bath 9-0x15-3

Kitchen 11-8x14-11

Laundry 11-6x7-6

Storage 11-6x7-10

Bath

Bedroom 11-10x11-6

Foyer

Dining 13-0x11-6

1/2 Bath

Garage 23-4x21-8

Porch 36-4x8-0

Rear View

Images provided by designer/architect.

Plan #381001

Dimensions: 37' W x 36' D
Levels: 2
Square Footage: 1,700
Main Level Sq. Ft.: 990
Upper Level Sq. Ft.: 710
Bedrooms: 3
Bathrooms: 2½
Foundation: Basement
Materials List Available: Yes
Price Category: C

This charming, compact home includes every feature you'll want in its friendly, open floor plan.

Features:

- **Porch:** Set out a couple of rockers, a table, and pots of herbs to make the porch a great place to relax.
- **Family Room:** Set up a media center in this room to make it a favorite with the children.
- **Living Room:** The fireplace welcomes friends and family into this spacious room.
- **Dining Room:** You'll love the extensive window area in this room, where you'll love to entertain.
- **Kitchen:** The U-shape saves steps and time.
- **Breakfast Room:** Cheerful natural light pours through the windows in this room.
- **Upper Floor:** The master bedroom has a desk in the dormer and private bath with a dual vanity. Large closets grace the other rooms.

Main Level Floor Plan

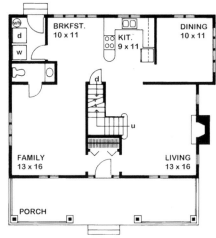

Upper Level Floor Plan

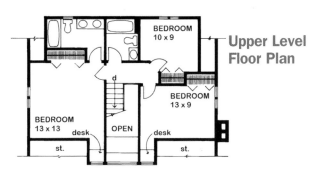

Copyright by designer/architect.

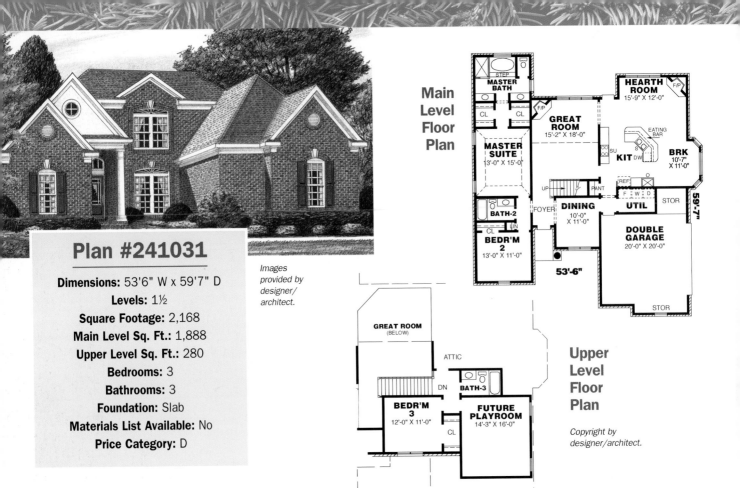

Plan #241031

Dimensions: 53'6" W x 59'7" D
Levels: 1½
Square Footage: 2,168
Main Level Sq. Ft.: 1,888
Upper Level Sq. Ft.: 280
Bedrooms: 3
Bathrooms: 3
Foundation: Slab
Materials List Available: No
Price Category: D

Images provided by designer/architect.

Main Level Floor Plan

Upper Level Floor Plan

Copyright by designer/architect.

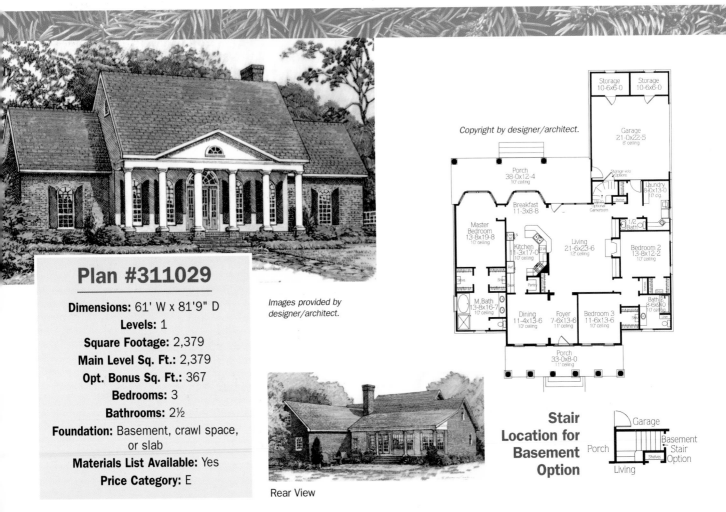

Plan #311029

Dimensions: 61' W x 81'9" D
Levels: 1
Square Footage: 2,379
Main Level Sq. Ft.: 2,379
Opt. Bonus Sq. Ft.: 367
Bedrooms: 3
Bathrooms: 2½
Foundation: Basement, crawl space, or slab
Materials List Available: Yes
Price Category: E

Images provided by designer/architect.

Rear View

Copyright by designer/architect.

Stair Location for Basement Option

Images provided by designer/architect.

Plan #141038

Dimensions: 40'4" W x 38' D
Levels: 2
Square Footage: 1,668
Main Level Sq. Ft.: 1,057
Upper Level Sq. Ft.: 611
Bedrooms: 3
Bathrooms: 2½
Foundation: Basement with drive-under garage
Materials List Available: No
Price Category: C

If you're looking for the ideal plan for a sloping site, this could be the home of your dreams.

Features:

• **Porch:** Set a couple of rockers on this large porch so you can enjoy the evening views.

• **Living Room:** A handsome fireplace makes a lovely focal point in this large room.

• **Dining Room:** Three large windows over looking the sundeck flood this room with natural light.

• **Kitchen:** The U-shaped, step-saving layout makes this kitchen a cook's dream.

• **Breakfast Room:** With an expansive window area and a door to the sundeck, this room is sure to be a family favorite in any season of the year.

• **Master Suite:** A large walk-in closet and a private bath with tub, shower, and double vanity complement this suite's spacious bedroom.

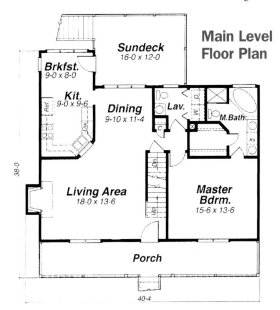

Main Level Floor Plan

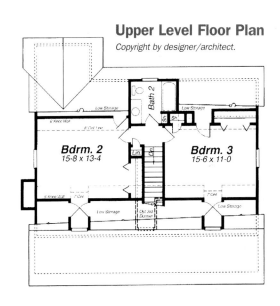

Upper Level Floor Plan

Copyright by designer/architect.

Plan #311005

Dimensions: 87' W x 57'3" D
Levels: 1
Square Footage: 2,497
Bedrooms: 3
Bathrooms: 3½
Foundation: Crawl space, slab
Materials List Available: Yes
Price Category: E

You'll love this home, which mixes practical features with a gracious appearance.

Features:

- **Great Room:** A handsome fireplace and flanking windows that give a view of the back patio are the highlights of this gracious room.

- **Kitchen:** A curved bar defines the perimeter of this well-planned kitchen.

- **Breakfast Room:** Open to both the great room and the kitchen, this sunny spot leads to the rear porch, which in turn, leads to the patio beyond.

- **Master Suite:** Vaulted ceilings, a huge walk-in closet, and deluxe bath create luxury here.

- **Bonus Room:** Finish this 966-sq.-ft. area as a huge game room, or divide it into a game room, study, and sewing or craft room.

- **Additional Bedrooms:** Each bedroom has a private bath and good closet space.

Images provided by designer/architect.

Main Level Floor Plan

Copyright by designer/architect.

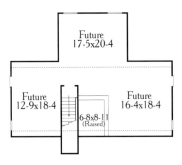

Bonus Area Floor Plan

SMARTtip

Front Porch

A front porch proclaims you to the outside world, so furnish it in a way that expresses what you want the world to know about you. Use the walls of your porch to hang interesting items such as sundials or old shutters. Set a mirror into an old window to reflect a portion of the garden.

Plan #241026

Dimensions: 59'11" W x 50'2" D

Levels: 1

Square Footage: 1,660

Bedrooms: 3

Bathrooms: 2

Foundation: Slab

Materials List Available: No

Price Category: C

Images provided by designer/architect.

59'-11"

50'-2"

Bonus Area

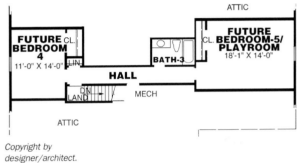

Copyright by designer/architect.

Plan #241028

Dimensions: 56' W x 63' D

Levels: 1

Square Footage: 1,970

Bedrooms: 3

Bathrooms: 2

Foundation: Slab

Materials List Available: No

Price Category: D

Images provided by designer/architect.

Copyright by designer/architect.

56'-0"

63'-0"

Plan #341041

Dimensions: 48' W x 56'8" D
Levels: 1
Square Footage: 1,454
Bedrooms: 3
Bathrooms: 2
Foundation: Crawl space, slab (basement option for fee)
Materials List Available: Yes
Price Category: B

This comfortable, one-story home is perfect for a family who enjoys hosting casual parties at home or simply relaxing there at the end of the day.

Features:

• Porches: Set rocking chairs on both porches, and add a grill on the rear porch for easy cooking.

• Family Room: A cozy fireplace and door to the rear porch are the focal points here.

• Kitchen/Dining Room: You'll love the pantry in this conveniently arranged room, which has plenty of space for a large table and chairs.

• Utility Room: This practical room opens from the garage, too, so you can use it as a mudroom when the weather's bad.

• Master Suite: The large walk-in closet and private bath will make this room a real retreat.

• Additional Bedrooms: Both rooms have huge closets and easy access to a shared bath.

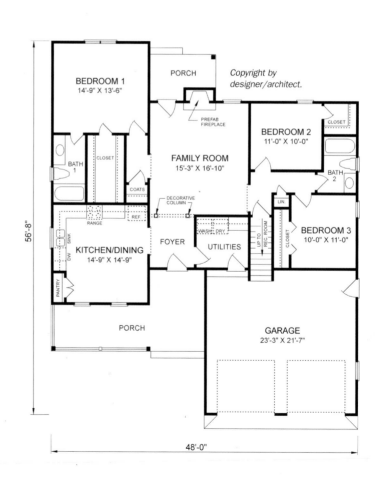

Plan #311030

Dimensions: 76'10" W x 55'6" D
Levels: 1
Square Footage: 2,286
Main Level Sq. Ft.: 2,286
Opt. Bonus Sq. Ft.: 443
Bedrooms: 3
Bathrooms: 2½
Foundation: Basement, crawl space, or slab
Materials List Available: No
Price Category: E

Images provided by designer/architect.

Rear Elevation

Bonus Area Floor Plan

Unfinished Attic space
12-0x20-0

Future Expansion
12-0x30-0
Sloped to 8'

Unfinished Attic Space

If you're looking for a home you can expand in coming years, this gorgeous plan might be the answer to your dreams.

Features:

• Foyer: A 10-ft. ceiling sets the tone for the fabulous spaces in this home.

• Great Room: You'll love the cathedral ceiling, great windows, and fireplace flanked by built-ins.

• Dining Room: Ample dimensions make it easy to create a somewhat formal dining area here.

• Kitchen: The family cook will love the angled work area and ample storage space.

• Breakfast Room: Expansive windows add a note of cheer to this room, which opens to the porch.

• Master Suite: A wall of windows and door to the backyard brighten the sizable bedroom, and the bath features two walk-in closets, two vanities, a garden tub, and a separate shower.

Copyright by designer/architect.

Porch
36-5x8-4
9' ceiling

Master Bedroom
14-0x16-6
9' ceiling

Breakfast
11-6x10-6
9' ceiling

Master Bath
9-1x15-4

Bedroom
13-5x11-6
9' ceiling

Greatroom
20-6x17-6
Cathedral Clg.

Laundry
9-10x9-6
9' ceiling

Kitchen
12-8x15-0
9' ceiling

Bath
9-9x5-2

Bedroom
13-5x11-7
9' ceiling

Foyer
6-7x11-4
10' clg.

Dining
15-9x11-7
9' ceiling

Garage
22-11x23-9
9' ceiling

1/2 Bath

Stor.
3-0x8-9

Porch
40-8x8-2

Plan #241019

Dimensions: 46'6" W x 34'2" D

Levels: 1

Square Footage: 1,397

Bedrooms: 3

Bathrooms: 2

Foundation: Slab

Materials List Available: No

Price Category: B

Images provided by designer/architect.

Plan #341043

Dimensions: 44'7" W x 50' D

Levels: 1

Square Footage: 1,213

Bedrooms: 3

Bathrooms: 2

Foundation: Crawl space, slab (basement option for fee)

Materials List Available: Yes

Price Category: B

Images provided by designer/architect.

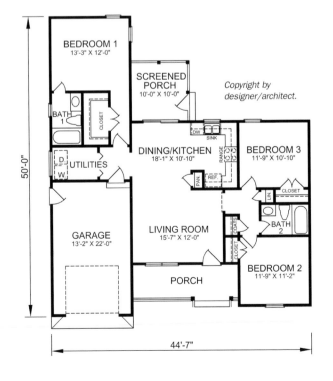

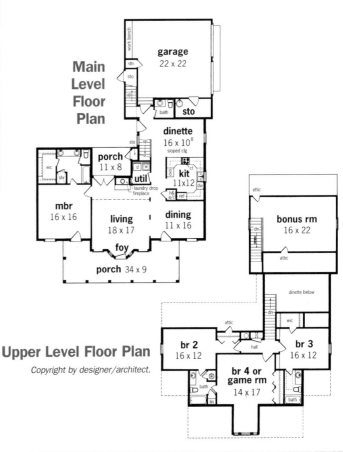

Main Level Floor Plan

garage
22 x 22

work bench

sto

sto

bath

sto

dinette
16 x 10⁸
sloped clg

porch
11 x 8

util

kit
11x12

laundry drop
fireplace

wic

shr

mbr
16 x 16

living
18 x 17

dining
11 x 16

foy

porch 34 x 9

attic

bonus rm
16 x 22

attic

dinette below

attic

wic

br 2
16 x 12

hall

br 3
16 x 12

br 4 or
game rm
14 x 17

bath

lin

bath

Upper Level Floor Plan

Copyright by designer/architect.

*Images provided by
designer/architect.*

Plan #211144

Dimensions: 52' W x 74' D

Levels: 2

Square Footage: 2,542

Main Level Sq. Ft.: 1,510

Upper Level Sq. Ft.: 1,032

Bedrooms: 4

Bathrooms: 3½

Foundation: Basement, crawl space,
or slab

Materials List Available: Yes

Price Category: E

Plan #241015

Dimensions: 67'2" W x 46'10" D

Levels: 1

Square Footage: 1,609

Bedrooms: 3

Bathrooms: 2

Foundation: Slab

Materials List Available: No

Price Category: C

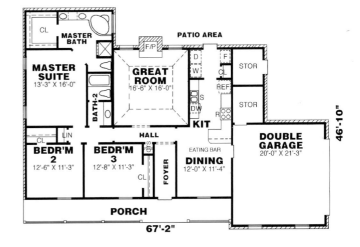

CL

MASTER
BATH

PATIO AREA

F/P

MASTER
SUITE
13'-3" X 16'-0"

BATH-2

GREAT
ROOM
16'-6" X 16'-0"

D
W

F

CL

STOR

REF

STOR

KIT

DOUBLE
GARAGE
20'-0" X 21'-3"

CL

LIN

BEDR'M
2
12'-6" X 11'-3"

BEDR'M
3
12'-8" X 11'-3"

HALL

CL

FOYER

EATING BAR

DINING
12'-0" X 11'-4"

46'-10"

PORCH

67'-2"

*Images provided by
designer/architect.*

Copyright by designer/architect.

Main Level Floor Plan

Upper Level Floor Plan

Copyright by designer/architect.

Images provided by designer/architect.

Plan #151184

Dimensions: 57'4" W x 55'10" D

Levels: 2

Square Footage: 2,755

Main Level Sq. Ft.: 2,084

Upper Level Sq. Ft.: 671

Bedrooms: 4

Bathrooms: 3

Foundation: Crawl space, slab (basement or walk-out basement option for fee)

Materials List Available: Yes

Price Category: F

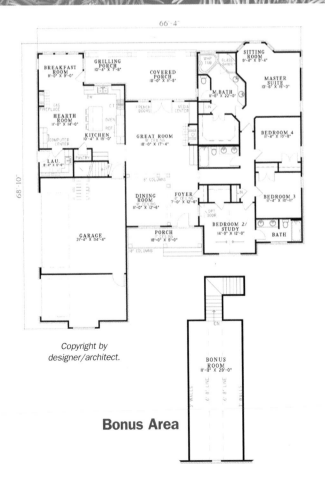

Bonus Area

Copyright by designer/architect.

Images provided by designer/architect.

Plan #151187

Dimensions: 66'4" W x 68'10" D

Levels: 1

Square Footage: 2,405

Main Level Sq. Ft.: 2,405

Bonus Sq. Ft.: 358

Bedrooms: 4

Bathrooms: 3

Foundation: Crawl space, slab (basement or walk-out basement option for fee)

Materials List Available: Yes

Price Category: E

Plan #311022

Dimensions: 73'1" W x 58'6" D

Levels: 1

Square Footage: 2,373

Main Level Sq. Ft.: 2,373

Opt. Bonus Sq. Ft. 1,178

Bedrooms: 3

Bathrooms: 2½

Foundation: Basement, crawl space, or slab

Materials List Available: Yes

Price Category: E

Images provided by designer/architect.

This spacious one-story home offers the option of adding living space in a basement as well as over the garage.

Features:

- Foyer: An 11-ft. ceiling welcomes guests into the spacious, open public rooms.

- Family Room: This lovely room is enhanced by a gorgeous fireplace and extensive window area.

- Dining Room: The dimensions of this room make entertaining here a true delight.

- Kitchen: All the family cooks will love the angled counter area, pantry, and snack bar here.

- Breakfast Room: Place a table by the windows, or step out to the sizable covered porch.

- Master Suite: In a wing by itself, this suite includes a large bedroom with wide window areas and a bath with a walk-in closet for two and a tub, shower, and dual vanity.

Rear Elevation

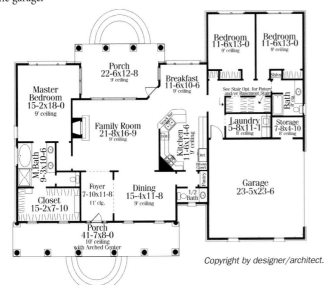

Copyright by designer/architect.

Plan #161067

Dimensions: 58' W x 44'4" D

Levels: 2

Square Footage: 2,160

Main Level Sq. Ft.: 1,541

Upper Level Sq. Ft.: 619

Bedrooms: 3

Bathrooms: 2½

Foundation: Basement

Materials List Available: Yes

Price Category: D

This traditional looking home holds a surprisingly contemporary and luxurious design inside.

Features:

- Great Room: The two-story ceiling, fireplace, and door to the rear porch lure everyone here.

- Dining Room: Just off the foyer, this room can be used formally or casually, as you wish.

- Kitchen: Designed for efficient work patterns, this room has a dining bar for total convenience.

- Breakfast Room: The deep bay lets natural light shine in to cheer your mornings.

- Master Suite: The sloped ceiling adds a luxurious feeling, and the bath has a walk-in closet, garden tub, separate shower, and double vanity.

- Upper Floor: Both bedrooms have large closets and easy access to the bath. The loft space is a special treat, as is the balcony, which is open to the great room below.

Rear Elevation

Main Level Floor Plan

Upper Level Floor Plan

Copyright by designer/architect.

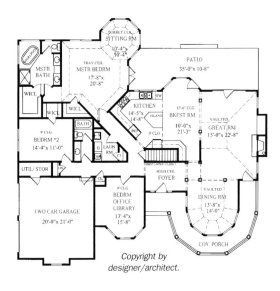

Copyright by designer/architect.

Images provided by designer/architect.

Plan #131052

Dimensions: 67' W x 63'10" D

Levels: 1

Square Footage: 2,171

Bedrooms: 2

Bathrooms: 2

Foundation: Basement, crawl space, or slab (walk-out option for fee)

Materials List Available: Yes

Price Category: D

Rear Elevation

Copyright by designer/architect.

Plan #151169

Dimensions: 51'6" W x 49'10" D

Levels: 1

Square Footage: 1,525

Bedrooms: 3

Bathrooms: 2

Foundation: Basement, daylight basement, crawl space, or slab

Materials List Available: Yes

Price Category: C

Images provided by designer/architect.

Rear Elevation

Plan #131002

Dimensions: 70'1" W x 60'7" D
Levels: 1
Square Footage: 1,709
Bedrooms: 3
Bathrooms: 2½
Foundation: Basement, crawl space, or slab
Materials List Available: Yes
Price Category: D

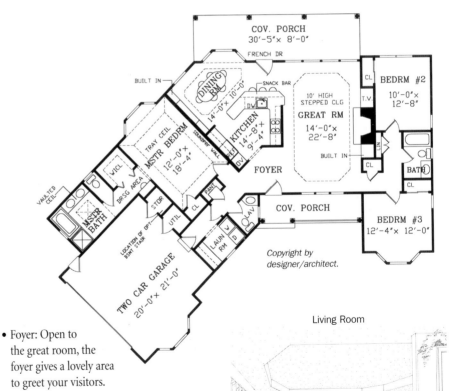

COV. PORCH
30'-5" x 8'-0"

FRENCH DR

BUILT IN

DINING RM
14'-0" x 10'-0"

SNACK BAR

KITCHEN
14'-8" x 9'-4"

10' HIGH STEPPED CLG
GREAT RM
14'-0" x 22'-8"

BEDRM #2
10'-0" x 12'-8"

CL

T.V.

TRAY CEIL
MSTR BEDRM
12'-0" x 18'-4"

FOYER

BUILT IN

CL

BATH

WICL

VAULTED CEIL

DRSG AREA

MSTR BATH

STOR

UTIL

CL

PANT

LAV

COV. PORCH

BEDRM #3
12'-4" x 12'-0"

LOCATION OF OPT'L BSMT STAIR

LAUN RM

CL

TWO CAR GARAGE
20'-0" x 21'-0"

Copyright by designer/architect.

Rear View

You'll love the way this angled ranch brings out the best in a corner lot or on a slope.

Features:

Ceiling Height: 8 ft.

- Front Porch: Hang baskets of plants from the roof of this porch, which is just the right size for a couple of rockers and a side table.

- Dining Room: Well-placed windows flood this room with sunlight during the day and a built-in cabinet gives ample storage space for all your china, linens, and collectables.

- Foyer: Open to the great room, the foyer gives a lovely area to greet your visitors.

- Great Room: A built-in media center surrounds the fireplace where friends and family are sure to gather.

- Master Suite: You'll love the privacy of this somewhat isolated but easily accessed room. Decorate to show off the large bay window and tray ceiling, and enjoy the luxury of a compartmented bathroom.

Living Room

Plan #271025

Dimensions: 62' W x 57' D
Levels: 2
Square Footage: 2,223
Main Level Sq. Ft.: 1,689
Upper Level Sq. Ft.: 534
Bedrooms: 3
Bathrooms: 2½
Foundation: Basement
Materials List Available: Yes
Price Category: E

Images provided by designer/architect.

This traditional home's unique design combines a dynamic, exciting exterior with a fantastic floor plan.

Features:

- **Living Room:** To the left of the column-lined, barrel-vaulted entry, this inviting space features a curved wall and corner windows.

- **Dining Room:** A tray ceiling enhances this formal meal room.

- **Kitchen:** This island-equipped kitchen includes a corner pantry and a built-in desk. Nearby, the sunny breakfast room opens onto a backyard deck via sliding glass doors.

- **Family Room:** A corner bank of windows provides a glassy backdrop for this room's handsome fireplace. Munchies may be served on the snack bar from the breakfast nook.

- **Master Suite:** This main-floor retreat is simply stunning, and includes a vaulted ceiling, access to a private courtyard, and of course, a sumptuous bath with every creature comfort.

Main Level Floor Plan

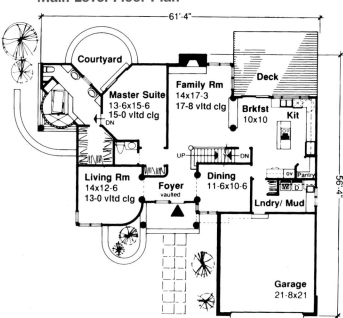

Upper Level Floor Plan

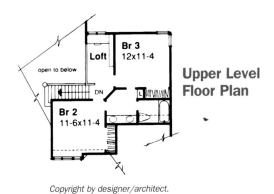

Copyright by designer/architect.

Plan #151177

Dimensions: 47'4" W x 58'8" D
Levels: 2
Square Footage: 2,470
Main Level Sq. Ft.: 1,595
Upper Level Sq. Ft.: 875
Bedrooms: 4
Bathrooms: 2½
Foundation: Crawl space, slab (basement or walk-out basement option for fee)
Materials List Available: Yes
Price Category: E

Designed for a busy family, this lovely home is also perfect for the family that loves to entertain.

Features:

- **Great Room:** You'll love the handsome fireplace and built-in media center in this two-story room that opens to the rear grilling porch.

- **Dining Room:** Use this lovely room for formal dinners or casual family meals.

- **Kitchen:** A huge walk-in pantry, U-shaped work zone, and snack bar will delight the family cook.

- **Breakfast Room:** Natural light pours into this large room that opens to the grilling porch.

- **Master Suite:** A computer room, door to the porch, and expansive windows highlight the bedroom, and the bath includes a huge walk-in closet, whirlpool tub, and double vanity.

- **Upper Floor:** The balcony, computer center, and bonus room add practical features to this home.

Main Level Floor Plan

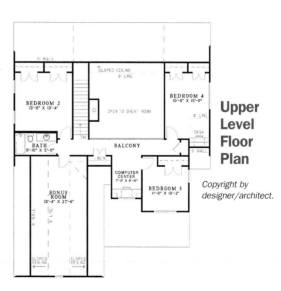

Upper Level Floor Plan

Plan #321055

Dimensions: 70' W x 40' D
Levels: 2
Square Footage: 2,505
Main Level Sq. Ft.: 1,436
Upper Level Sq. Ft.: 1,069
Bedrooms: 3
Bathrooms: 2½
Foundation: Basement
Materials List Available: Yes
Price Category: E

You'll love the many conveniences and amenities inside this gracious, comfortable home.

Features:

- Outdoor spaces: The friendly wraparound porch and rear patio integrate this home with its site.

- Family Room: A fireplace and sloped ceiling give character to this spacious room.

- Living Room: Natural light on two sides cheers this room in every season of the year.

- Dining Room: It's easy to serve in this room because it's adjacent to the kitchen.

- Kitchen: You'll love the walk-in pantry, center cook and dining island, and U-shaped counter.

- Breakfast Room: A pass-through from the kitchen is convenient, and doors here open to the patio.

- Master Suite: Two walk-in closets, a raised tub, and separate shower make this suite a luxury.

Images provided by designer/architect.

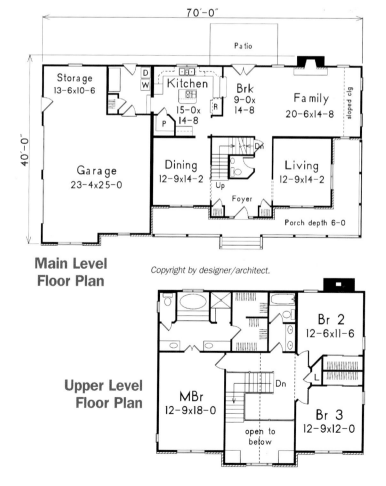

Main Level Floor Plan

Copyright by designer/architect.

Upper Level Floor Plan

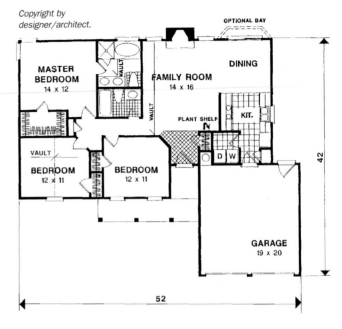

Copyright by designer/architect.

Images provided by designer/architect.

Plan #101023

Dimensions: 52' W x 42' D

Levels: 1

Square Footage: 1,197

Bedrooms: 3

Bathrooms: 2

Foundation: Crawl space, slab

Materials List Available: No

Price Category: B

Images provided by designer/architect.

Plan #241025

Dimensions: 59'9" W x 44'3" D

Levels: 1

Square Footage: 1,487

Bedrooms: 3

Bathrooms: 2

Foundation: Slab

Materials List Available: No

Price Category: B

Copyright by designer/architect.

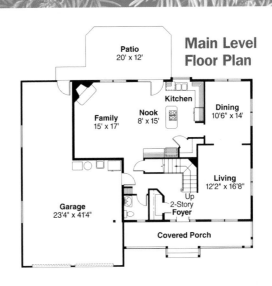

Main Level Floor Plan

Patio 20' x 12'

Family 15' x 17'

Kitchen

Nook 8' x 15'

Dining 10'6" x 14'

Living 12'2" x 16'8"

Garage 23'4" x 41'4"

Up 2-Story Foyer

Covered Porch

Images provided by designer/architect.

Plan #361024

Dimensions: 54' W x 42' D
Levels: 2
Square Footage: 2,296
Main Level Sq. Ft.: 1,186
Upper Level Sq. Ft.: 1,110
Bedrooms: 3
Bathrooms: 2½
Foundation: Crawl space
Materials List Available: No
Price Category: E

Upper Level Floor Plan

Copyright by designer/architect.

Bedroom 12' x 11'

Bedroom 11'8" x 11'

Dn

Master Suite 12'2" x 16'8"

Open to Foyer Below

Utility

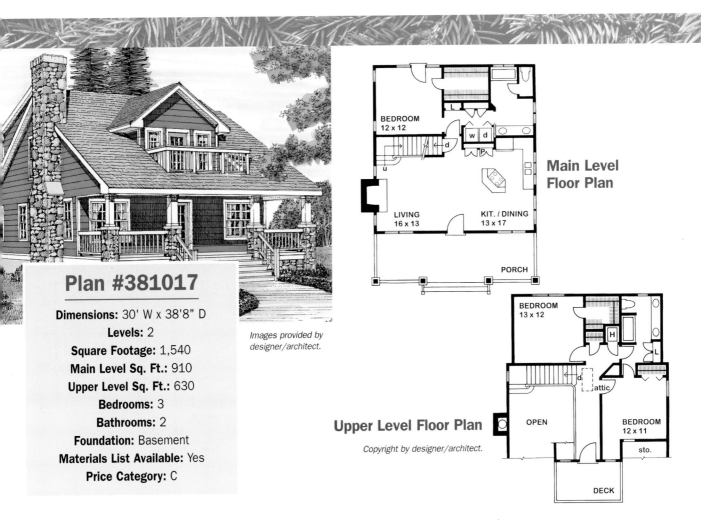

Main Level Floor Plan

BEDROOM 12 x 12

w d

LIVING 16 x 13

KIT. / DINING 13 x 17

PORCH

Plan #381017

Dimensions: 30' W x 38'8" D
Levels: 2
Square Footage: 1,540
Main Level Sq. Ft.: 910
Upper Level Sq. Ft.: 630
Bedrooms: 3
Bathrooms: 2
Foundation: Basement
Materials List Available: Yes
Price Category: C

Images provided by designer/architect.

Upper Level Floor Plan

Copyright by designer/architect.

BEDROOM 13 x 12

H

attic

OPEN

BEDROOM 12 x 11

sto.

DECK

Plan #321052

Dimensions: 57' W x 48'8" D
Levels: 2
Square Footage: 2,182
Main Level Sq. Ft.: 1,112
Upper Level Sq. Ft.: 1,070
Bedrooms: 3
Bathrooms: 3½
Foundation: Basement
Materials List Available: Yes
Price Category: D

The friendly wraparound porch gives a hint of the comfort you'll find in this large, impressive home.

Features:

- Great Room: Create a cozy sitting area near the masonry fireplace so you can watch the children come in and out through the door to the back.

- Dining Room: This spacious room makes a lovely place to entertain, but you'll enjoy it just as much for private family meals.

- Breakfast Room: A deep bay window here creates a frame for your table and chairs.

- Kitchen: This pretty room has an L-shaped counter and a central work and dining island.

- Master Suite: You'll be spoiled by the handsome fireplace, vaulted ceiling, two walk-in closets, and bath with tub, shower, and double vanity.

- Additional Bedrooms: Both have private baths and large closets, and one has a vaulted ceiling.

Main Level Floor Plan

Upper Level Floor Plan

Copyright by designer/architect.

Plan #321050

Dimensions: 49' W x 42' D
Levels: 2
Square Footage: 2,336
Main Level Sq. Ft.: 1,291
Upper Level Sq. Ft.: 1,045
Bedrooms: 4
Bathrooms: 2½
Foundation: Basement
Materials List Available: Yes
Price Category: E

Images provided by designer/architect.

This traditional-looking home has an interior filled with up-to-date design elements and amenities.

Features:

- Family Room: The spacious family room is lit by a wall of windows punctuated by a handsome fireplace.

- Living Room: The vaulted ceiling emphasizes the sunken floor in this spacious room.

- Dining Room: Convenient to the kitchen, this room is also isolated enough for formal parties.

- Kitchen: The L-shaped work area and center island make this room an efficient work space.

- Breakfast Room: You'll find a doorway to the backyard in the bayed area of this friendly, comfortable room.

- Master Suite: The bedroom has a vaulted ceiling and two walk-in closets, and the bath has a tub, two vanities, and a separate shower.

Main Level Floor Plan

Upper Level Floor Plan

Copyright by designer/architect.

Plan #321060

Dimensions: 36' W x 46'8" D
Levels: 2
Square Footage: 1,575
Main Level Sq. Ft.: 802
Upper Level Sq. Ft.: 773
Bedrooms: 3
Bathrooms: 2½
Foundation: Basement
Materials List Available: Yes
Price Category: C

Images provided by designer/architect.

This stylish home is designed for a narrow lot but can complement any setting.

Features:

- **Living Room:** A masonry fireplace and large window area are the focal points in this spacious room.

- **Dining Room:** Open to the living room, the dining room has a large bay window that lets you enjoy the scenery as you dine.

- **Breakfast Room:** A bay window here lets morning sunlight help you greet the day.

- **Kitchen:** The center island gives extra work space as well as a snack bar. The adjacent laundry room and built-in pantry add to the convenience you'll find here.

- **Master Suite:** A vaulted ceiling and large walk-in closet make this room a treat, and the bath features a double vanity, tub, and separate shower.

Main Level Floor Plan

36'-0"

46'-8"

Brkfst
Kit 10-0x11-0
9-0x11-7
D W P

Dining
12-0x11-0

Living
15-7x14-4

Dn
Up

Garage
19-4x20-4

Upper Level Floor Plan

MBr
12-0x14-8
vaulted clg

Br 2
12-0x11-0

Dn

Br 3
12-0x11-3
vaulted clg

plant shelf

Copyright by designer/architect.

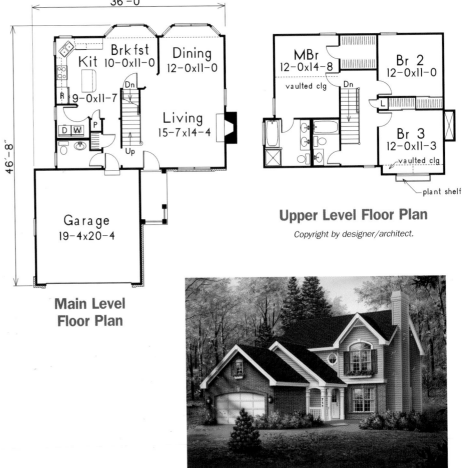

Images provided by designer/architect.

Plan #271074

Dimensions: 68' W x 86' D
Levels: 1
Square Footage: 2,400
Bedrooms: 4
Bathrooms: 3
Foundation: Crawl space or slab
Materials List Available: No
Price Category: E

Perfect for families with aging relatives or boomerang children, this home includes a completely separate suite at the rear.

Features:

- **Living Room:** A corner fireplace casts a friendly glow over this gathering space.
- **Kitchen:** This efficient space offers a serving bar that extends toward the eating nook

and the formal dining room.

- **Master Suite:** A cathedral ceiling presides over this deluxe suite, which boasts a whirlpool tub, dual-sink vanity, and walk-in closet.
- **In-law Suite:** This separate wing has its own vaulted living room, plus a kitchen, a dining room, and a bedroom suite.

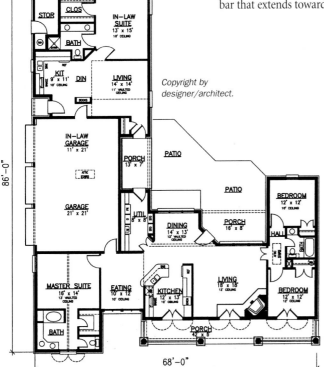

Copyright by designer/architect.

SMARTtip

Adding Professional Flair to Window Treatments

You can give your window treatment designs a professional look by using decorator tricks to customize readymades or dress your own home-sewn designs. These could include contrast linings, tassels, cording, ribbons, or couture trimmings such as buttons, coins, or bows applied to edges. Another trick is to sew a fine wire into the hem of curtains or valances to create a pliable edge that you can shape yourself. Small weights that you can sew into the hem of drapery panels or jabots will make them hang better. For more inspiration look at fashion magazines and visit showrooms.

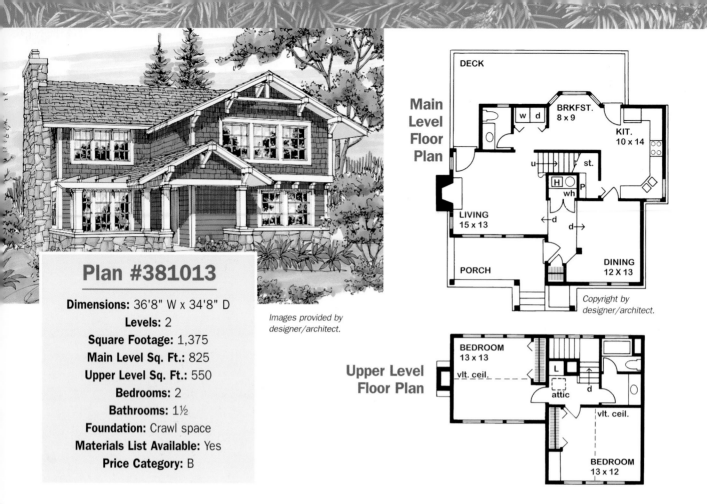

Plan #381013

Dimensions: 36'8" W x 34'8" D
Levels: 2
Square Footage: 1,375
Main Level Sq. Ft.: 825
Upper Level Sq. Ft.: 550
Bedrooms: 2
Bathrooms: 1½
Foundation: Crawl space
Materials List Available: Yes
Price Category: B

Images provided by designer/architect.

Copyright by designer/architect.

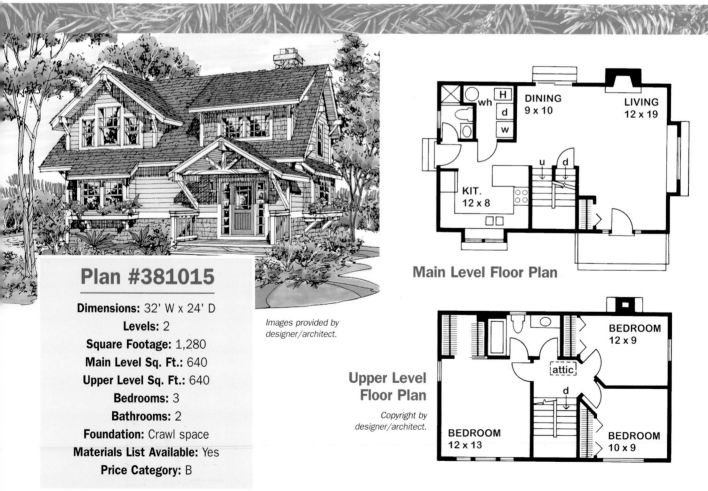

Plan #381015

Dimensions: 32' W x 24' D
Levels: 2
Square Footage: 1,280
Main Level Sq. Ft.: 640
Upper Level Sq. Ft.: 640
Bedrooms: 3
Bathrooms: 2
Foundation: Crawl space
Materials List Available: Yes
Price Category: B

Images provided by designer/architect.

Copyright by designer/architect.

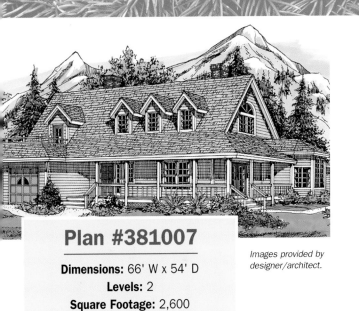

Main Level Floor Plan

Images provided by designer/architect.

Plan #381007

Dimensions: 66' W x 54' D
Levels: 2
Square Footage: 2,600
Main Level Sq. Ft.: 1,700
Upper Level Sq. Ft.: 900
Bedrooms: 4
Bathrooms: 2½
Foundation: Crawl space
Materials List Available: Yes
Price Category: F

Upper Level Floor Plan
Copyright by designer/architect.

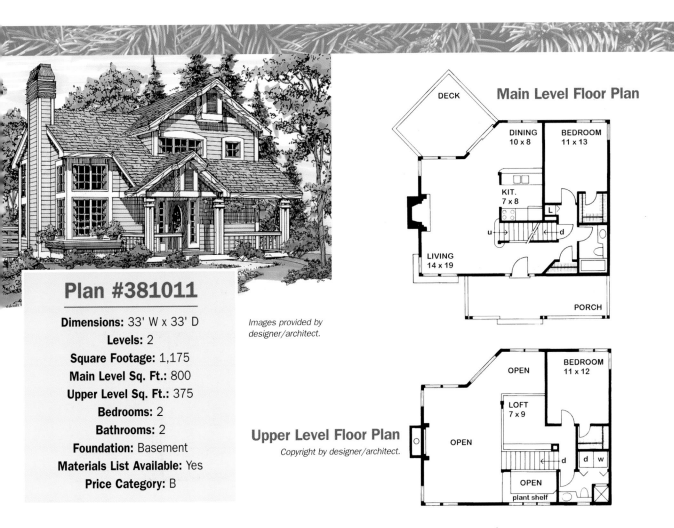

Plan #381011

Dimensions: 33' W x 33' D
Levels: 2
Square Footage: 1,175
Main Level Sq. Ft.: 800
Upper Level Sq. Ft.: 375
Bedrooms: 2
Bathrooms: 2
Foundation: Basement
Materials List Available: Yes
Price Category: B

Images provided by designer/architect.

Main Level Floor Plan

Upper Level Floor Plan
Copyright by designer/architect.

Plan #261010

Dimensions: 61' W x 38'4" D

Levels: 2

Square Footage: 2,724

Main Level Sq. Ft.: 1,450

Upper Level Sq. Ft.: 1,274

Bedrooms: 3

Bathrooms: 2½

Foundation: Basement

Materials List Available: No

Price Category: F

The minute you see this lovely house with its corner turret, you'll know you've found the home of your dreams.

Features:

- **Great Room:** A vaulted ceiling and fireplace make this room a natural gathering spot.
- **Office:** Built-in shelves and a window seat are luxurious touches in this practical room.
- **Kitchen:** A work island and ample counter and cabinet space make this kitchen a cook's delight.
- **Dinette:** Two skylights give this rear-facing room extra light in every season of the year.
- **Master Suite:** Located on the first floor for privacy, this bedroom is endlessly versatile. French doors open to this room, and the master bath has twin sinks, a whirlpool tub, a walk-in shower, and a huge walk-in closet.

Optional Floor Plan for Master Suite

Main Level Floor Plan

Upper Level Floor Plan

Plan #261004

Dimensions: 82' W x 48'8" D
Levels: 2
Square Footage: 2,707
Main Level Sq. Ft.: 1,484
Upper Level Sq. Ft.: 1,223
Bedrooms: 3
Bathrooms: 2½
Foundation: Basement
Materials List Available: No
Price Category: F

Inside the classic Victorian exterior is a spacious home filled with contemporary amenities that the whole family is sure to love.

Features:

- Porch: This wraparound porch provides space for entertaining or sitting out to enjoy the evening.

- Foyer: Two stories high, the foyer opens to the formal dining room and front parlor.

- Family Room: French doors open from the parlor into this room, with its cozy fireplace.

- Sunroom: A cathedral ceiling adds drama to this versatile room.

- Kitchen: A pantry and a work island make this well-planned kitchen even more convenient.

- Master Suite: A tray ceiling and French doors to the bath give the bedroom elegance, while the sumptuous bath features a deluxe tub, walk-in shower, and split vanities.

Images provided by designer/architect.

Main Level Floor Plan

Copyright by designer/architect.

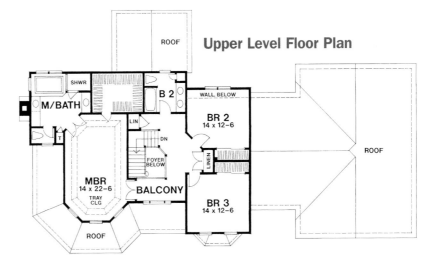

Upper Level Floor Plan

Plan #131030

Dimensions: 51' W x 41'10" D
Levels: 2
Square Footage: 2,470
Main Level Sq. Ft.: 1,290
Upper Level Sq. Ft.: 1,180
Bedrooms: 4
Bathrooms: 2½
Foundation: Crawl space, slab, basement, or walk-out basement
Materials List Available: Yes
Price Category: F

Master Bedroom

Master Bathroom

Entry

If high ceilings and spacious rooms make you happy, you'll love this gorgeous home.

Features:

- **Family Room:** An 18-ft. vaulted ceiling that's open to the balcony above, a corner fireplace, and a wall of windows make this room feel special.

- **Dining Room:** This formal room, which flows into the living room, also opens to the front porch and optional backyard deck.

- **Kitchen:** A bright breakfast room joins with this kitchen and opens to the backyard deck.

- **Master Suite:** You'll smile when you see the 11-ft. vaulted ceiling, stunning arched window, and two walk-in closets in the bedroom. A skylight lets natural light into the private bath, with its spa tub, separate shower, and dual-sink vanity.

- **Bedrooms:** To reach these three charming bedrooms, you'll admire the view into the family room below as you walk along the balcony hall.

Main Level Floor Plan

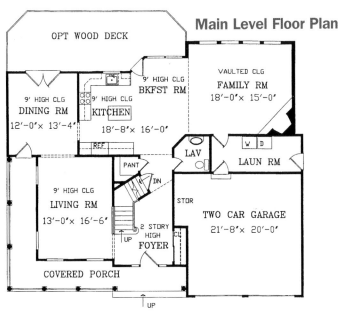

OPT WOOD DECK

9' HIGH CLG
DINING RM
12'-0" x 13'-4"

9' HIGH CLG
KITCHEN
18'-8" x 16'-0"

BKFST RM

VAULTED CLG
FAMILY RM
18'-0" x 15'-0"

REF

PANT

9' HIGH CLG
LIVING RM
13'-0" x 16'-6"

LAV

DN

UP

2 STORY
HIGH
FOYER

W D
LAUN RM

STOR

TWO CAR GARAGE
21'-8" x 20'-0"

COVERED PORCH

UP

Upper Level Floor Plan

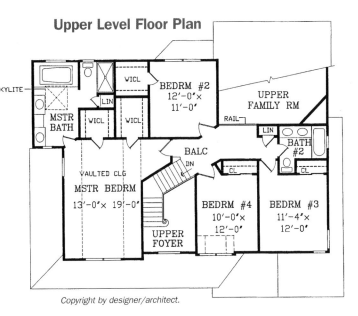

SKYLITE

MSTR
BATH

WICL

LIN

WICL

WICL

BEDRM #2
12'-0" x
11'-0"

UPPER
FAMILY RM

RAIL

LIN

BATH
#2

VAULTED CLG
MSTR BEDRM
13'-0" x 19'-0"

BALC

DN

CL

CL

UPPER
FOYER

BEDRM #4
10'-0" x
12'-0"

BEDRM #3
11'-4" x
12'-0"

Copyright by designer/architect.

Kitchen/Breakfast Area

Dining Room

Living Room

Kitchen/Breakfast Area

Planning Your Landscape

Landscapes change over the years. As plants grow, the overall look evolves from sparse to lush. Trees cast cool shade where the sun used to shine. Shrubs and hedges grow tall and dense enough to provide privacy. Perennials and ground covers spread to form colorful patches of foliage and flowers. Meanwhile, paths, arbors, fences, and other structures gain the patina of age.

Constant change over the years—sometimes rapid and dramatic, sometimes slow and subtle—is one of the joys of landscaping. It is also one of the challenges. Anticipating how fast plants will grow and how big they will eventually get is difficult, even for professional designers.

To illustrate the kinds of changes to expect in a planting, these pages show a landscape design at three different "ages." Even though a new planting may look sparse at first, it will soon fill in. And because of careful spacing, the planting will look as good in 10 to 15 years as it does after 3 to 5. It will, of course, look different, but that's part of the fun.

At Planting

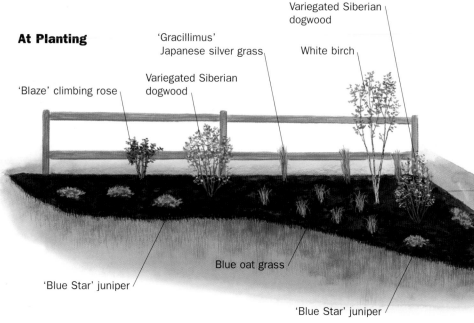

'Blaze' climbing rose

Variegated Siberian dogwood

'Gracillimus' Japanese silver grass

Variegated Siberian dogwood

White birch

'Blue Star' juniper

Blue oat grass

'Blue Star' juniper

Three to Five Years

At Planting—Here's how the corner might appear in early summer immediately after planting. The white birch tree is only 5 to 6 ft. tall, with trunks no thicker than broomsticks. The variegated Siberian dogwoods each have a few main stems about 3 to 4 ft. tall. The 'Blaze' rose has just short stubs where the nursery cut back the old stems, but it will grow fast and may bloom the first year. The 'Blue Star' junipers are low mounds about 6 to 10 in. wide. The blue oat grass forms small, thin clumps of sparse foliage. The 'Gracillimus' Japanese silver grass may still be dormant, or it may have a short tuft of new foliage. Both grasses will grow vigorously the first year.

Three to Five Years—The birch tree has grown 1 to 2 ft. taller every year but is still quite slender. Near the base, it's starting to show the white bark typical of maturity. The variegated Siberian dogwoods are well established now. If you cut them to the ground every year or two in spring, they grow back 4 to 6 ft. tall by midsummer, with strong, straight stems. The 'Blaze' rose covers the fence, and you need to prune out a few of its older stems every spring. The slow-growing 'Blue Star' junipers make a series of low mounds; you still see them as individuals, not a continuous patch. The grasses have reached maturity and form lush, robust clumps. It would be a good idea to divide and replant them now, to keep them vigorous.

Ten to Fifteen Years—The birch tree is becoming a fine specimen, 20 to 30 ft. tall, with gleaming white bark on its trunks. Prune away the lower limbs up to 6 to 8 ft. above ground to expose its trunks and to keep it from crowding and shading the other plants. The variegated dogwoods and 'Blaze' rose continue to thrive and respond well to regular pruning. The 'Blue Star' junipers have finally merged into a continuous mass of glossy foliage. The blue oat grass and Japanese silver grass will still look good if they have been divided and replanted over the years. If you get tired of the grasses, you could replace them with cinnamon fern and astilbe, as shown here, or other perennials or shrubs.

Ten to Fifteen Years

Cinnamon fern

Astilbe

A Warm Welcome
Make a Pleasant Passage to Your Front Door

Why wait until a visitor reaches the front door to extend a cordial greeting? Have your landscape offer a friendly welcome and a helpful "Please come this way." Well-chosen plants and a revamped walkway not only make a visitor's short journey a pleasant one, but they can also enhance your home's most public face.

This simple arrangement of plants and paving produces an elegant entrance that deftly mixes formal and informal elements.

A wide walk of neatly fitted flagstones and a rectangular bed of roses have the feel of a small formal courtyard, complete with a pair of "standard" roses in planters, each displaying a mound of flowers atop a single stem. Clumps of ornamental grass rise from the paving like leafy fountains.

Gently curving beds of low-growing evergreens and shrub roses edge the flagstones, softening the formality and providing a comfortable transition to the lawn.

Morning glories and clematis climb simple trellises to brighten the walls of the house.

Flowers in pink, white, purple, and violet are abundant from early summer until frost. They are set off by the rich green foliage of the junipers and roses and the gray leaves of the catmint edging.

Add a bench, as shown here, so you can linger and enjoy the scene; in later years, the lovely star magnolia behind it will provide comfortable dappled shade.

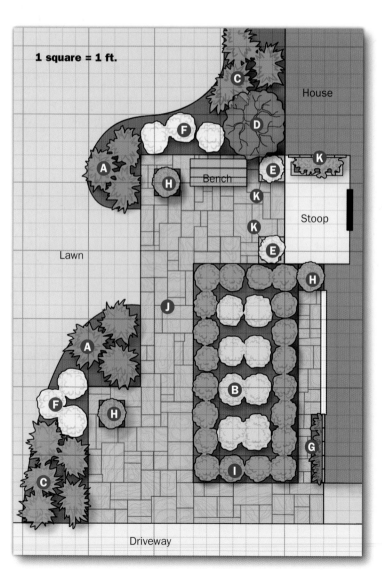

1 square = 1 ft.

House

Bench

Stoop

Lawn

Driveway

Plants and Projects

Once established, these shrubs and perennials require little care beyond deadheading and an annual pruning. Ask the nursery where you buy the standard roses for advice on how to protect the plants in winter.

A 'Blue Star' juniper *Juniperus squamata* (use 6 plants)
The sparkly blue foliage of this low-growing evergreen shrub neatly edges the opening onto the lawn.

B 'Bonica' rose *Rosa* (use 8)
This deciduous shrub blooms from June until frost, producing clusters of double, soft pink flowers.

C Dwarf creeping juniper *Juniperis procumbens* 'Nana' (use 8)
This low, spreading evergreen with prickly green foliage makes a tough, handsome ground cover.

D Star magnolia *Magnolia stellata* (use 1)
This small, multitrunked deciduous tree graces the entry with lightly scented white flowers in early spring.

E 'The Fairy' rose *Rosa* (use 2)
Clusters of small, double, pale pink roses appear in abundance from early summer to frost. Buy plants

trained as standards at a nursery. Underplant with impatiens.

F 'White Meidiland' rose *Rosa* (use 6)
A low, spreading shrub, it is covered with clusters of lovely single white flowers all summer.

G Jackman clematis *Clematis* x *Jackmanii* (use 2)
Trained to a simple lattice, this deciduous vine produces large, showy, dark purple flowers for weeks in summer.

H 'Gracillimus' Japanese silver grass *Miscanthus* (use 3)
The arching leaves of this perennial grass are topped by fluffy seed heads from late summer through winter.

I 'Six Hills Giant' catmint *Nepeta* x *faassenii* (use 20)
A perennial with violet-blue flowers and aromatic gray-green foliage edges the roses.

J Flagstone paving
Rectangular flagstones in random sizes.

K Planters
Simple wooden boxes contain blue-flowered annual morning glories (on the stoop, trained to a wooden lattice) and standard roses (in front of the stoop).

K Morning glories in planter

H 'Gracillimus' Japanese silver grass

E 'The Fairy' rose

D Star magnolia

C Dwarf creeping juniper

H 'Gracillimus' Japanese silver grass

A 'Blue Star' juniper

F 'White Meidiland' rose

C Dwarf creeping juniper

H 'Gracillimus' Japanese silver grass

J Flagstone paving

I 'Six Hills Giant' catmint

B 'Bonica' rose

G Jackman clematis on lattice support

Site: Sunny

Season: Summer

Concept: Easy-care plantings and flagstone paving make an attractive entryway to the house.

Note: All plants are appropriate for USDA Hardiness Zones 4, 5, and 6.

A Step Up
Plant a Foundation Garden

'Techny' American **C** arborvitae

Germander **H**

'Blue Star' juniper **D**

'Sarah Bernhardt' **F** peony

Rare is the home without foundation plantings. These simple skirtings of greenery hide unattractive concrete block underpinnings and help overcome the impression that the house is hovering a few feet above the ground. Useful as these plantings are, they are too often just monochromatic expanses of clipped yews, dull as dishwater. But, as this design shows, a durable, low-maintenance foundation planting can be more varied, more colorful, and more fun.

Broad-leaved and coniferous evergreen shrubs anchor this planting and provide four-season cover for the foundation. But they also offer contrasting shapes and textures and a range of colors from icy blue through a variety of greens to maroon.

What makes this design special is the smaller plants fronting the foundation shrubs. Including perenni-als, grasses, and low shrubs in the mix expands the foundation planting into a small front-yard garden. From spring until frost, flowers in white, pink, magenta, and mauve stand out against the blue-and-green backdrop. When the last flower fades in autumn, the evergreen foliage takes center stage, serving through the winter as a welcome reminder that the world will green up again.

Plants and Projects

Eye-catching as the flowers in this planting are, the foliage is the key to its success in every season. The evergreens are attractive year-round. And each of the perennials has been chosen as much for its foliage as for its flowers. A thorough cleanup and maintenance pruning spring and fall will keep the planting looking its best.

A **'Wichita Blue' juniper** *Juniperus scopulorum* (use 1 plant)
This slow-growing, upright evergreen shrub has a neat pyramidal form and lovely silver-blue foliage and blue berries to add year-round color at the corner of the house.

B **'PJM' rhododendron**
Rhododendron (use 5)
An informal row of these hardy evergreen shrubs beautifully conceals the foundation. Vivid magenta flowers in early spring, small dark green leaves that turn maroon in winter, all on a compact plant.

C **'Techny' American arborvitae**
Thuja occidentalis (use 1)
This cone-shaped, slow-growing evergreen fills the corner near the front steps with fragrant, rich green, fine-textured foliage.

D **'Blue Star' juniper** *Juniperus squamata* (use 3)
The sparkly blue foliage and irregular mounded form of this low-growing evergreen shrub look great next to the peony and germander.

E **'Sea Urchin' blue fescue grass**
Festuca ovina var. *glauca* (use 3)
The very fine blue leaves of this perennial grass contrast handsomely with the dark green rhododendrons behind. Flower spikes rise above the neat, soft-looking mounds in early summer.

F **'Sarah Bernhardt' peony**
Paeonia (use 3)
A sentimental favorite, this perennial offers fragrant pink double flowers in early summer. Forms a multistemmed clump with attractive foliage that will look nice next to the steps through the summer.

G **White astilbe** *Astilbe* (use 3)
The lacy dark green foliage and fluffy white flower plumes of this tough perennial stand out against the blue foliage of its neighbors. Flowers in June or July.

H **Germander** *Teucrium chamaedrys* (use 1)
This rugged little shrub forms a tidy mound of small, dark, shiny evergreen leaves next to the walk. Mauve flowers bloom in late summer.

I **'Sheffield' chrysanthemum**
Dendranthema × *grandiflorum* (use 1)
A longtime regional favorite, this hardy perennial forms a broad mound of fragrant gray-green foliage. Small, clear pink, daisylike blossoms cover the plant from September until frost.

I 'Sheffield' chrysanthemum

E 'Sea Urchin' blue fescue grass

B 'PJM' rhododendron

G White astilbe

A 'Wichita Blue' juniper

Note: All plants are appropriate for USDA Hardiness Zones 4, 5, and 6.

Site: Sunny

Season: Fall

Concept: A mixture of easy-care perennials and shrubs provides a colorful setting for a home's public face.

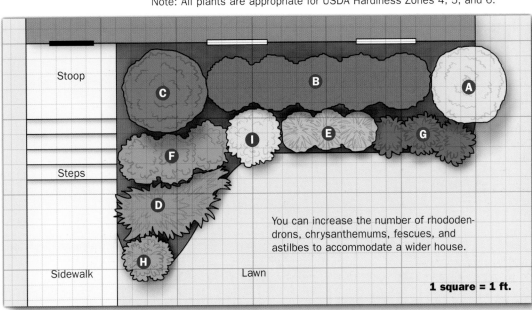

You can increase the number of rhododendrons, chrysanthemums, fescues, and astilbes to accommodate a wider house.

1 square = 1 ft.

Up Front and Formal

Greet Visitors with Classic Symmetry

Formal gardens have a special appeal. Their simple geometry can be soothing in a hectic world, and the look is timeless, never going out of style. The front yard of a classical house, like the one shown here, invites a formal makeover. (A house with a symmetrical facade in any style has similar potential.)

In this design, a paved courtyard and a planting of handsome trees, shrubs, and ground covers have transformed a site typically given over to lawn and a cement walkway. The result is a more dramatic entry, but also one where you can happily linger with guests on a fine day.

Tall hedges on the borders of the design and the centrally placed redbud provide a modicum of privacy in this otherwise public space. Lower hedges along the sidewalk and front of the driveway allow a view of the street and make these approaches more welcoming.

A matched pair of viburnums make a lovely setting for the front door. To each side, layered groups of shrubs give depth and interest to the house's facade. From spring through fall, the planting's flowers and foliage make the courtyard a comfortable spot, and there is ample evergreen foliage to keep up appearances in winter. Completing the scene is an ornamental focal point and a bench for enjoying the results of your landscaping labors.

Site: Sunny

Season: Early summer

Concept: Wide paving, hedges, trees, and shrubs create an appealing entry courtyard.

'Janet Blair' **F**
rhododendron

Japanese holly **C**

Dwarf **G**
creeping juniper

D 'Crimson Pygmy'
Japanese barberry

Plants and Projects

Spring is the season for flowers in this planting, with redbud, rhododendron, and candytuft blossoms in shades of pink and white. The colorful leaves and berries of viburnum, redbud, and barberry brighten the fall. While the hedge plants are dependable and problem-free, you'll need to shear them at least once a year to maintain the formal shapes.

A **Redbud** *Cercis canadensis*
(use 1 plant)
Small pink flowers line the branches of this deciduous tree in early spring before the foliage appears. The heart-shaped leaves emerge reddish, mature to a lustrous green, and turn gold in fall. Bare branches form an attractive silhouette in winter, especially as the tree ages.

Note: All plants are appropriate for USDA Hardiness Zones 4, 5, and 6.

Plan labels: House, Stoop, Lawn, Driveway, Sidewalk, 1 square = 1 ft.

E Dwarf double-file viburnum

H Evergreen candytuft

C Japanese holly

K Bench

See site plan for **J**.

B Pachysandra

D 'Crimson Pygmy' Japanese barberry

A Redbud

I Pavers

B **Pachysandra** *Pachysandra terminalis* (use 250)
Hardy, adaptable evergreen ground cover that will spread in the shade of the redbud, forming an attractive, weed-smothering, glossy green carpet.

C **Japanese holly** *Euonymus alatus* 'Compactus' (use 19)
Choose an upright cultivar of this evergreen shrub to form a hedge of dark green leaves. In Zones 4 and 5 substitute the hardier compact burning bush, *Euonymus alatus* 'Compactus.'

D **'Crimson Pygmy' Japanese barberry** *Berberis thunbergii* (use 34)
This rugged deciduous shrub puts on a colorful show, with small maroon leaves that turn red in fall when they're joined by bright red berries. A small rounded plant, it can be sheared, as shown here, or pruned lightly into an informal low hedge.

E **Dwarf double-file viburnum** *Viburnum*

plicatum var. *tomentosum* (use 2)
A pair of these deciduous shrubs make an elegant frame for the door. Tiers of horizontal branches are smothered with small clusters of pure white flowers from May through fall. Large, crinkled leaves are medium green.

F **'Janet Blair' rhododendron** *Rhododendron* (use 6)
The wonderful evergreen foliage and light pink flowers of this compact shrub anchor the planting at the corners of the house. Blooms in late spring. 'Mist Maiden' and 'Anna Hall' rhododendrons are good substitutes.

G **Dwarf creeping juniper** *Juniperus procumbens* 'Nana' (use 10)
Layered sprays of this evergreen shrub's prickly bright green foliage lay like thick rugs on the edge of the lawn. A lovely contrast to the dark green rhododendrons behind. For extra color in spring, plant handfuls of crocuses, snowdrops, or

grape hyacinths next to the junipers.

H **Evergreen candytuft** *Iberis sempervirens* (use 12)
An evergreen perennial ground cover, it forms a low, sprawling mound of glossy foliage next to the viburnums. Bears small white flowers for weeks in the spring.

I **Pavers**
The courtyard is surfaced with 2-ft.-square precast pavers. Use two complementary colors to create patterns, if you choose. Substitute flagstones or bricks if they would look better with your house.

J **Ornament**
An ornament centered in the courtyard paving provides a focal point. Choose a sculpture, sundial, reflecting ball, birdbath, or large potted plant to suit your taste.

K **Bench**
Enjoy the courtyard garden from a comfortable bench in a style that complements the garden and the house.

Angle of Repose

Make a Back-Door Garden for a Sheltered Niche

Many homes offer the opportunity to tuck a garden into a protected corner. In the front yard, such spots are ideal for an entry garden or a landscaping display that showcases your house when viewed from the sidewalk or the street. If the planting is in the backyard, like the site shown here, it can be more intimate, part of a comfortable outdoor room you can enjoy from a nearby patio or window.

The curved bed wraps around the small patio, increasingly shaded by the neighboring crab apple as the years pass. The planting has been designed with spring especially in mind, so we're showing that season here. Dozens of bulbs light up the corner in April and May, assisted by several early-blooming trees and shrubs. Flowers in white, pink, yellow, purple, and blue carpet the ground

or twinkle on bare branches above. Several impart a delicious scent to the fresh spring air.

Early flowers aren't the only pleasures of spring in the garden. Watch buds fatten and burst into leaf on the deciduous trees and shrubs, and mark the progress of the season as new, succulent shoots of summer perennials emerge.

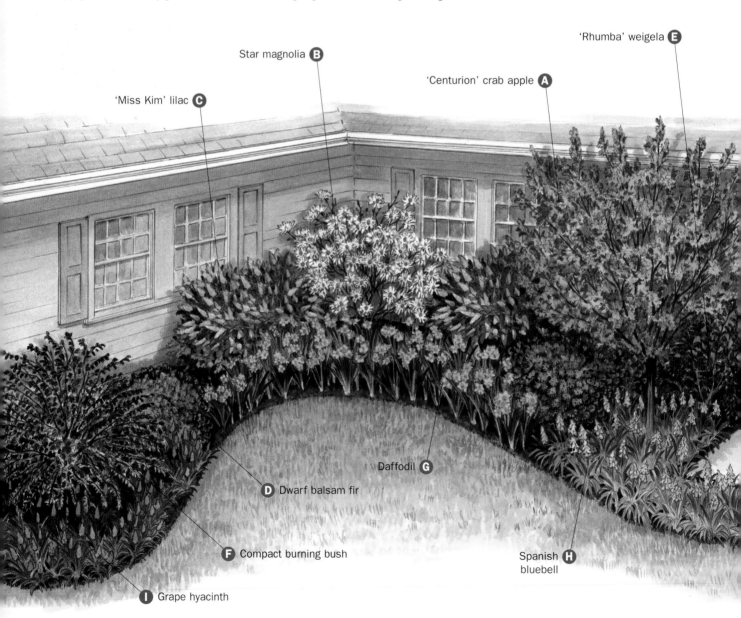

'Rhumba' weigela **E**

Star magnolia **B**

'Centurion' crab apple **A**

'Miss Kim' lilac **C**

Daffodil **G**

D Dwarf balsam fir

F Compact burning bush

Spanish **H**
bluebell

I Grape hyacinth

Note: All plants are appropriate for USDA Hardiness Zones 4, 5, and 6.

Plants and Projects

Once established, these plants require little maintenance. The shrubs won't overgrow nearby windows, and the trees will need little pruning. Every few years you will have to divide the bulbs.

A **'Centurion' crab apple**
Malus (use 1 plant)
A small deciduous tree with cheerful rosy pink flowers in May, attractive summer foliage, and glossy little fruits that last into winter. Will broaden to shade the terrace as it ages.

B **Star magnolia** *Magnolia stellata* (use 1)
This small, rounded, multi-trunked deciduous tree won't outgrow the corner. Delightful white flowers bloom in early spring, before leaves appear.

C **'Miss Kim' lilac** *Syringa patula* (use 2)
This well-behaved, compact deciduous shrub has clusters of purple flowers in May. Open nearby windows to enjoy their wonderful scent.

D **Dwarf balsam fir** *Abies balsamea* 'Nana' (use 1)
Lustrous dark green needles and a compact rounded form make this low-growing evergreen shrub an ideal companion for the taller deciduous shrubs and a good backdrop for spring bulbs.

E **'Rhumba' weigela** *Weigela florida* (use 1)
With dark red flowers in summer and dark green-and-purple leaves, this compact deciduous shrub is eye-catching throughout the growing season.

F **Compact burning bush** *Euonymus alatus* 'Compacta' (use 1)
This deciduous shrub lights up the end of the planting with its dependable fall color: the dark green leaves turn pale copper and then bright crimson red.

G **Daffodil** *Narcissus* (use 35)
One of the cheeriest spring sights is the butter yellow trumpets of this prince of flowering bulbs. To keep the flowers coming each year, you must let the foliage die down naturally, but the daylilies will hide it as they grow.

H **Spanish bluebell** *Endymion hispanica* (use 24)
Dangling above attractive grassy foliage, the pretty blue bell-like flowers of this spring bulb dapple the ground beneath the crab apple. When its foliage gets ragged, you can pull or trim it.

I **Grape hyacinth** *Muscari armeniacum* (use 35 or more)
These little bulbs will spread happily beneath the burning bush, making a carpet of grassy foliage topped with fragrant dark blue-purple flowers arranged in grapelike clusters.

J **Planter**
Extend springtime color onto the patio with Darwin tulips and pansies in the large planter next to the door. Plant tulip bulbs in fall; replace them every few years. Add a few dozen pansy plants in early spring.

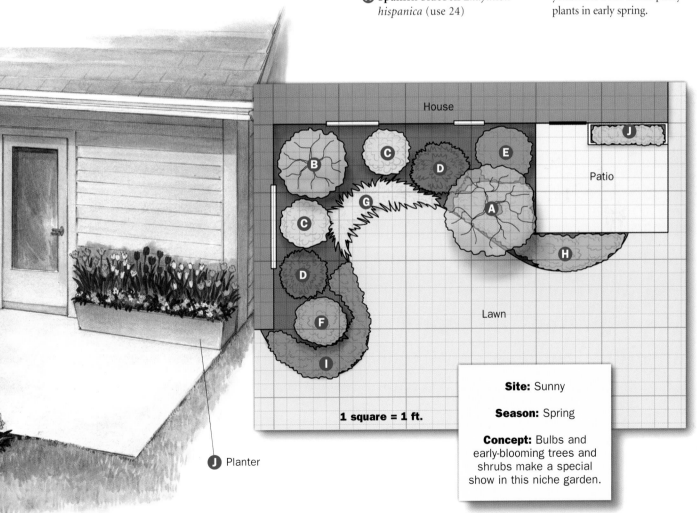

House

Patio

Lawn

1 square = 1 ft.

J Planter

Site: Sunny

Season: Spring

Concept: Bulbs and early-blooming trees and shrubs make a special show in this niche garden.

A Neighborly Corner
Beautify a Boundary with Easy-Care Plants

The corner where your property meets your neighbor's and the sidewalk can be a kind of grassy no-man's-land. This design defines the boundary with a planting that can be enjoyed by the property owners as well as by people passing by.

Because of its exposed location, remote from the house and close to the street, this is a less personal planting than those in other more private parts of your property.

It is meant to be appreciated from a distance. Anchored by a multitrunked birch tree, attractive grasses and shrubs are arrayed in large masses at several heights. An existing split-rail fence on the property line now serves as a scaffold for a rose trained around its rails. While not intended as a barrier, the planting also provides a modest physical and psychological screen from activity on the street.

Site: Sunny

Season: Summer

Concept: Enhance the property line with a low-care, neighbor-friendly planting of trees and shrubs.

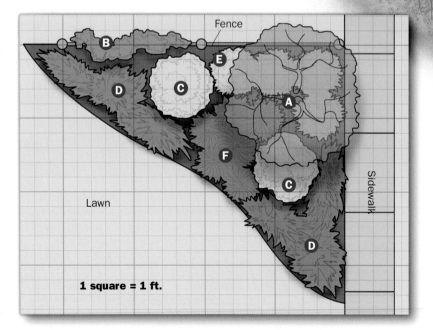

Variegated Siberian **C** dogwood

'Blaze' **B** climbing rose

'Blue Star' juniper **D**

Plants and Projects

These plants all have a four-season presence, including the grasses, whose foliage stands up as well as many shrubs to the rigors of winter. Good gardens make good neighbors, so we've used well-behaved plants that won't make extra work for the person next door—or for you. The rose will need training throughout the summer, there will be some birch leaves to rake in fall, and the grasses must be trimmed back in late winter or early spring.

A **White birch** *Betula platyphylla* 'White Spire' (use 1 plant)

Fence

B

E

D

C

A

F

C

D

Lawn

Sidewalk

1 square = 1 ft.

Note: All plants are appropriate for USDA Hardiness Zones 4, 5, and 6.

124   order direct: 1-800-523-6789

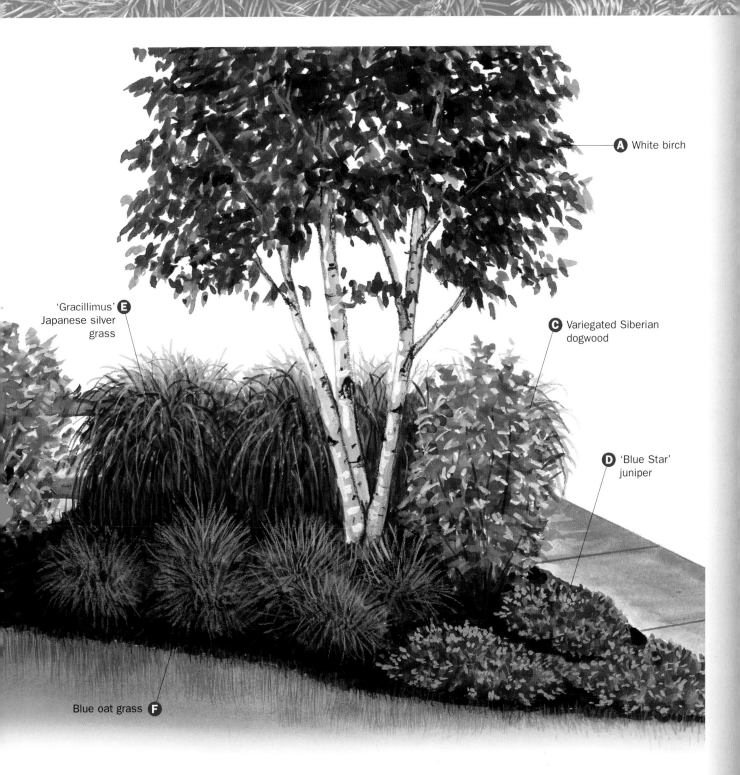

A White birch

E 'Gracillimus' Japanese silver grass

C Variegated Siberian dogwood

D 'Blue Star' juniper

Blue oat grass **F**

A deciduous tree grown for its graceful upright form and striking white bark. Green leaves dance in the summer breezes and turn a pretty yellow in fall. Buy a multi-trunked specimen, and keep the lower limbs pruned so it won't cast too much shade on the shrubs and grasses underneath.

B **'Blaze' climbing rose** *Rosa* (use 1)
This vigorous climbing rose has long flexible canes that can be trained horizontally. Tied to or wrapped around the rails, they'll cover the fence quickly. Bears lots of red semidouble flowers in June; blooms off and on until frost. The flowers are only mildly fragrant.

C **Variegated Siberian dogwood** *Cornus alba* 'Elegantissima' (use 2)
A deciduous shrub with eye-catching features year-round: white flowers in spring, white-and-green leaves in summer, and pale blue berries in fall. In winter, dark red stems provide a lovely contrast to the blue foliage of the juniper.

D **'Blue Star' juniper** *Juniperus squamata* (use 6)
This evergreen shrub forms an irregular sparkling blue mass. It grows slowly and never needs pruning. An excellent ground cover, it is a nice counterpoint to the flowing grasses.

E **'Gracillimus' Japanese silver grass** *Miscanthus* (use 4)
This perennial grass is always beautiful, but never more so than in fall and winter, when silvery plumes of tiny seeds wave above an arching clump of tan foliage. Earlier, the narrow leaves are green striped with white.

F **Blue oat grass** *Helictotrichon sempervirens* (use 6)
Less than half as tall as the silver grass, this perennial is just as lovely. Dense compact mounds bristle with wiry blue leaves, which often live through the winter. Thin stalks carry slender seed heads that turn tan in winter.

Streetwise and Stylish

Give Your Curbside Strip a New Look

Homeowners seldom think much about the area that runs between the sidewalk and street. At best it is a tidy patch of lawn; at worst, a weed-choked eyesore. But it is one of the most public parts of your property. The colorful planting shown here and a weekend's work can transform the area, warmly welcoming visitors and adding a touch of beauty to your yard and the entire neighborhood.

A handsome cobblestone path splits the planting, allowing visitors who park on the street easy access to the sidewalk. On each side lie plants tough enough to stand up to life on the street, where masses of concrete keep things hot in summer and snow and road salt can make winter brutal.

Attractive evergreen shrubs form the backbone of the design, surrounded by perennials chosen for their bold, long-blooming flowers or striking foliage. All of these plants are short, and the overall effect is like laying a bright carpet at the foot of your property.

Curbside strips are often city-owned, so check local ordinances for restrictions before you begin to dig. It is easy to extend the planting to fill a larger space by repeating plants shown here or adding other tough, low-growing favorites.

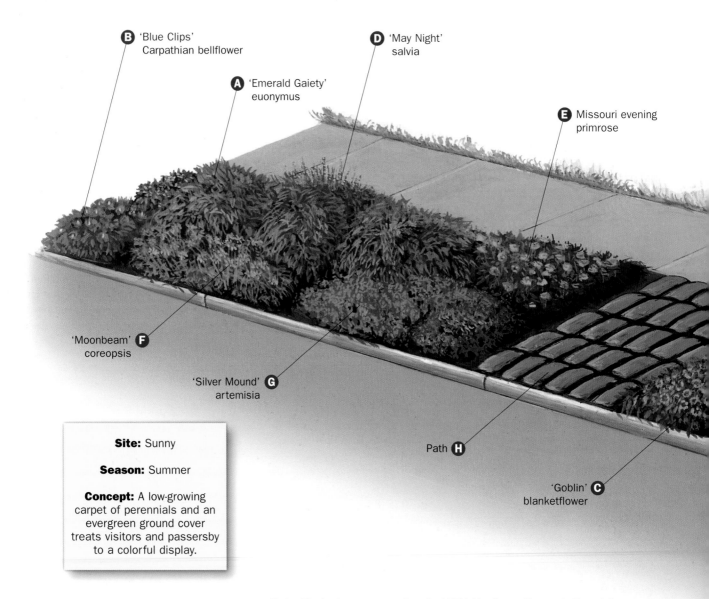

B 'Blue Clips' Carpathian bellflower

A 'Emerald Gaiety' euonymus

D 'May Night' salvia

E Missouri evening primrose

F 'Moonbeam' coreopsis

G 'Silver Mound' artemisia

H Path

C 'Goblin' blanketflower

Site: Sunny

Season: Summer

Concept: A low-growing carpet of perennials and an evergreen ground cover treats visitors and passersby to a colorful display.

Note: All plants are appropriate for USDA Hardiness Zones 4, 5, and 6.

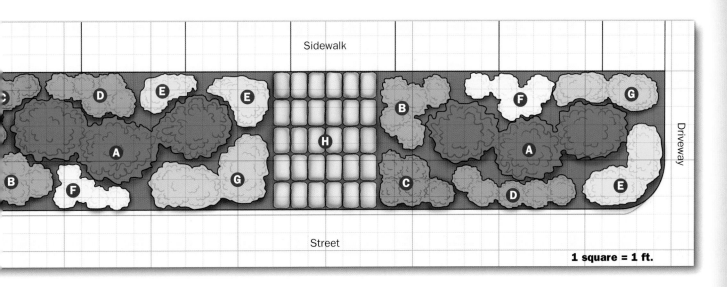

Sidewalk

Street

Driveway

1 square = 1 ft.

Plants and Projects

Mound the soil in the beds so the center is about a foot higher than the edges. The euonymus cascades down this little hill, providing a backdrop for the flowering plants at its feet. Use a layer of bark mulch to conserve soil moisture, inhibit weeds, and make the bed look neat in this highly visible location. Cut all the perennials to the ground in early spring and rake or renew the mulch at the same time.

A **'Emerald Gaiety' euonymus** *Euonymus fortunei* (use 6 plants) A small evergreen shrub with trailing stems that won't be harmed by a heavy load of snow. The small leathery leaves are dark green edged with white and frequently turn pinkish purple in winter.

B **'Blue Clips' Carpathian bellflower** *Campanula carpatica* (use 10) Small spreading mounds of delicate glossy green leaves look pretty beneath this perennial's summer-long display of blue cuplike flowers.

C **'Goblin' blanketflower** *Gaillardia* x *grandiflora* (use 10) The cheerful red-and-yellow daisylike flowers of this native perennial keep coming from June until frost, and it thrives in the heat radiating from the pavement.

D **'May Night' salvia** *Salvia* x *superba* (use 10) These dark indigo-purple flower spikes rise like exclamation points between brightly colored blanketflowers and cup-shaped primroses. This hardy perennial blooms from late spring to frost if spent flowers are clipped.

E **Missouri evening primrose** *Oenothera missouriensis* (use 4)

This perennial spreads a mat of glossy deep green leaves that is covered with large, glowing yellow flowers from mid- to late summer.

F **'Moonbeam' coreopsis** *Coreopsis verticillata* (use 10) Clouds of tiny lemon yellow flowers float above this perennial's dark green foliage from July into September.

G **'Silver Mound' artemisia** *Artemisia schmidtiana* (use 4) The mounded soft silvery foliage of this perennial contrasts with and sets off the foliage and flowers of nearby plants.

H **Path** A combination landing and path, it is wide enough to accommodate open car doors and disembarking visitors. The surface shown here is precast pavers made to resemble cobblestones.

B 'Blue Clips' Carpathian bellflower

F 'Moonbeam' coreopsis

A 'Emerald Gaiety' euonymus

G 'Silver Mound' artemisia

E Missouri evening primrose

D 'May Night' salvia

Landscaping a Low Wall
Two-Tier Garden Replaces a Short Slope

Some things may not love a wall, but plants and gardeners do. For plants, walls offer warmth for an early start in spring and good drainage for roots. Gardeners appreciate the rich visual potential of composing a garden on two levels, as well as the practical advantage of working on two relatively flat surfaces instead of a single sloping one. If you have a wall, or have a place to put one, grasp the opportunity for some handsome landscaping.

This design places two complementary perennial borders above and below a wall bounded at one end by a set of stairs. While each bed is narrow enough for easy maintenance, when viewed from the lower level they combine to form a border almost 8 ft. deep, with plants rising to eye level. The planting can be easily extended on both sides of the steps.

Building the wall that makes this impressive sight possible doesn't require the time or skill it once did. Nor is it necessary to scour the countryside for tons of fieldstone or to hire an expensive contractor. Thanks to precast retaining-wall systems, a knee-high do-it-yourself wall can be installed in as little as a weekend. More experienced or ambitious wall builders may want to tackle a natural stone wall, but anyone with a healthy back (or access to energetic teenagers) can succeed with a prefabricated system.

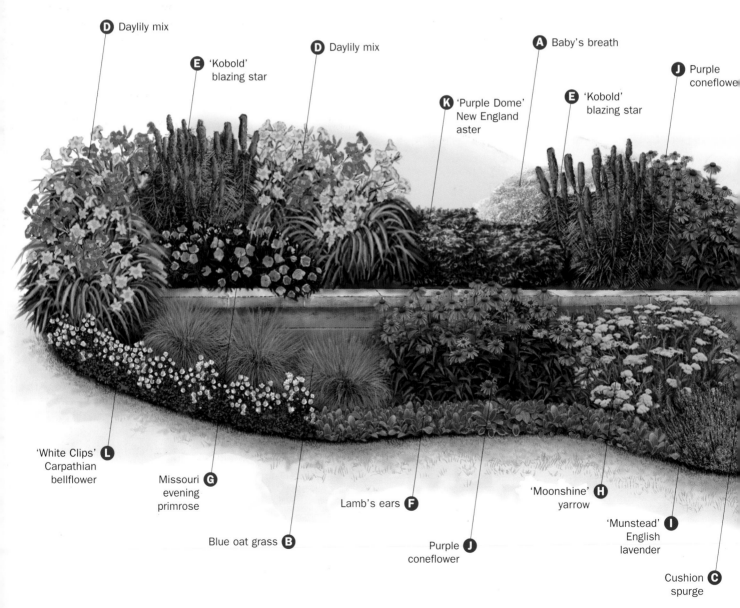

D Daylily mix

E 'Kobold' blazing star

D Daylily mix

A Baby's breath

J Purple coneflower

K 'Purple Dome' New England aster

E 'Kobold' blazing star

'White Clips' **L** Carpathian bellflower

Missouri **G** evening primrose

Lamb's ears **F**

'Moonshine' **H** yarrow

'Munstead' **I** English lavender

Blue oat grass **B**

Purple **J** coneflower

Cushion **C** spurge

Plants and Projects

These plants provide color from spring until frost with little care from you. All are perennials or grasses that need minimal maintenance beyond clipping of spent blooms and a fall or spring clean-up. Several offer excellent flowers for cutting or drying.

A Baby's breath *Gypsophila paniculata* (use 3 plants)
This popular perennial produces a cloud of tiny white flowers in June and July that add an airy texture to the garden and are excellent for cutting. A good foil to the stronger colors and textures of the adjacent plants.

B Blue oat grass *Helictotrichon sempervirens* (use 3)
A carefree grass, it forms a neat, dense clump of thin blue leaves that maintain their color through winter.

C Cushion spurge *Euphorbia polychroma* (use 1)
The electric-yellow spring color of this showy perennial is produced by long-lasting flower bracts, not petals, so it serves as a garden focal point for weeks. Its mound of foliage neatly fills the corner by the steps and turns red in fall.

D Daylily mix *Hemerocallis* (use 6)
For an extended show of lovely lilylike flowers, combine early- and late-blooming cultivars in a selection of your favorite colors. The grassy foliage of this perennial covers the end of the wall.

E 'Kobold' blazing star *Liatris spicata* (use 6)
Magenta flower spikes of this durable perennial rise from a clump of dark green foliage from late July through August. A good mate for its prairie companion, purple cone-flower. Flowers are great for cutting and drying, and butterflies love them.

F Lamb's ears *Stachys byzantina* (use 6)
The large soft leaves of this spreading perennial ground cover are a season-long presence; their silvery color is a nice foil to the blues and yellows nearby. Bears small purple flowers in early summer.

G Missouri evening primrose *Oenothera missouriensis* (use 6)
Large, glowing yellow flowers cover the glossy foliage of this low spreading perennial, which will cascade over the wall. Blooms from late June through August.

H 'Moonshine' yarrow *Achillea* (use 3)
This perennial's flat heads of lemon yellow flowers light up the center of the garden much of the summer. Grayish foliage is fragrant, surprisingly tough despite its lacy looks. Flowers are good for drying.

I 'Munstead' English lavender *Lavandula angustifolia* (use 3)
The gray foliage of this classic bushy herb seems to deepen the greens nearby. Bears a profusion of fragrant pale lavender flower spikes in July, a pretty combination with the yellow yarrow and primroses.

J Purple coneflower *Echinacea purpurea* (use 6)
In July and August, stiff stalks carrying large daisylike pink flowers with dark brown cone-shaped centers rise above this native perennial's basal clump of rich green leaves. Leave some flower stalks standing for winter interest and to provide seeds for songbirds.

K 'Purple Dome' New England aster *Aster novaeangliae* (use 2)
This native perennial makes a mound of foliage and is covered with purple flowers in the fall, when the garden needs a shot of color.

L 'White Clips' Carpathian bellflower *Campanula carpatica* (use 6)
A hardy little perennial with tufts of glossy green leaves and white cuplike flowers that stand out beside the blue oat grass from July until frost.

M Wall and steps
This wall and steps are built from a readily available prefabricated wall system. It is 15 ft. long and 24 in. high. Select a system to match the colors and style of your home.

N Walkway
This is built from flagstone dressed to random rectangular sizes. Precast concrete pavers or gravel would also go well with a prefabricated wall.

> **Site:** Sunny
>
> **Season:** Summer
>
> **Concept:** Low retaining wall creates easy-to-maintain beds for a distinctive two-level planting.

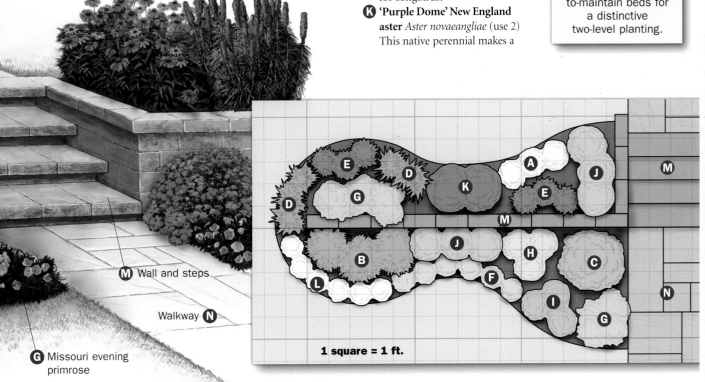

M Wall and steps

Walkway N

G Missouri evening primrose

1 square = 1 ft.

Note: All plants are appropriate for USDA Hardiness Zones 4, 5, and 6.

Plan #151010

Dimensions: 38'4" W x 68'6" D

Levels: 1

Square Footage: 1,379

Bedrooms: 3

Bathrooms: 2

Foundation: Crawl, slab

Materials List Available: Yes

Price Category: B

This French Country home has a spacious great room for friends and family to gather, but you can sneak away to the covered rear porch or patio off the master suite for cozy tête-à-têtes.

Features:

- Entry: Take advantage of the marvelous 10-ft. ceilings to hang groups of potted flowering plants.

- Great Room: This spacious room, with an optional 10-ft. boxed ceiling, is the place to curl up by the gas fireplace on a cold winter night.

- Kitchen: The kitchen includes a bar for casual meals, and is open to the breakfast room.

- Rear Porch: Enjoy leisurely meals on the covered rear porch that you can access from both the master suite and the breakfast room.

- Master Suite: The 10-ft. boxed ceiling in the bedroom and the master bath with a whirlpool tub and separate shower make this suite a luxurious place to end a long day.

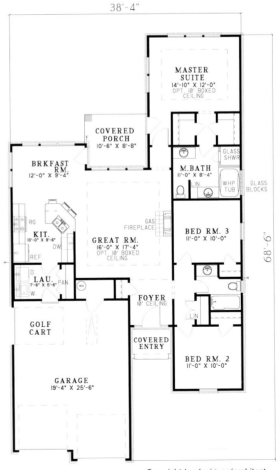

Plan #151004

Dimensions: 64'8" W x 62'1" D
Levels: 1
Square Footage: 2,158
Bedrooms: 4
Bathrooms: 2½
Foundation: Basement, slab, crawl space
Materials List Available: Yes
Price Category: D

Images provided by designer/architect.

You'll love the spacious feeling in this comfortable home designed for a family.

Features:

- Foyer: A 10-ft. ceiling greets you in this home.

- Great Room: A 10-ft. ceiling complements this large room, with its fireplace, built-in cabinets, and easy access to the rear covered porch.

- Dining Room: The 9-ft. boxed ceiling in this large room helps to create a beautiful formal feeling.

- Kitchen: The island in this kitchen is open to the breakfast room for true convenience.

- Breakfast Room: Morning light will stream through the bay window here.

- Master Suite: A 9-ft. pan ceiling adds a distinctive note to this room with access to the rear porch. In the bath, you'll find a whirlpool tub, separate shower, double vanities, and two walk-in closets.

Copyright by designer/architect.

Plan #201034

Dimensions: 66'10" W x 46'10" D
Levels: 1
Square Footage: 1,660
Bedrooms: 3
Bathrooms: 2
Foundation: Crawl space, slab
Materials List Available: Yes
Price Category: C

Images provided by designer/architect.

This warm and inviting traditional country-style home, which features a delightful front porch that's perfect for relaxing on warm evenings, is a great choice for a growing family.

Features:

• Ceiling Height: 9 ft.

• Den: From the covered front porch, guests proceed through an entry foyer to this spacious den, which features a vaulted ceiling, built-in bookshelves and cabinets, and a handsome fireplace.

• Kitchen: This kitchen which is designed for convenience and easy work patterns, features abundant counter space, a breakfast bar, a large eating area, and access to the covered rear patio.

• Master Bedroom: Separated for privacy, this master bedroom features a whirlpool tub, separate shower, and large closet.

• Garage: The two-bay attached garage features a large storage room and has immediate access to the utility room.

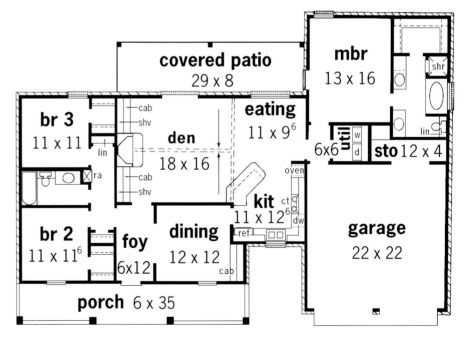

Copyright by designer/architect.

Plan #261008

Dimensions: 68' W x 64'6" D
Levels: 2
Square Footage: 2,226
Main Level Sq. Ft.: 1,689
Upper Level Sq. Ft.: 537
Bedrooms: 4
Bathrooms: 3
Foundation: Basement
Materials List Available: No
Price Category: E

Images provided by designer/architect.

You'll love the elements that transform this design into an amenity-filled home.

Features:

- Great Room: The upper-story balcony looking onto the foyer in the front and this great room in the rear adds elegance, while the high ceilings add to the spacious feeling.

- Sunroom: Adjoining the dining room and kitchen, this room is ideal for an indoor garden, extra dining area, or sitting space.

- Kitchen: This well-designed kitchen is open to the main living spaces and features a breakfast bar, walk-in pantry, and double sink in the corner.

- Master Suite: Privacy is assured in this suite. The double vanities, huge walk-in closet, whirlpool tub, and walk-in shower are luxurious touches.

- Garage: The angled design of this front entrance garage is as attractive as it is practical. You'll find space for two cars and a workshop here.

Main Level Floor Plan

Copyright by designer/architect.

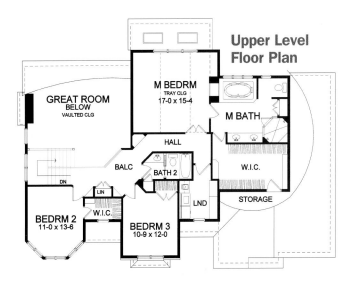

Upper Level Floor Plan

Plan #201103

Dimensions: 57'10" W x 56'10" D
Levels: 2
Square Footage: 2,490
Main Level Sq. Ft.: 1,911
Upper Level Sq. Ft.: 579
Bedrooms: 4
Bathrooms: 3
Foundation: Crawl space, slab
Materials List Available: Yes
Price Category: E

Thoughtful details are built into every corner of this grand yet comfortable home.

Features:

- Den: A fireplace and built-in shelves grace this room, which looks out to the large rear porch.

- Dining Room: Columns define this spacious room, which is open to the roomy den and two-story foyer.

- Kitchen: A U-shaped work area, island cooktop, and handy snack bar will delight the family cook.

- Eating Nook: The deep bay lights this room and makes the perfect spot for a table and chairs.

- Master Suite: A decorative ceiling highlights the bedroom, and a walk-in closet, bath with tub, a shower, and dual vanity add luxury to this suite.

- Additional Bedrooms: Dormer spaces make wonderful hideaways in these rooms with adjacent walk-in closets, private vanities, and a shared bath.

Images provided by designer/architect.

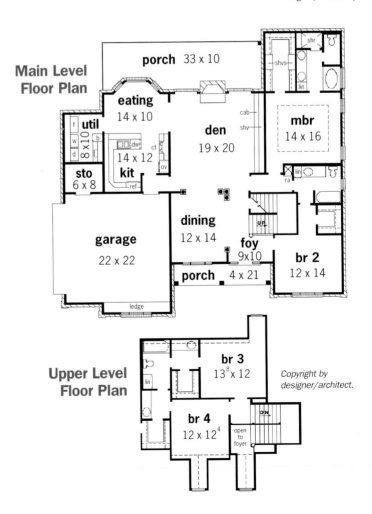

Main Level Floor Plan

Upper Level Floor Plan

Copyright by designer/architect.

Images provided by designer/architect.

Plan #321035

Dimensions: 55'8" W x 46' D
Levels: 1
Square Footage: 1,384
Bedrooms: 2
Bathrooms: 2
Foundation: Basement
Materials List Available: Yes
Price Category: B

You'll love the way the two-story atrium windows meld this home with your sloped site.

Features:

- **Great Room:** A masonry fireplace, vaulted ceiling, huge bayed area, and stairs to the atrium below make this room a natural gathering spot.

- **Dining Area:** You'll love sitting here and admiring the view by sunlight or starlight.

- **Kitchen:** An angled bar is both a snack bar and work space in this well-designed kitchen with an attached laundry room.

- **Master Suite:** Double doors open into the spacious bedroom with a huge walk-in closet. The bath has a garden tub, separate shower, and double vanity.

- **Optional Basement Plan:** Take advantage of this space to build a family room, media room, or home studio that's lit by the huge atrium windows and opens to the patio.

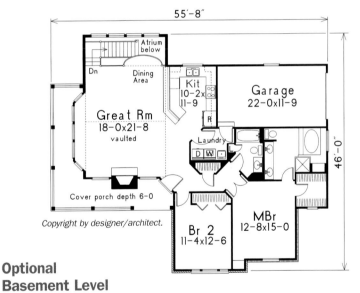

Copyright by designer/architect.

**Optional
Basement Level
Floor Plan**

Rear View

Plan #381003

Dimensions: 63' W x 38'8" D

Levels: 2

Square Footage: 1,925

Main Level Sq. Ft.: 1,000

Upper Level Sq. Ft.: 925

Bedrooms: 3

Bathrooms: 2½

Foundation: Basement, crawl space

Materials List Available: Yes

Price Category: D

Images provided by designer/architect.

Main Level Floor Plan

Upper Level Floor Plan

Copyright by designer/architect.

Plan #381004

Dimensions: 44' W x 48' D

Levels: 2

Square Footage: 1,860

Main Level Sq. Ft.: 1,155

Upper Level Sq. Ft.: 705

Bedrooms: 3

Bathrooms: 2½

Foundation: Basement

Materials List Available: Yes

Price Category: D

Images provided by designer/architect.

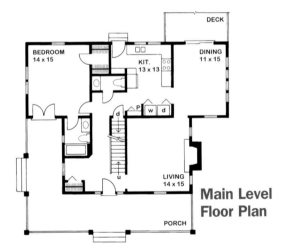

Main Level Floor Plan

Copyright by designer/architect.

Upper Level Floor Plan

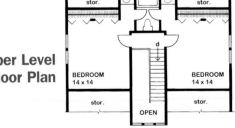

Upper Level Floor Plan

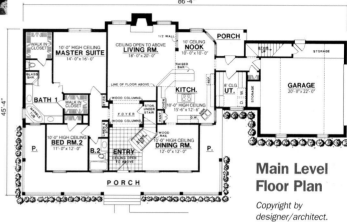

Images provided by designer/architect.

Main Level Floor Plan

Copyright by designer/architect.

Plan #371008

Dimensions: 86'4" W x 45'4" D

Levels: 2

Square Footage: 2,656

Main Level Sq. Ft: 1,969

Upper Level Sq. Ft.: 687

Bedrooms: 4

Bathrooms: 3

Foundation: Slab
(crawl space option for fee)

Materials List Available: No

Price Category: F

Plan #381002

Dimensions: 68'4" W x 42'4" D

Levels: 2

Square Footage: 2,225

Main Level Sq. Ft.: 1,125

Upper Level Sq. Ft.: 1,100

Bedrooms: 3

Bathrooms: 2½

Foundation: Basement, crawl space

Materials List Available: Yes

Price Category: E

Images provided by designer/architect.

Main Level Floor Plan

Upper Level Floor Plan

Copyright by designer/architect.

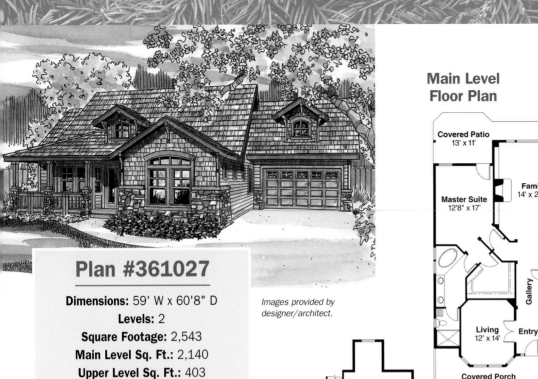

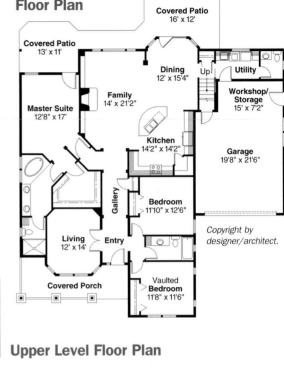

Main Level Floor Plan

Covered Patio
16' x 12'

Covered Patio
13' x 11'

Master Suite
12'8" x 17'

Dining
12' x 15'4"

Family
14' x 21'2"

Up

Utility

Workshop/ Storage
15' x 7'2"

Kitchen
14'2" x 14'2"

Garage
19'8" x 21'6"

Gallery

Bedroom
11'10" x 12'6"

Living
12' x 14'

Entry

Vaulted Bedroom
11'8" x 11'6"

Covered Porch

Images provided by designer/architect.

Copyright by designer/architect.

Plan #361027

Dimensions: 59' W x 60'8" D
Levels: 2
Square Footage: 2,543
Main Level Sq. Ft.: 2,140
Upper Level Sq. Ft.: 403
Bedrooms: 3
Bathrooms: 2 full, 2 half
Foundation: Crawl space
Materials List Available: No
Price Category: E

Bonus Room
15' x 16'

Dn

Upper Level Floor Plan

Plan #371006

Dimensions: 49'9" W x 48'6" D
Levels: 1
Square Footage: 1,374
Bedrooms: 3
Bathrooms: 2
Foundation: Slab
(crawl space option for fee)
Materials List Available: No
Price Category: B

Images provided by designer/architect.

49'-9"

48'-6"

W.I.C.

B.1

W.I.C.

SHR.

NOOK
9'-0" x 10'-0"

PORCH

BED RM.2
11'-0" X 9'-6"

MASTER SUITE
16'-0" x 11'-0"

KIT.
9' x 10'

LIVING RM.
12'-0" x 15'-0"

LIN.

B.2

W/H

SHLVS.

DINING
10'-0" x 12'-0"

ENT

BED RM.3
11'-0" X 9'-6"

STORAGE

UTIL

PANT.

PORCH

GARAGE
20'-0" x 20'-0"

Copyright by designer/architect.

Plan #341040

Dimensions: 74'6" W x 50'6" D

Levels: 2

Square Footage: 2,624

Main Level Sq. Ft.: 1,800

Upper Level Sq. Ft.: 824

Bedrooms: 3

Bathrooms: 2½

Foundation: Crawl space, slab (basement option for fee)

Materials List Available: Yes

Price Category: F

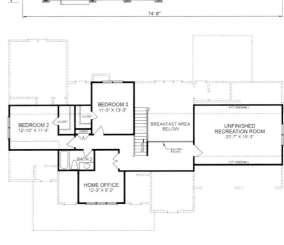

Images provided by designer/architect.

Copyright by designer/architect.

Plan #361025

Dimensions: 48' W x 52' D

Levels: 2

Square Footage: 1,904

Main Level Sq. Ft.: 1,430

Upper Level Sq. Ft.: 474

Bedrooms: 3

Bathrooms: 2½

Foundation: Crawl space

Materials List Available: No

Price Category: D

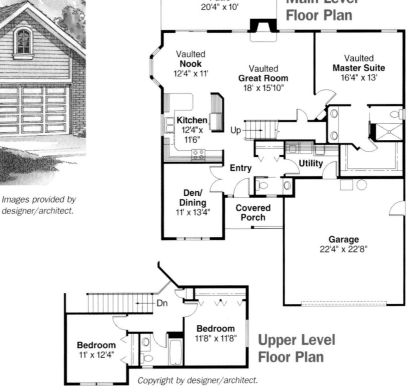

Images provided by designer/architect.

Copyright by designer/architect.

Plan #321030

Dimensions: 61' W x 51' D
Levels: 1
Square Footage: 2,029
Bedrooms: 4
Bathrooms: 2
Foundation: Basement
Materials List Available: Yes
Price Category: D

Images provided by designer/architect.

Two covered porches and a rear patio make this lovely home fit right into a site with a view.

Features:

- Great Room: Boxed entryway columns, a vaulted ceiling, corner fireplace, widowed wall, and door to the patio are highlights in this spacious room.

- Study: Tucked into the back of the house for privacy, the study also opens to the rear patio.

- Dining Area: The windowed alcove lets natural light flow into this room, which adjoins the kitchen.

- Kitchen: A central island, deep pantry, and ample counter area make this room a cook's delight.

- Master Suite: You'll love the two walk-in closets, decorative bedroom window, and double doors opening to the private porch. The bath includes a garden tub, a separate shower, and two vanities.

- Additional Bedrooms: Both bedrooms have a walk-in closet.

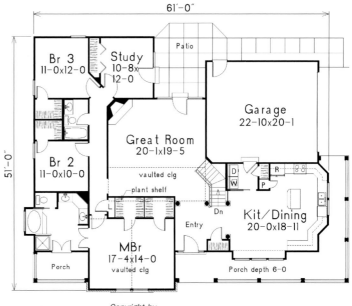

Copyright by designer/architect.

Plan #321001

Dimensions: 83' W x 42' D
Levels: 1
Square Footage: 1,721
Bedrooms: 3
Bathrooms: 2
Foundation: Basement, crawl space, or slab
Materials List Available: Yes
Price Category: C

Images provided by designer/architect.

You'll love the atrium that creates a warm, naturally lit space inside this gracious home, as well as the roof dormers that give it wonderful curb appeal from the outside.

Features:

- Great Room: Bathed in light from the atrium window wall, this room, with its vaulted ceiling, will be the hub of your family life.

- Dining Room: This room also has a vaulted ceiling and is lit by the atrium, but you can draw drapes at night to create a cozy, warm feeling.

- Kitchen: Designed for functionality, this step-saving kitchen is easy to organize and makes cooking a pleasure.

- Breakfast Room: For convenience, this room is located between the kitchen and the rear covered porch.

- Master Suite: Retire with pleasure to this lovely retreat, with its luxurious bath.

Rear View

Copyright by designer/architect.

Plan #341048

Dimensions: 58' W x 39' D

Levels: 1

Square Footage: 1,471

Bedrooms: 3

Bathrooms: 2

Foundation: Crawl space, slab (basement option for fee)

Materials List Available: Yes

Price Category: B

Images provided by designer/architect.

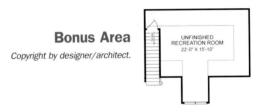

Bonus Area
Copyright by designer/architect.

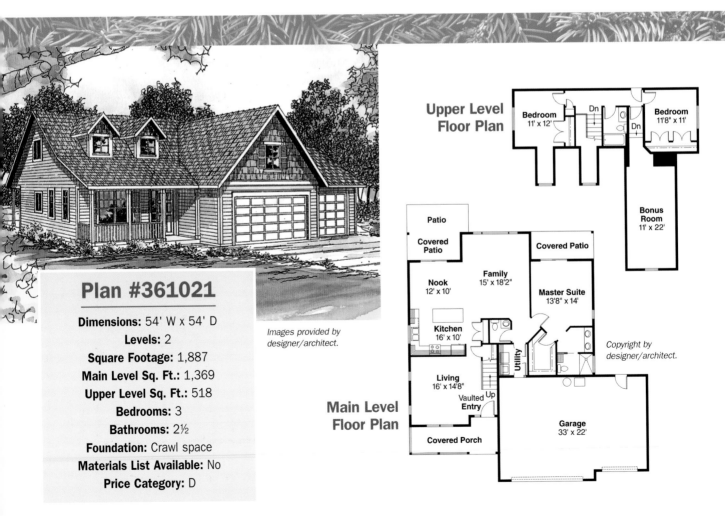

Plan #361021

Dimensions: 54' W x 54' D

Levels: 2

Square Footage: 1,887

Main Level Sq. Ft.: 1,369

Upper Level Sq. Ft.: 518

Bedrooms: 3

Bathrooms: 2½

Foundation: Crawl space

Materials List Available: No

Price Category: D

Images provided by designer/architect.

Copyright by designer/architect.

Images provided by designer/architect.

Plan #341042

Dimensions: 52'8" W x 28'6" D

Levels: 1

Square Footage: 1,055

Bedrooms: 3

Bathrooms: 2

Foundation: Crawl space, slab (basement option for fee)

Materials List Available: Yes

Price Category: B

Copyright by designer/architect.

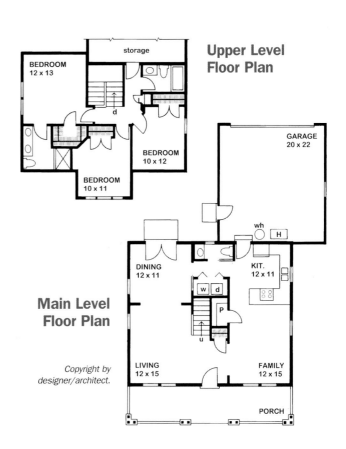

Images provided by designer/architect.

Plan #381018

Dimensions: 38'6" W x 56' D

Levels: 2

Square Footage: 1,540

Main Level Sq. Ft.: 865

Upper Level Sq. Ft.: 675

Bedrooms: 3

Bathrooms: 2½

Foundation: Crawl space

Materials List Available: Yes

Price Category: C

Upper Level Floor Plan

Main Level Floor Plan

Copyright by designer/architect.

Plan #121076

Dimensions: 64' W x 60'8" D
Levels: 2
Square Footage: 3,067
Main Level Sq. Ft.: 2,169
Upper Level Sq. Ft.: 898
Bedrooms: 4
Bathrooms: 3½
Foundation: Basement
Materials List Available: Yes
Price Category: G

You'll love the combination of formal features and casual, family-friendly areas in this spacious home with an elegant exterior.

Features:

• Entry: The elegant windows in this two-story area are complemented by the unusual staircase.

• Family Room: This family room features an 11-ft. ceiling, wet bar, fireplace, and trio of windows that look out to the covered porch.

• Living Room: Columns set off both this room and the dining room. Decorate to accentuate their formality, or make them blend into a more casual atmosphere.

• Master Suite: Columns in this suite highlight a bayed sitting room where you'll be happy to relax at the end of the day or on weekend mornings.

• Bedrooms: Bedroom 2 has a private bath, making it an ideal guest room, and you'll find private vanities in bedrooms 3 and 4.

Main Level Floor Plan

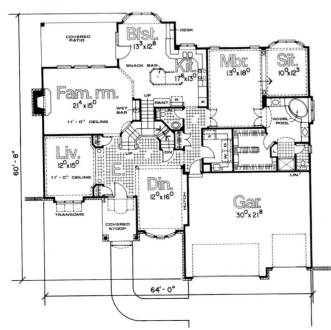

Upper Level Floor Plan

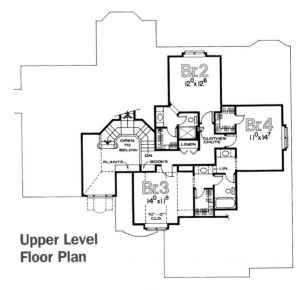

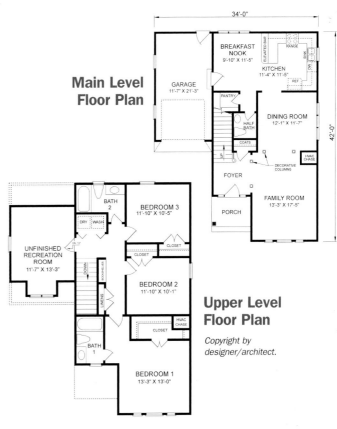

Main Level Floor Plan

Images provided by designer/architect.

Upper Level Floor Plan

Copyright by designer/architect.

Plan #341044

Dimensions: 34' W x 42' D

Levels: 2

Square Footage: 1,704

Main Level Sq. Ft.: 852

Upper Level Sq. Ft.: 852

Bedrooms: 3

Bathrooms: 2½

Foundation: Crawl space, slab (basement option for fee)

Materials List Available: Yes

Price Category: C

Images provided by designer/architect.

Plan #341046

Dimensions: 50'8" W x 51' D

Levels: 1

Square Footage: 1,495

Bedrooms: 3

Bathrooms: 2

Foundation: Crawl space, slab (basement option for fee)

Materials List Available: Yes

Price Category: B

Copyright by designer/architect.

Plan #211002

Dimensions: 68' W x 62' D
Levels: 1
Square Footage: 1,792
Bedrooms: 3
Bathrooms: 2
Foundation: Crawl space
Materials List Available: Yes
Price Category: C

Arched windows on the front of this home give it a European style that you're sure to love.

SMARTtip

Water Features

Water features create the ambiance of a soothing oasis on a deck. A water-filled urn becomes a mirror that reflects the sky—making a small deck look larger. Fish flashing in an ornamental pool add color and act as a focal point for a deck with no view.

A water fountain introduces a pleasant rhythmical sound that helps drown out the background noises of traffic and nearby neighbors.

Features:

- **Living Room:** The 12-ft. ceiling in this large, open room enhances its spacious feeling. A fireplace adds warmth on chilly days and cool evenings.

- **Dining Room:** Decorate to accentuate the 12-ft. ceiling and formal feeling of this room.

- **Kitchen:** Designed for comfort and efficiency, this room also has a 12-ft. ceiling. The cozy breakfast bar is a natural gathering spot for friends and family.

- **Master Suite:** A split design guarantees privacy here. A sloped cathedral ceiling adds elegance, and a walk-in closet makes it practical. The bath has two vanities, a tub, and a walk-in shower.

- **Garage:** Park two cars here, and use the balance of this 520 sq. ft. area as a handy storage area.

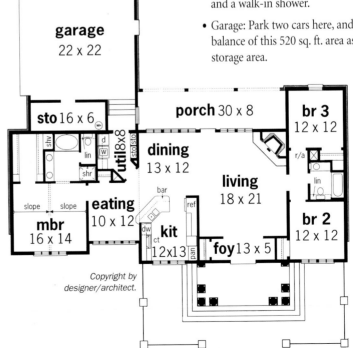

Copyright by designer/architect.

Plan #141031

Dimensions: 58'4" W x 30' D
Levels: 2
Square Footage: 2,367
Main Level Sq. Ft.: 1,025
Upper Level Sq. Ft.: 1,342
Bedrooms: 4
Bathrooms: 2½
Foundation: Basement
Materials List Available: No
Price Category: E

Images provided by designer/architect.

This inviting home combines traditional exterior lines, luxurious interior amenities, and innovative design to present a package that will appeal to all members of your family.

Features:

• **Foyer:** Formal living and dining rooms flank this impressive two-story foyer, which welcomes you to this delightful home with a staircase leading to a balcony.

• **Command Center:** You will enjoy the open flow of the main floor from the family room to this command center, beyond the kitchen, where you can plan your family activities.

• **Master Suite:** This master bedroom with optional window seat features a stepped tray ceiling. The master bath with cathedral ceiling offers an optional radius window.

• **Additional Bedrooms:** The secondary bedroom, next to the master, offers an over look to the foyer, well suited for a sitting room or study.

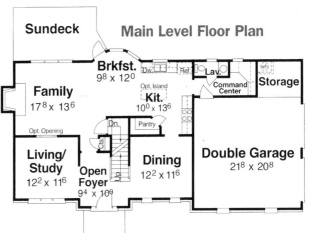

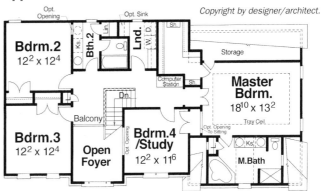

Plan #231015

Dimensions: 63' W x 42' D
Levels: 2
Square Footage: 2,360
Main Level Sq. Ft.: 1,054
Upper Level Sq. Ft.: 1,306
Bedrooms: 4
Bathrooms: 2½
Foundation: Crawl space
Materials List Available: No
Price Category: E

The wraparound front porch and upper-level balcony are just two of the touches that make this home a very special place.

Features:

- **Foyer:** Designed for convenience, this foyer includes a closet and opens to the stairs as well as the living and family rooms.

- **Living Room:** This sunken room is lit by windows looking out to the front porch.

- **Family Room:** You'll enjoy the fireplace in chilly weather and step through the sliding doors to the patio when it's warm.

- **Kitchen:** A central island and bayed breakfast nook make the kitchen inviting and practical.

- **Dining Room:** Boxed columns separate this room from the living room, and large windows light it.

- **Master Suite:** The balcony makes a sitting area in this suite with walk-in closet and private bath.

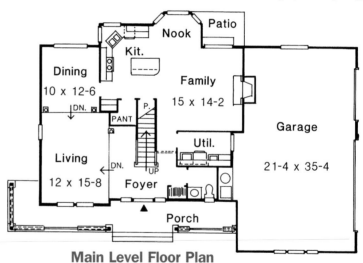

Main Level Floor Plan

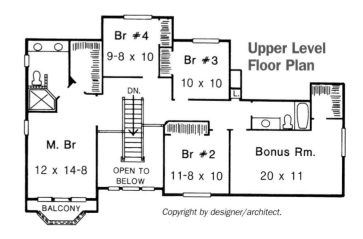

Upper Level Floor Plan

Plan #231009

Dimensions: 111'6" W x 77'1" D
Levels: 1
Square Footage: 2,765
Bedrooms: 3
Bathrooms: 2½
Foundation: Crawl space
Materials List Available: No
Price Category: F

Images provided by designer/architect.

If your family loves contemporary designs, this spacious, angled home could be the house of your dreams.

Features:

- Foyer: This open space is separated from the dining and living rooms by boxed columns.

- Living Room: A large window area is the focal point of this spacious room.

- Family Room: With a corner fireplace and sliding glass doors that lead to the patio, this room invites company.

- Kitchen: A central work island and ample pantry add convenience to this room.

- Breakfast Nook: Nestled into a corner, windows in this nook look out to the patio.

- Master Suite: A huge walk-in closet, angled walls, sliding door to a private patio, luxury bath, and access to the den make a true retreat.

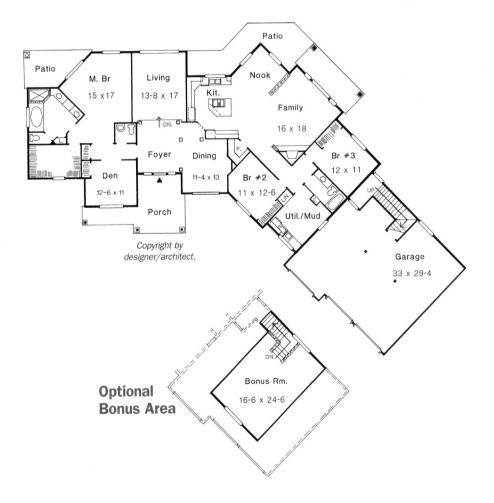

Optional Bonus Area

Plan #341047

Dimensions: 50' W x 54'9" D

Levels: 1

Square Footage: 1,670

Bedrooms: 3

Bathrooms: 2

Foundation: Crawl space, slab (basement option for fee)

Materials List Available: Yes

Price Category: C

Images provided by designer/architect.

Copyright by designer/architect.

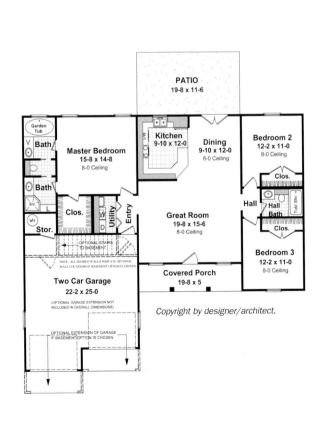

Plan #351009

Dimensions: 54' W x 47' D

Levels: 1

Square Footage: 1,400

Bedrooms: 3

Bathrooms: 2

Foundation: Crawl space, slab (basement option for fee)

Materials List Available: Yes

Price Category: B

Images provided by designer/architect.

Copyright by designer/architect.

Plan #351010

Dimensions: 61'8" W x 45'8" D

Levels: 1

Square Footage: 1,502

Bedrooms: 3

Bathrooms: 2

Foundation: Basement, crawl space, or slab

Materials List Available: Yes

Price Category: C

Images provided by designer/architect.

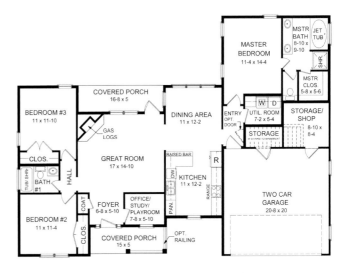

Copyright by designer/architect.

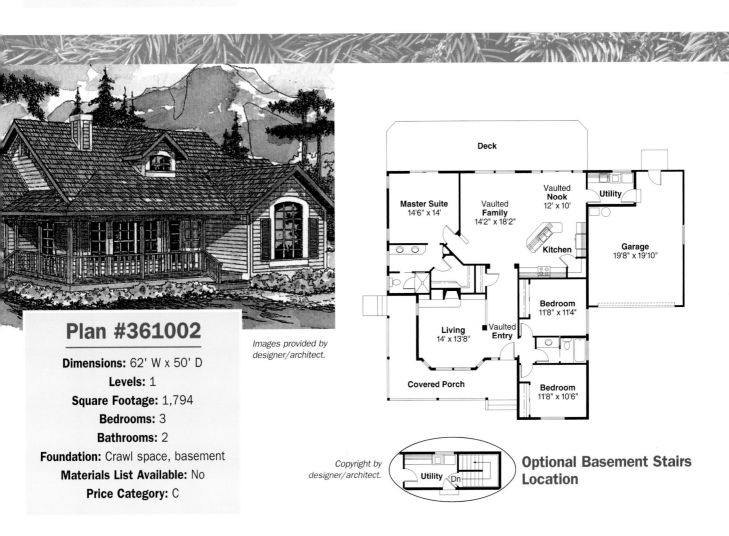

Plan #361002

Dimensions: 62' W x 50' D

Levels: 1

Square Footage: 1,794

Bedrooms: 3

Bathrooms: 2

Foundation: Crawl space, basement

Materials List Available: No

Price Category: C

Images provided by designer/architect.

Copyright by designer/architect.

Optional Basement Stairs Location

Plan #231008

Dimensions: 60' W x 62' D
Levels: 1
Square Footage: 1,941
Bedrooms: 3
Bathrooms: 2½
Foundation: Crawl space
Materials List Available: No
Price Category: D

The interesting dimensions and roof lines on this house hint at its fresh interior layout.

Features:

- Great Room: A two-story ceiling, built-in media center and bookshelves, large fireplace, and doorway to the deck make this a room a family favorite.

- Kitchen: The central island here includes a cooktop. Ample counter and cabinet space face it on the opposite wall.

- Eating Nook: With windows on three sides, this area is a cheery place to sit at any time of day.

- Utility Room: Opening into the garage, this area includes a laundry and half bath for everyone's convenience.

- Master Suite: A bank of windows and glass door leading to the deck make the bedroom light and airy. It also has a huge walk-in closet and bath with garden tub, double vanity, and shower.

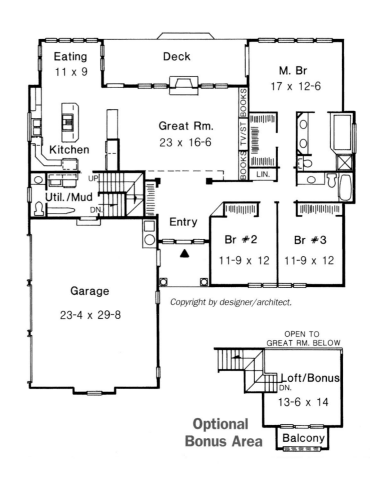

Copyright by designer/architect.

Plan #121073

Dimensions: 70' W x 52' D
Levels: 2
Square Footage: 2,579
Main Level Sq. Ft.: 1,933
Upper Level Sq. Ft.: 646
Bedrooms: 4
Bathrooms: 2½
Foundation: Basement
Materials List Available: Yes
Price Category: E

Images provided by designer/architect.

Luxury will surround you in this home with contemporary styling and up-to-date amenities at every turn.

Features:

- **Great Room:** This large room shares both a see-through fireplace and a wet bar with the adjacent hearth room. Transom-topped windows add both light and architectural interest to this room.

- **Den:** Transom-topped windows add visual interest to this private area.

- **Kitchen:** A center island and corner pantry add convenience to this well-planned kitchen, and a lovely ceiling treatment adds beauty to the bayed breakfast area.

- **Master Suite:** A built-in bookcase adds to the ambiance of this luxury-filled area, where you're sure to find a retreat at the end of the day.

Main Level Floor Plan

Upper Level Floor Plan

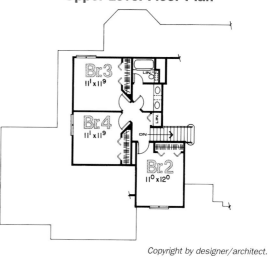

Copyright by designer/architect.

Plan #361010

Dimensions: 49' W x 48' D

Levels: 2

Square Footage: 2,372

Main Level Sq. Ft.: 1,116

Upper Level Sq. Ft.: 1,256

Bedrooms: 3

Bathrooms: 2½

Foundation: Crawl space

Materials List Available: No

Price Category: E

Images provided by designer/architect.

Main Level Floor Plan

Copyright by designer/architect.

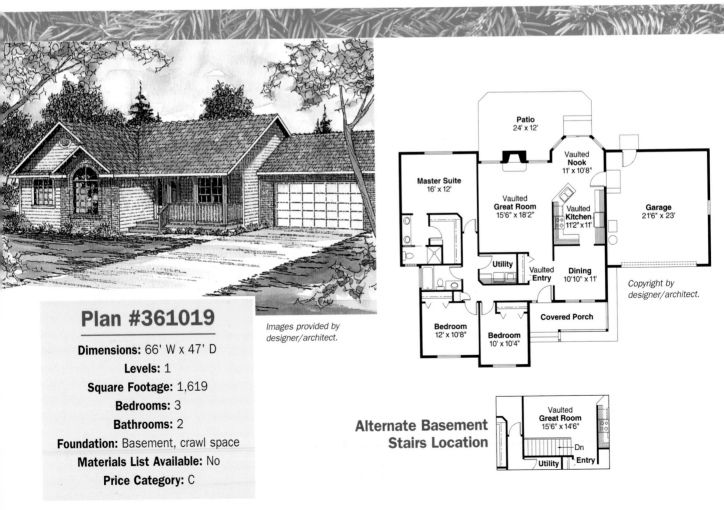

Plan #361019

Dimensions: 66' W x 47' D

Levels: 1

Square Footage: 1,619

Bedrooms: 3

Bathrooms: 2

Foundation: Basement, crawl space

Materials List Available: No

Price Category: C

Images provided by designer/architect.

Copyright by designer/architect.

Alternate Basement Stairs Location

Plan #101004

Dimensions: 55'8" W x 56'6" D

Levels: 1

Square Footage: 1,787

Bedrooms: 3

Bathrooms: 2

Foundation: Slab, crawl space, or basement

Materials List Available: No

Price Category: C

Images provided by designer/architect.

SITTING

TRAY CEILING

DECK

MASTER BDRM
21'-4" x 15'-0"

SCREEN PORCH

BEDROOM 3
13'-0" x 12'-0"

SKYLIGHT   SKYLIGHT

HERS   HIS

FAMILY ROOM
18'-0" x 16'-2"

LINEN

56'-6"

BRKFST BAR

BRKFST
9'-4" x 10'-0"

KITCHEN
12'-4" x 11'-0"

SERVING BAR

11' HIGH CEILING

DW

DESK

K/S

STAIRS TO BONUS ROOM

35'-0"

STAIRS TO BASEMENT

PANTRY

HP

BEDROOM 2
13'-0" x 12'-0"

BONUS ROOM
12'-2" x 20'-4"

DINING
11'-0" x 12'-0"

ENTRY
11' HIGH CEILING

GARAGE
21'-4" x 20'-4"

PORCH

55'-8'

Copyright by designer/architect.

Plan #101005

Dimensions: 63' W x 57'2" D

Levels: 1

Square Footage: 1,992

Bedrooms: 3

Bathrooms: 2½

Foundation: Slab, crawl space, or basement

Materials List Available: Yes

Price Category: D

Images provided by designer/architect.

Copyright by designer/architect.

SCREENED PORCH
15'4" x 13'10"

DECK
11'0" x 7'6"

14' CEILING

SITTING

VLT   VLT

VLT   VLT

BEDROOM 3
13'0" x 11'0"

BRKFST
11'0" x 10'10"

MASTER SUITE
21'4" x 15'0"

8' HIGH OPENING

KITCHEN
13'8" x 9'6"

LINEN

LINEN COATS

FAMILY ROOM
16'0" x 24'1"

VLT   VLT

PANTRY

DW

13'10" CEILING

10' CEILING

OPTIONAL STAIRS TO BASEMENT

57'-2"

13'4" CEILING

DINING
11'0" x 12'0"

9' CEILING

TRAY CEILING

BEDROOM 2
13'0" x 11'0"

VLT   VLT

LIVING
11'0" x 12'0"

PORCH
15'4" x 5'4"

3 CAR GARAGE
21'4" x 29'10"

2 CAR GARAGE OPTION

63'-0'

Rear View

Images provided by designer/architect.

Plan #121001

Dimensions: 56' W x 58' D
Levels: 1
Square Footage: 1,911
Bedrooms: 3
Bathrooms: 2
Foundation: Basement
Materials List Available: Yes
Price Category: D

Detailed, soaring ceilings and top-notch amenities set this distinctive home apart.

Features:

- Ceiling Height: 8 ft. except as noted.

- Great Room: A soaring ceiling and six tall transom-topped windows make this a light and airy spot for entertaining.

- Formal Dining Room: The entry enjoys a pleasing view of this dining room's detailed 12-ft. ceiling and picture window.

- Great Room: At the back of the home, a see-through fireplace in this great room is joined by a built-in entertainment center.

- Hearth Room: This bayed room shares the see-through fireplace with the great room.

- Master Suite: Enjoy the stars and the sun in the private bath's whirlpool and separate shower. The bath features the same decorative ceiling as the dining room.

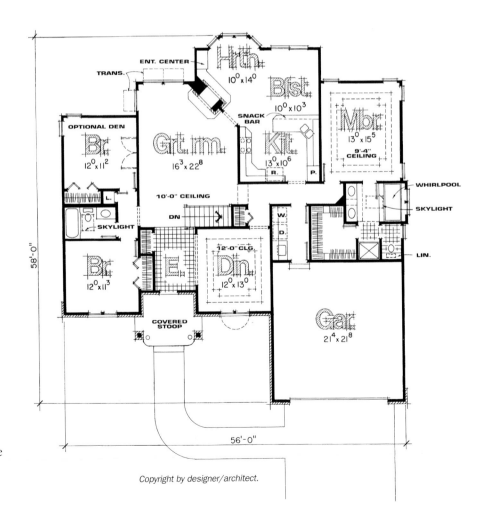

Copyright by designer/architect.

Plan #201067

Dimensions: 68'10" W x 67'4" D

Levels: 1

Square Footage: 2,735

Bedrooms: 4

Bathrooms: 3

Foundation: Crawl space, slab

Materials List Available: Yes

Price Category: F

Images provided by designer/architect.

If your family has as much fun staying at home as they do entertaining or going out, this lovely home with an open floor plan could be ideal.

Features:

- **Den:** Separated from the foyer by boxed columns, this room has a raised ceiling and fireplace flanked by windows.

- **Dining Room:** You can save this elegant room for formal parties, thanks to the eating nook.

- **Kitchen:** An angled bar doubles as work space and snack bar here. A walk-in pantry and ample counter space make this room a delight.

- **Eating Nook:** With sliding doors leading to the porch, this room is ideal for family meals or entertaining a crowd.

- **Master Suite:** A raised ceiling adds to the luxurious feeling here. The enormous bath has two walk-in closets, a garden tub, two vanities, and a shower.

Copyright by designer/architect.

Rear View

Kitchen

Images provided by designer/architect.

Plan #141030

Dimensions: 38' W x 32' D
Levels: 2
Square Footage: 2,323
Main Level Sq. Ft.: 1,179
Upper Level Sq. Ft.: 1,144
Bedrooms: 4
Bathrooms: 2½
Foundation: Basement
Materials List Available: Yes
Price Category: E

This European-style home provides visual excitement, with its many rooflines and multiple gables. Its distinctive design creates a rich, solid appearance.

Features:

- Living Room: Your guests will appreciate the elegance and style that characterize this formal living room.

- Dining Room: A fitting complement to the living room, this formal dining room is well suited for special occasions.

- Kitchen: The well-designed kitchen, with ample cabinet and counter space, makes food preparation a pleasure.

- Master Suite: Enjoy the quiet luxury of this large master suite, sure to become your favorite retreat at the end of the day.

- Bonus Room: This impressive home features an optional bonus room above the garage.

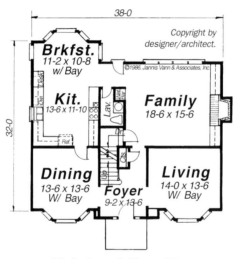
Main Level Floor Plan

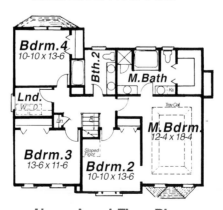
Upper Level Floor Plan

Living Room

Plan #271030

Dimensions: 56' W x 45' D
Levels: 2
Square Footage: 1,926
Main Level Sq. Ft.: 1,490
Upper Level Sq. Ft.: 436
Bedrooms: 3
Bathrooms: 2½
Foundation: Basement
Materials List Available: Yes
Price Category: D

Images provided by designer/architect.

This traditional home's main-floor master suite is hard to resist, with its inviting window seat and delightful bath.

Features:

- Master Suite: Just off from the entry foyer, this luxurious oasis is entered through double doors, and offers an airy vaulted ceiling, plus a private bath that includes a separate tub and shower, dual-sink vanity, and walk-in closet.

- Great Room: This space does it all in style, with a breathtaking wall of windows and a charming fireplace.

- Kitchen: A cooktop island makes dinnertime tasks a breeze. You'll also love the roomy pantry. The adjoining breakfast room, with its deck access and built-in desk, is sure to be a popular hangout for the teens.

- Secondary Bedrooms: Two additional bedrooms reside on the upper floor and allow the younger family members a measure of desired—and necessary—privacy.

Main Level Floor Plan

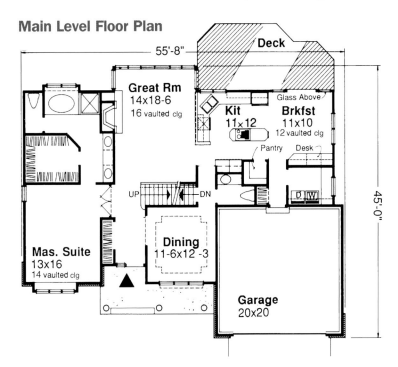

Upper Level Floor Plan

Copyright by designer/architect.

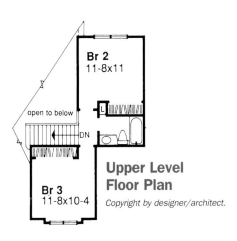

Plan #381008

Dimensions: 43' W x 36' D
Levels: 2
Square Footage: 1,465
Main Level Sq. Ft.: 895
Upper Level Sq. Ft.: 570
Bedrooms: 3
Bathrooms: 2
Foundation: Basement
Materials List Available: Yes
Price Category: B

Images provided by designer/architect.

The wraparound porch adds to the friendly, comfortable feeling in this well-designed home.

Features:

- **Porch:** Doors from both the entry and the dining room make this porch an easy place to entertain or simply relax at the end of the day.

- **Living Room:** This spacious room is naturally lit by four windows on one wall and two windows flanking the handsome fireplace.

- **Dining Room:** The whole family will gather here because it's so convenient to the kitchen and the porch.

- **Kitchen:** The U-shaped counter area provides plenty of space for working, and you'll find enough storage in top and bottom cabinets.

- **Bedrooms:** Each room showcases a large closet and easy access to a nearby bath. On the second floor, the dormer space is given to one bedroom and the adjoining, open study.

Main Level Floor Plan

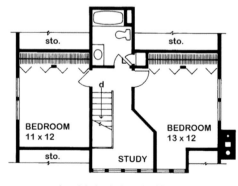

Copyright by designer/architect.

Upper Level Floor Plan

Plan #261007

Dimensions: 58' W x 44' D

Levels: 2

Square Footage: 2,635

Main Level Sq. Ft.: 1,435

Upper Level Sq. Ft.: 1,200

Bedrooms: 4

Bathrooms: 2½

Foundation: Basement

Materials List Available: No

Price Category: F

You'll love the dramatic roofline of this gracious home, which is as carefully designed inside as it is on the exterior.

Features:

- Foyer: This 2-story area opens to the formal dining and living rooms.

- Living Room: A pocket door between this room and the family room allows for plenty of space for large gatherings.

- Dining Room: Convenient to the kitchen, this room can be used for family meals as well as formal parties.

- Family Room: Enjoy the fireplace in this comfortable room.

- Den: You'll love the quiet and privacy here.

- Master Suite: This luxurious suite features a large walk-in closet and bath with two vanities, a corner whirlpool tub, and a separate shower.

Images provided by designer/architect.

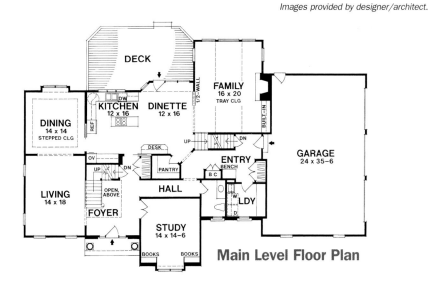

Main Level Floor Plan

Copyright by designer/architect.

Upper Level Floor Plan

Plan #161001

Dimensions: 67'2" W x 47' D

Levels: 1

Square Footage: 1,782

Bedrooms: 3

Bathrooms: 2

Foundation: Basement

Materials List Available: Yes

Price Category: C

Images provided by designer/architect.

An all-brick exterior displays the solid strength that characterizes this gracious home.

Features:

- Gathering Area: A feeling of spaciousness permeates this gathering area, created by the foyer, great room, and dining room. Multiple windows provide natural light that dances along a sloped ceiling, spilling onto decorative columns and a fireplace.

- Breakfast Area: A continuation of the sloped ceiling leads to this breakfast area, where French doors open to a screened porch.

- Kitchen: An abundance of cabinets and counter space are the hallmarks of this large kitchen, with its easy access to a spacious laundry room and storage area.

- Master Suite: A tray ceiling and spacious walk-in closet in the master bedroom, along with a whirlpool tub and double-bowl vanity in the bathroom, enable you to pamper yourself.

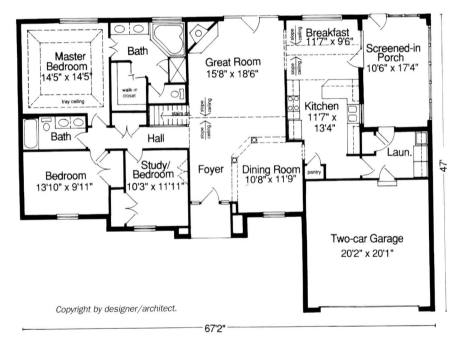

Copyright by designer/architect.

Rear Elevation

Left Side Elevation

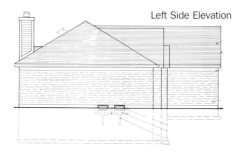

Right Side Elevation

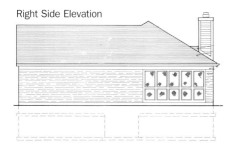

Front View

Great Room / Foyer

Color

No other decorating component has more power and greater effect at such little cost than color. It can fill a space and make furnishings look fresh and new. Color can also show off fine architectural details or downplay a room's structural flaws. A particular color can make a cold room cozy, while another hue can cool down a sunny cooker. And color comes cheap, giving a tremendous impact for your decorating dollar: elbow grease, supplies, prep work, and paint will all cost pretty much the same if you choose a gorgeous hue over plain white.

But finding the color—the right color—isn't easy. Where do you begin to look? Like the economy, color has leading indicators. You have a market basket full of choices, and there are lots of signposts to direct you where to go.

The Lay of the Land

For the past 200 years, white has been the most popular choice for American home exteriors. And it still is, followed by tan, brown, and beige. You can play it safe and follow the leader. But you should also think about the architecture of your house and where you live when you're considering exterior color. For example, traditional Colonials have a color-combination range of about two that look appropriate: white with black or green shutters and gray with white trim. Mediterranean-style houses typically pick up the colors of terra-cotta and the tile that are indigenous to the regions that developed the architecture—France, Italy, and Spain. A ranch-style house shouldn't be overdone—it is, after all, usually a modest structure. On the other hand, a cottage can be fanciful. Whimsical colors also look charming on Victorian houses in San Francisco, but they would be out of place in conservative Scarsdale, New York, where you must

check with the local building board even when you want to change the exterior color of your house.

How's the Weather?

Like exteriors, interiors often take their color cues from their environs and local traditions. In the rainy and often chilly Pacific Northwest, cozy blanket plaids in strong reds and black abound. In the hot-and-arid climate of the West, indigo or brown ticking-stripes and faded denim look appropriately casual and cool. Subtle grays and neutrals, reflecting steel, limestone, and concrete, look apropos for sophisticated city life. In extremely warm southern climates, the brilliant sun tends to overpower lighter colors. That explains the popularity of strong hues in tropical, sun-drenched locales.

Natural Light. That's the one you don't pay for. Its direction and intensity greatly affects color. A room with a window that faces trees will look markedly different in summer, when warm white sunlight is filtered through the leaves, than in winter, when the trees are bare and the color of natural light takes on a cool blue cast. Time of day affects color, too. Yellow walls that are pleasant and cheerful in the early morning can be stifling and blinding in the afternoon. That's because afternoon

The yellow-colored wall, above, complements the antique painted dresser.

Warm neutral-color walls, opposite, and touches of red make this bedroom cozy.

sun is stronger than morning sun.

When you're choosing a color for an interior, always view it at different times of day, but especially during the hours in which you will inhabit the room.

Artificial Light. Because artificial light affects color rendition as much as natural light, don't judge a color in the typically chilly fluorescence of a hardware store. The very same color chip will look completely different when you bring it home, which is why it's so important to test out a paint color in your own home. Most fluorescent light is bluish and distorts colors. It depresses red and exaggerates green, for example. A romantic faded rose on your dining room walls will just wash out in the kitchen if your use a fluorescent light there. Incandescent light, the type produced by the standard bulbs you probably use in your chandelier and in most of your home's light fixtures, is warm but slightly yellow. Halogen light, which comes from another newer type of incandescent bulb, is white and the closest to natural sunlight. Of all three types of bulbs, halogen is truest in rendering color.

 # red

RED is powerful, dramatic, motivating. Red is also hospitable, and it stimulates the appetite, which makes it a favorite choice for dining rooms. Some studies have indicated that a red room actually makes people feel warmer.

yellow

YELLOW illuminates the colors it surrounds. It warms rooms that receive northern light but can be too bright in a sunny room. It's best for daytime rooms, not bedrooms. It has a short range, which means as white is added to yellow, it disappears. Yellow highlights and calls attention to features—think of bright taxicabs.

green

GREEN is tranquil, nurturing, rejuvenating. It is a psychological primary, and because it is mixed from yellow and blue, it can appear both warm and cool. Time seems to pass more quickly in green rooms. Perhaps that's why waiting rooms off-stage are called "green rooms."

 # neutrals

GRAY goes with all colors—it is a good neighbor. Various tones of gray range from dark charcoal to pale oyster.

BLACK (technically the absence of color) enhances and brightens other colors, making for livelier decorating schemes when used as an accent.

 **pink**

PINK is perceived as outgoing and active. It's also a color that flatters skin tones. Hot shades are invigorating, while soft, toned-down versions can be relaxed and charming.

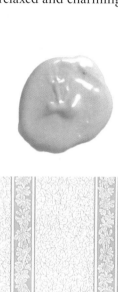

 # blue

BLUE, with its associations of sea and sky, offers serenity, which is why it is a favorite in bedrooms. Studies have shown that people think better in blue rooms. Perhaps that explains the popularity of the navy blue suit. Cooler blues show this color's melancholy side, however.

Plan #161033

Dimensions: 78'2" W x 74'6" D
Levels: 2
Square Footage: 5,125
Main Level Sq. Ft.: 2,782
Upper Level Sq. Ft.: 1,027
Optional Basement Level Sq. Ft.: 1,316
Bedrooms: 4
Bathrooms: 3½
Foundation: Basement
Materials List Available: Yes
Price Category: I

Images provided by designer/architect.

The dramatic design of this home, combined with its comfort and luxuries, suit those with discriminating tastes.

Features:

• **Great Room:** Let the fireplace and 14-ft. ceilings in this room set the stage for all sorts of gatherings, from causal to formal.

• **Dining Room:** Adjacent to the great room and kitchen fit for a gourmet, the dining room allows you to entertain with ease.

• **Music Room:** Give your music the space it deserves in this specially-designed room.

• **Library:** Use this room as an office, or reserve it for quiet reading and studying.

• **Master Suite:** You'll love the separate dressing area and walk-in closet in the bedroom.

• **Lower Level:** A bar and recreational area give even more space for entertaining.

Rear View

Main Level Floor Plan

Copyright by designer/architect.

Upper Level Floor Plan

Optional Basement Level Floor Plan

Color Wheel Combinations

The color wheel is the designer's most useful tool for pairing colors. Basically, it presents the spectrum of pigment hues as a circle. The primary colors (yellow, blue, and red) are combined in the remaining hues (orange, green, and purple). The following are the most often used configurations for creating color schemes.

Dining Room

Living Room

Plan #321061

Dimensions: 55' W x 49'4" D
Levels: 2
Square Footage: 3,169
Main Level Sq. Ft.: 1,679
Upper Level Sq. Ft.: 1,490
Bedrooms: 4
Bathrooms: 2½
Foundation: Basement
Materials List Available: Yes
Price Category: G

Images provided by designer/architect.

You'll love the spacious interior of this gorgeous home, which is built for comfortable family living but includes amenities for gracious entertaining.

Features:

• Entry: This large entry gives a view of the handcrafted staircase to the upper floor.

• Living Room: Angled French doors open into this generously sized room with a vaulted ceiling.

• Family Room: You'll love to entertain in this huge room with a masonry fireplace, built-in entertainment area, gorgeous bay window, and well-fitted wet bar.

• Breakfast Room: A door in the bayed area opens to the outdoor patio for dining convenience.

• Kitchen: The center island provides work space and a snack bar, and the walk-in pantry is a delight.

• Master Suite: Enjoy the vaulted ceiling, two walk-in closets, and luxurious bath in this suite.

Main Level Floor Plan

Upper Level Floor Plan

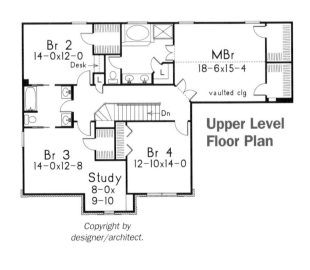

Copyright by designer/architect.

Plan #321054

Dimensions: 70'6" W x 55'6" D
Levels: 2
Square Footage: 2,828
Main Level Sq. Ft.: 2,006
Upper Level Sq. Ft.: 822
Bedrooms: 5
Bathrooms: 3½
Foundation: Basement
Materials List Available: Yes
Price Category: F

Images provided by designer/architect.

The wraparound porch welcomes visitors to this spacious home built for a large family.

Features:

- **Foyer:** Flanked by the study on one side and the dining room on the other, the foyer leads to the staircase, breakfast room, and family room.

- **Family Room:** You'll feel comfortable in this room, with its vaulted ceiling, wet bar, ample window area, and door to the patio.

- **Kitchen:** A center island adds work space to this well-planned room with large corner windows and a convenient door to the outside patio.

- **Master Suite:** Doors to the covered porch flank the fireplace here, and the luxurious bath includes a corner tub, two vanities, and separate shower. A huge walk-in closet is in the hall.

- **Upper Floor:** You'll find four bedrooms, each with a large closet, and two full baths here. Bay windows grace the two front bedrooms.

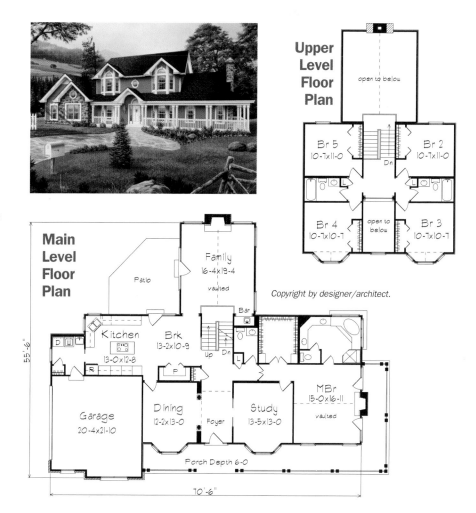

Copyright by designer/architect.

Plan #261014

Dimensions: 78'10" W x 43' D
Levels: 2
Square Footage: 3,471
Main Level Sq. Ft.: 1,873
Upper Level Sq. Ft.: 1,598
Bedrooms: 4
Bathrooms: 3½
Foundation: Basement
Materials List Available: No
Price Category: G

Images provided by designer/architect.

You'll love this stately home if you're looking for a traditional exterior appearance mixed with a contemporary interior layout.

Features:

- Family Room: Columns define the entry to this spacious room, where you'll find a fireplace, built-in shelves, and extensive window area.

- Living Room: The windowed alcoves here and in the dining room add elegance to the rooms.

- Den: Decorate this room to be a quiet reading area, or turn it into a media room for the children.

- Kitchen: This roomy kitchen has a center work island; plenty of counter space; and a large, attached walk-in pantry.

- Family Dining Area: Sliding doors here open to the rear wood deck for dining convenience.

- Master Suite: You'll love the two walk-in closets and luxury bath in this suite.

Main Level Floor Plan

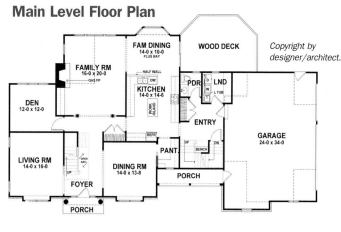

Copyright by designer/architect.

Rear Elevation

Upper Level Floor Plan

Plan #261013

Dimensions: 81'8" W x 34' D
Levels: 2
Square Footage: 3,193
Main Level Sq. Ft.: 1,735
Upper Level Sq. Ft.: 1,458
Bedrooms: 4
Bathrooms: 3½
Foundation: Basement
Materials List Available: No
Price Category: G

This gracious family home has space for a busy family life and diverse sorts of entertaining, too.

Features:

- Family Room: A gas fireplace and extensive window area are highlights in this spacious room.

- Living Room: Pocket doors to the family room let you close off this room for privacy.

- Dining Room: Adjacent to the kitchen and foyer, this room is an ideal spot for entertaining guests.

- Kitchen: You'll love the L-shaped counter and central island for both dining and cooking.

- Dinette: You can host a crowd in this open space, which leads to the screened porch and wood deck.

- Den: Use this room for a library or separate media room for times you want to be quiet.

- Master Suite: Pamper yourself with the walk-in closet and bath with whirlpool tub and shower.

Images provided by designer/architect.

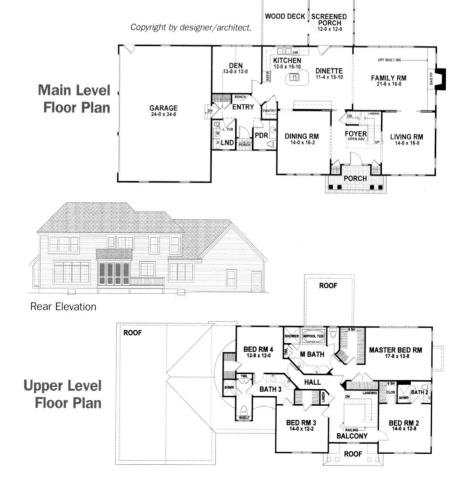

Plan #241021

Dimensions: 60' W x 77'2" D

Levels: 2

Square Footage: 3,509

Main Level Sq. Ft.: 2,135

Upper Level Sq. Ft.: 1,374

Bedrooms: 4

Bathrooms: 3½

Foundation: Slab

Materials List Available: No

Price Category: H

Images provided by designer/architect.

This elegant home is designed with the grandeur of the past and the convenience of the present.

Features:

- Great Room: It's a treat to entertain here, thanks to the wet bar, fireplace, and sliders to the yard.

- Living Room: Bookshelves set the gracious tone in this slightly formal room.

- Dining Room: You'll love the decorative ceiling in this well-positioned room.

- Kitchen: The angled bar has space for eating and working, and there's a desk and pantry here.

- Breakfast Room: The interesting line and bright windows here add beauty to the space.

- Master Suite: A boxed ceiling, door to the yard, two walk-in closets, and bath with two vanities, a glass shower, and separate tub make true luxury.

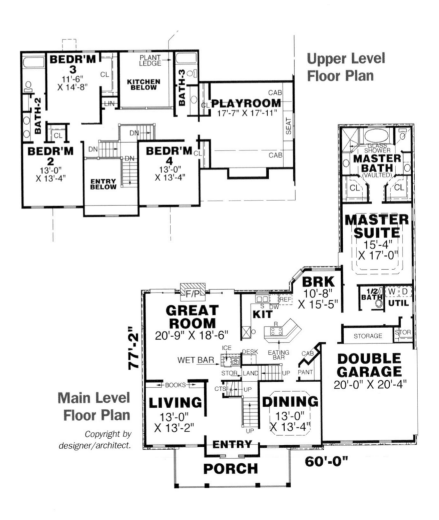

Upper Level Floor Plan

Main Level Floor Plan

Copyright by designer/architect.

Plan #151185

Dimensions: 58'10" W x 57' D
Levels: 2
Square Footage: 2,955
Main Level Sq. Ft.: 2,245
Upper Level Sq. Ft.: 710
Bedrooms: 4
Bathrooms: 3
Foundation: Crawl space, slab (basement or walk-out basement option for fee)
Materials List Available: Yes
Price Category: F

Images provided by designer/architect.

You'll love the design elements that give this home both elegance and practicality.

Features:

• Great Room: A fireplace and wall of windows emphasize the beauty of this two-story room, which is visible from the theater balconies above.

• Guest Room: The deep bay and walk-in closet are highlights of this lovely room.

• Kitchen: An angled bar serves as snack bar and counter in this well-designed kitchen.

• Hearth Room: This room has a lovely corner fireplace and a door to the grilling porch beyond.

• Breakfast Room: You'll love to sit near the large window area in this comfortable room.

• Master Suite: Who could resist the bedroom, with its 16-ft. boxed ceiling, door to the grilling porch, and bath with two walk-in closets, a whirlpool and standard tub, shower, and double vanity.

Copyright by designer/architect.

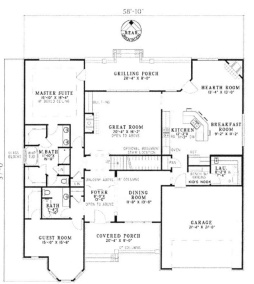

Main Level Floor Plan

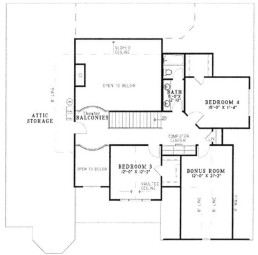

Upper Level Floor Plan

Plan #141034

Dimensions: 77' W x 66' D
Levels: 2
Square Footage: 3,588
Main Level Sq. Ft.: 2,329
Upper Level Sq. Ft.: 1,259
Bedrooms: 4
Bathrooms: 3½
Foundation: Basement
Materials List Available: Yes
Price Category: H

The elegance and style of the exterior design is only a preview of the many luxurious amenities found inside this exciting home.

Features:

- Foyer: A formal dining room and private library flank this two-story foyer, which features a staircase leading to a second-floor balcony.

- Living Room: The balcony overlooks this formal living room, well-suited for special-occasion entertaining.

- Kitchen: This spacious kitchen, with ample cabinets and counter space, is designed for easy work patterns and has easy access to both the formal dining and living rooms.

- Master Suite: This elaborate master suite will be your ultimate hideaway. It features a vaulted master bath, a sitting room with a fireplace, and a large walk-in closet. You will also enjoy easy access to the private library for relaxing reading.

Images provided by designer/architect.

Main Level Floor Plan

Rear View

Kitchen

Upper Level Floor Plan

Copyright by designer/architect.

Plan #161030

Dimensions: 98'6" W x 61'5" D
Levels: 2
Square Footage: 4,562
Main Level Sq. Ft.: 3,364
Upper Level Sq. Ft.: 1,198
Bedrooms: 4
Bathrooms: 3½
Foundation: Basement
Materials List Available: Yes
Price Category: I

You'll be charmed by this impressive home, with its stone-and-brick exterior.

Features:

- **Great Room:** The two-story ceiling here adds even more dimension to this expansive space.

- **Hearth Room:** A tray ceiling and molding help to create a cozy feeling in this room, which is located so your guests will naturally gravitate to it.

- **Dining Room:** This formal room features columns at the entry and a butler's pantry for entertaining.

- **Master Suite:** A walk-in closet, platform whirlpool tub, and 2-person shower are only a few of the luxuries in the private bath, and tray ceilings and moldings give extra presence to the bedroom.

- **Upper Level:** A balcony offers a spectacular view of the great room and leads to three large bedrooms, each with a private bath.

Images provided by designer/architect.

Main Level Floor Plan

Upper Level Floor Plan

Copyright by designer/architect.

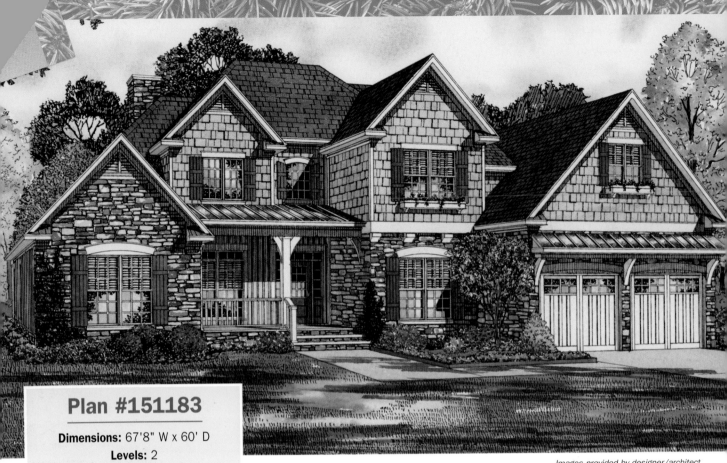

Plan #151183

Dimensions: 67'8" W x 60' D
Levels: 2
Square Footage: 2,952
Main Level Sq. Ft.: 2,266
Upper Level Sq. Ft.: 686
Bedrooms: 4
Bathrooms: 3
Foundation: Crawl space, slab (basement or walk-out basement option for fee)
Materials List Available: Yes
Price Category: F

Images provided by designer/architect.

This lovely home includes private spaces as well as large rooms that invite everyone to gather.

Features:

- **Great Room:** Look out to the grilling porch from the bank of windows in this two-story room with a fireplace and built-in media center.

- **Dining Room:** Columns set off this room, but it's an easy walk from the adjacent kitchen.

- **Kitchen:** Designed for a gourmet cook, the kitchen features an angled snack bar.

- **Breakfast Room:** Lit by expansive windows, this room opens to the rear grilling porch.

- **Master Suite:** A fireplace, expansive windows, and door to the porch accent this suite, which includes a private study, two walk-in closets, and bath with whirlpool tub, shower, and bidet.

- **Upper Floor:** Look down to the foyer and great room from the theater balconies here.

Main Level Floor Plan

Upper Level Floor Plan

Copyright by designer/architect.

Plan #151180

Dimensions: 67'3" W x 68'6" D
Levels: 2
Square Footage: 3,167
Main Level Sq. Ft.: 2,486
Upper Level Sq. Ft.: 681
Bedrooms: 4
Bathrooms: 3
Foundation: Crawl space, slab (basement or walk-out basement option for fee)
Materials List Available: Yes
Price Category: G

Images provided by designer/architect.

From one end to the other, this home is designed to give your friends and family total comfort.

Features:

• Great Room: This spacious room is visible from the second floor balconies, has a fabulous fireplace, and opens to the grilling porch.

• Dining Room: The columns here add a touch of formality around which you can decorate.

• Kitchen: The kitchen is designed for convenience and shares a snack bar with the breakfast room.

• Guest Room: The walk-in closet and bank of windows will welcome all of your friends.

• Breakfast Room: You'll love the natural lighting in this room, which leads to the grilling porch beyond.

• Master Suite: The high boxed ceiling and door to the grilling porch highlight the bedroom. The bath includes a walk-in closet, whirlpool tub, separate shower, and double vanity.

Main Level Floor Plan

Copyright by designer/architect.

Upper Level Floor Plan

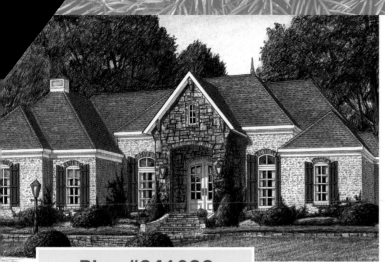

Main Level Floor Plan

BRK 13'-8" X 12'-0"

HEARTH ROOM 20'-0" X 13'-0"

EATING BAR

KIT

GREAT ROOM 17'-0" X 16'-0"

MASTER SUITE 13'-0" X 16'-0"

STOR

UTIL
D W F

UP

DINING 11'-0" X 15'-1" 13' CLG.

BEDR'M 2 11'-0" X 12'-9" 13' CLG.

MASTER BATH

BATH-2

W.I.C.

54'-4"

DOUBLE GARAGE 21'-0" X 20'-0"

FOYER

UP

POR

71'-0"

BEDR'M 3 13'-0" X 14'-0"

GREAT ROOM BELOW

LIN CL

BATH-3

DN

GAME ROOM 17'-4" X 21'-6"

CL

BALCONY

DN

FOYER BELOW

Upper Level Floor Plan

Copyright by designer/architect.

Plan #241032

Images provided by designer/architect.

Dimensions: 71' W x 54'4" D

Levels: 1½

Square Footage: 3,274

Main Level Sq. Ft.: 2,368

Upper Level Sq. Ft.: 906

Bedrooms: 3

Bathrooms: 3

Foundation: Slab

Materials List Available: No

Price Category: G

Copyright by designer/architect.

Master Bedroom 14-6x18-3 9' ceiling

M.Bath

T.V.

Family/ Breakfast 15-8x28-10 9' ceiling

Porch 20-10x12-0 9' ceiling

Storage 7-6x9-11

Laun. 7-6x9-11

Bedroom 15-11x11-3 9' ceiling

Bath

Kitchen 15-9x20-6 9' ceiling

Living 15-9x20-4 9' ceiling

Island

Garage 23-5 x 23-5

Bedroom 12-0x13-3 9' ceiling

Pantry

Dining 13-5x15-2 11' ceiling

Foyer 11' ceiling

Study/ Bedroom 13-5x15-2 11' ceiling

Plan #311027

Images provided by designer/architect.

Dimensions: 79' W x 65'4" D

Levels: 1

Square Footage: 3,175

Bedrooms: 4

Bathrooms: 2½

Foundation: Basement, crawl space, or slab

Materials List Available: Yes

Price Category: G

Rear View

Plan #151186

Dimensions: 59'6" W x 81'10" D

Levels: 1½

Square Footage: 2,975

Main Level Sq. Ft.: 2,530

Upper Level Sq. Ft.: 445

Bedrooms: 4

Bathrooms: 4

Foundation: Crawl space, slab (basement or walk-out basement option for fee)

Materials List Available: Yes

Price Category: F

Images provided by designer/architect.

Main Level Floor Plan

Upper Level Floor Plan

Copyright by designer/architect.

Plan #241020

Dimensions: 82'6" W x 78'7" D

Levels: 2

Square Footage: 4,058

Main Level Sq. Ft.: 2,570

Upper Level Sq. Ft.: 1,488

Bedrooms: 4

Bathrooms: 3 full, 2 half

Foundation: Slab

Materials List Available: No

Price Category: I

Images provided by designer/architect.

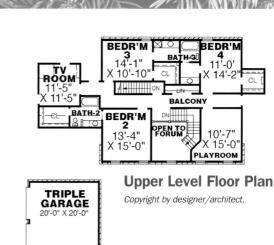

Upper Level Floor Plan

Copyright by designer/architect.

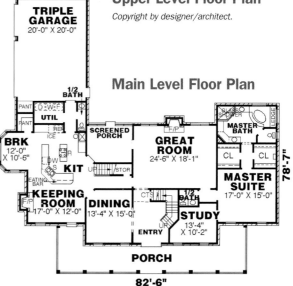

Main Level Floor Plan

Images provided by designer/architect.

Plan #321063

Dimensions: 87'8" W x 46'10" D
Levels: 2
Square Footage: 3,222
Main Level Sq. Ft.: 2,276
Upper Level Sq. Ft.: 946
Bedrooms: 4
Bathrooms: 3½
Foundation: Basement
Materials List Available: Yes
Price Category: G

This home will thrill any family looking for an elegant setting and plenty of space for entertaining as well as family time.

Features:

- Foyer: With a two-story ceiling and a central staircase to the upper level, this foyer also leads to the dining and living rooms.

- Great Room: This two-story room has a large fireplace and arched openings to the second floor. A door leads to the rear terrace, where it's easy to host parties for friends and family.

- Kitchen: This room will delight all the cooks in the family with its ample work and storage space and attached breakfast booth.

- Master Suite: This elegant suite includes a separate reading room with bookshelves and a fireplace as well as a luxury bath.

- Additional Bedrooms: Each bedroom has a walk-in closet. Bedroom 4 has a private bath.

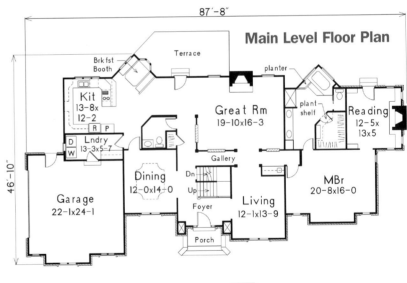

Main Level Floor Plan

Upper Level Floor Plan

Copyright by designer/architect.

Plan #261001

Dimensions: 77'8" W x 49' D
Levels: 2
Square Footage: 3,746
Main Level Sq. Ft.: 1,965
Upper Level Sq. Ft.: 1,781
Bedrooms: 4
Bathrooms: 3½
Foundation: Basement
Materials List Available: No
Price Category: H

If contemporary designs appeal to you, you're sure to love this stunning home.

Features:

- **Foyer:** A volume ceiling here announces the spaciousness of this gracious home.

- **Great Room:** Also with a volume ceiling, this great room features a fireplace where you can create a cozy sitting area.

- **Kitchen:** Designed for the pleasure of the family cooks, this room features a large pantry, ample counter and cabinet space, and a dining bar.

- **Dinette:** Serve the family in style, or host casual, informal dinners for friends in this dinette with its gracious volume ceiling.

- **Master Suite:** A fireplace makes this suite a welcome retreat on cool nights, but even in warm weather you'll love its spaciousness and the walk-in closet. The bath features dual vanities, a whirlpool tub, and a separate shower.

Images provided by designer/architect.

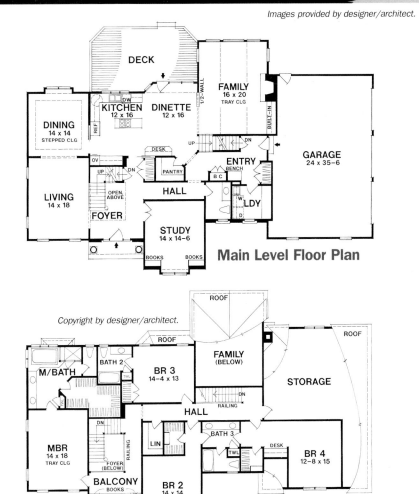

Main Level Floor Plan

Copyright by designer/architect.

Upper Level Floor Plan

Plan #121062

Dimensions: 70' W x 62' D
Levels: 2
Square Footage: 3,448
Main Level Sq. Ft.: 2,375
Upper Level Sq. Ft.: 1,073
Bedrooms: 4
Bathrooms: 3½
Foundation: Basement
Materials List Available: Yes
Price Category: G

Images provided by designer/architect.

You'll love this design if you're looking for a comfortable home with dimensions and details that create a sense of grandeur.

Features:

• Entry: A soaring ceiling, curved staircase, and balcony that overlooks a tall plant shelf combine to create your first impression of grandeur in this home.

• Great Room: A transom-topped bowed window highlights this room, with its 11-ft., beamed ceiling, built-in wet bar, and see-through fireplace.

• Kitchen: Designed for the gourmet cook, this kitchen has every amenity you could desire.

• Breakfast Room: Adjacent to the great room and the kitchen, this gazebo-shaped breakfast area lights both the kitchen and hearth room.

Main Level Floor Plan

Upper Level Floor Plan

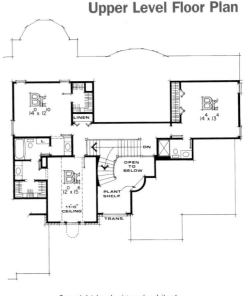

Copyright by designer/architect.

Plan #121061

Dimensions: 56' W x 52' D
Levels: 2
Square Footage: 3,025
Main Level Sq. Ft.: 1,583
Upper Level Sq. Ft.: 1,442
Bedrooms: 4
Bathrooms: 3 ½
Foundation: Basement
Materials List Available: Yes
Price Category: G

Images provided by designer/architect.

This large home with a contemporary feeling is ideal for the family looking for comfort and amenities.

Features:

- **Entry:** Stacked windows bring sunlight into this two-story entry, with its stylish curved staircase.
- **Library:** French doors off the entry lead to this room, with its built-in bookcases flanking a large, picturesque window.
- **Family Room:** Located in the rear of the home, this family room is sunken to set it apart. A spider-beamed ceiling gives it a contemporary feeling, and a bay window, wet bar, and pass-through fireplace add to this impression.
- **Kitchen:** The island in this kitchen makes working here a pleasure. The corner pantry joins a breakfast area and hearth room to this space.

Main Level Floor Plan

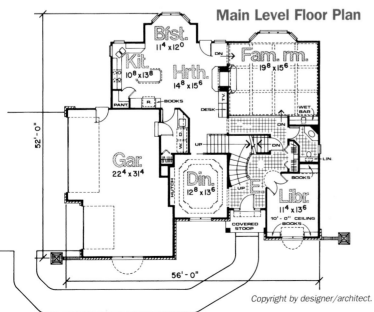

Copyright by designer/architect.

Upper Level Floor Plan

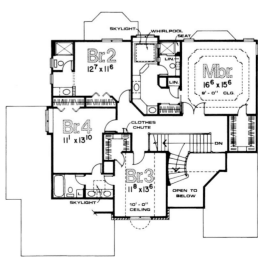

Plan #261009

Dimensions: 90' W x 46' D
Levels: 2
Square Footage: 4,048
Main Level Sq. Ft.: 2,388
Upper Level Sq. Ft.: 1,660
Bedrooms: 5
Bathrooms: 4½
Foundation: Basement
Materials List Available: No
Price Category: I

You'll love the elegant exterior of this classic Tudor manor and luxuriate in its amenity-filled, contemporary interior design.

Features:

- **Ceiling Heights:** High, volume ceilings give an airy feeling in the foyer, family room, and living room. All other rooms feature 9-ft. ceilings.

- **Family Room:** Gather around the fireplace here or in the living room in chilly weather.

- **Den:** Use this well-positioned first-floor room for a bedroom, guestroom, or home office.

- **Dining Room:** Everyone will love the pocket door here that leads to the kitchen.

- **Kitchen:** With a pantry and large work island, this kitchen is designed for efficiency and comfort.

- **Master Suite:** French doors open to the bedroom, and the private bath has double vanities, a corner whirlpool tub, and a walk-in shower.

Images provided by designer/architect.

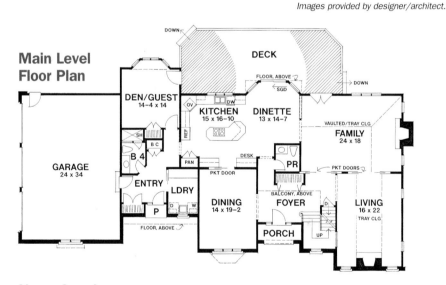

Main Level Floor Plan

Copyright by designer/architect.

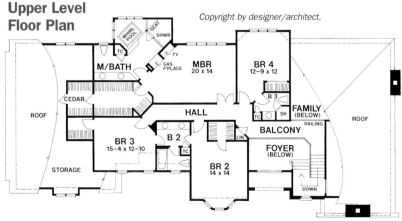

Upper Level Floor Plan

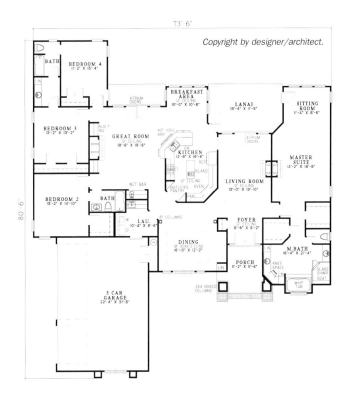

Copyright by designer/architect.

Plan #151057

Dimensions: 73'6" W x 80'6" D

Levels: 1

Square Footage: 2,951

Bedrooms: 4

Bathrooms: 3

Foundation: Crawl space, slab, or basement

Materials List Available: Yes

Price Category: F

Images provided by designer/architect.

Main Level Floor Plan

Plan #151174

Dimensions: 57'4" W x 55'10" D

Levels: 2

Square Footage: 2,815

Main Level Sq. Ft.: 2,142

Upper Level Sq. Ft.: 673

Bedrooms: 4

Bathrooms: 3

Foundation: Crawl space, slab (Basement or walk-out basement option for fee)

Materials List Available: Yes

Price Category: F

Images provided by designer/architect.

Copyright by designer/architect.

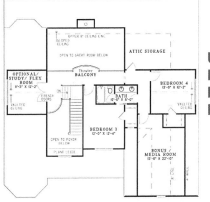

Upper Level Floor Plan

Plan #321016

Dimensions: 88' W x 70'8" D
Levels: 1
Square Footage: 3,814
Main Level Sq. Ft.: 3,566
Lower Level Sq. Ft.: 248
Bedrooms: 3
Bathrooms: 2½
Foundation: Daylight basement
Materials List Available: Yes
Price Category: H

Images provided by designer/architect.

Rear View

If you're looking for a design that makes the most of a sloped site, you'll love this gorgeous home.

Features:

- Great Room: This fabulous room has a vaulted ceiling, sunken floor, and masonry fireplace, and it opens to the two-story atrium.

- Dining Room: Both this room and the living room opposite are naturally lit by two-story arched windows.

- Kitchen: Open to the hearth room and breakfast room, this kitchen has a central island, too.

- Hearth Room/Breakfast Room: A vaulted ceiling, corner fireplace, and door to one deck highlight this angled space.

- Master Suite: The bedroom has a coffered ceiling, corner fireplace, door to one deck, and huge walk-in closet. The bath includes a step-down tub with windows and a fireplace, a linen closet, a separate shower, and two vanities.

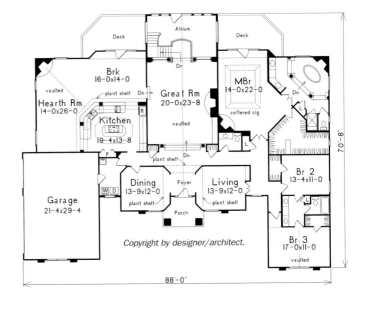

Copyright by designer/architect.

Plan #321011

Dimensions: 83' W x 50'4" D

Levels: 1

Square Footage: 2,874

Bedrooms: 4

Bathrooms: 2½

Foundation: Basement

Materials List Available: Yes

Price Category: F

Images provided by designer/architect.

The traditional good looks of the exterior of this home are matched by the practical yet beautiful interior design.

Features:

- Family Room: A fireplace flanked by windows creates a focal point in this room, while the wet bar and doors to the backyard are practical.

- Living Room: Double doors open from the foyer into this lovely room you can use formally.

- Dining Room: The windowed alcove makes an ideal spot for a table in this lovely room.

- Kitchen: A central island and large pantry add convenience to this well-planned room.

- Breakfast Area: A bank of windows floods this room with cheery morning light.

- Master Suite: The bedroom has a windowed alcove, walk-in closet, and bath with a tub in the bayed area, double vanity, and shower.

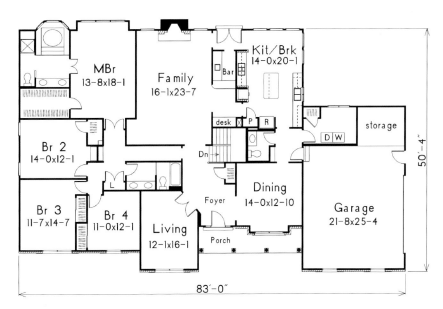

Copyright by designer/architect.

Plan #161029

Dimensions: 87' W x 82' D

Levels: 2

Square Footage: 4,470

Main Level Sq. Ft.: 3,300

Upper Level Sq. Ft.: 1,170

Bedrooms: 4

Bathrooms: 3 Full; 2 Half

Foundation: Basement

Materials List Available: Yes

Price Category: I

Images provided by designer/architect.

This gracious home is so impressive — inside and out — that it suits the most discriminating tastes.

Features:

- Foyer: A balcony overlooks this gracious area decorated by tall columns.

- Hearth Room: Visually open to the kitchen and the breakfast area, this room is ideal for any sort of gathering.

- Great Room: Colonial columns also form the entry here, and a magnificent window treatment that includes French doors leads to the terrace.

- Library: Built-in shelving adds practicality to this quiet retreat.

- Kitchen: Spread out on the oversized island with a cooktop and seating.

- Additional Bedrooms: Walk-in closets and private access to a bath define each bedroom.

Main Level Floor Plan

Copyright by designer/architect.

Upper Level Floor Plan

Rear View

Living Room

Ideas for Entertaining

Whether an everyday family meal or a big party for 50, make it memorable and fun. With a world of options, it's easier than you think. Be imaginative with food and decoration. Although it is true that great hamburgers and hot dogs will taste good even if served on plain white paper plates, make the meal more fun by following a theme of some sort — color, occasion, or seasonal activity, for example. Be inventive with the basic elements as well as the extraneous touches, such as flowers and lighting. Here are some examples to get you started.

· For an all-American barbecue, set a picnic table with a patchwork quilt having red, white, and blue in it. Use similar colors for the napkins, and perhaps even bandannas. Include a star-studded centerpiece.

· Make a children-size dining set using an old door propped up on crates, and surround it with appropriate-size benches or chairs. Cover the table with brightly colored, easy-to-clean waxed or vinyl-covered fabric.

· If you're planning an elegant dinner party, move your dining room table outside and set it with your best linens, china, silver, and crystal. Add romantic lighting with candles in fabulous candelabras, and set a beautiful but small floral arrangement at each place setting.

· Design a centerpiece showcasing the flowers from your garden. Begin the arrangement with a base of purchased flowers, and fill in with some of your homegrown blooms. That way your flower beds will still be full of blossoms when the guests arrive.

· Base your party theme on the vegetables growing in your yard, and let them be the inspiration for the menu. When your zucchini plants are flowering, wow your family or guests by serving steamed squash blossoms. Or if the vegetables are starting to develop, lightly grill them with other young veggies — they have a much more delicate flavor than mature vegetables do.

· During berry season, host an elegant berry brunch. Serve mixed-berry crepes on your prettiest plates.

Living Room/Kitchen

Plan #121082

Dimensions: 68'8" W x 60' D

Levels: 2

Square Footage: 2,932

Main Level Sq. Ft.: 2,084

Upper Level Sq. Ft.: 848

Bedrooms: 4

Bathrooms: 3½

Foundation: Basement

Materials List Available: Yes

Price Category: F

Enjoy the spacious covered veranda that gives this house so much added charm.

Features:

• Great Room: A volume ceiling enhances the spacious feeling in this room, making it a natural gathering spot for friends and family. Transom-topped windows look onto the veranda, and French doors open to it.

• Den: French doors from the entry lead to this room, with its unusual ceiling detail, gracious fireplace, and transom-topped windows.

• Hearth Room: Three skylights punctuate the cathedral ceiling in this room, giving it an extra measure of light and warmth.

• Kitchen: This kitchen is a delight, thanks to its generous working and storage space.

Main Level Floor Plan

Upper Level Floor Plan

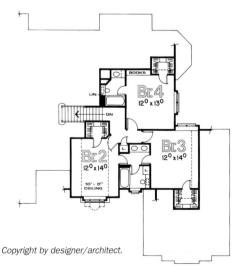

Plan #121065

Dimensions: 62' W x 55'4" D
Levels: 2
Square Footage: 3,407
Main Level Sq. Ft.: 1,719
Upper Level Sq. Ft.: 1,688
Bedrooms: 4
Bathrooms: 2½
Foundation: Basement
Materials List Available: Yes
Price Category: G

If you love contemporary design, the unusual shapes of the rooms in this home will delight you.

Features:

- Entry: You'll see a balcony from the upper level that overlooks this entryway, as well as the lovely curved staircase to this floor.

- Great Room: This room is sunken to set it apart. A fireplace, wet bar, spider-beamed ceiling, and row of arched windows give it character.

- Dining Room: Columns define this lovely octagon room, where you'll love to entertain guests or create lavish family dinners.

- Master Suite: A multi-tiered ceiling adds a note of grace, while the fireplace and private library create a real retreat. The gracious bath features a gazebo ceiling and a skylight.

Main Level Floor Plan

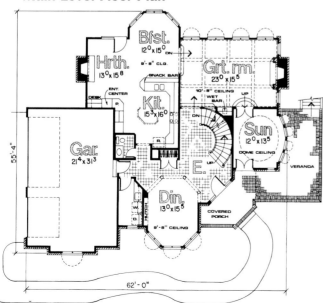

Upper Level Floor Plan

Copyright by designer/architect.

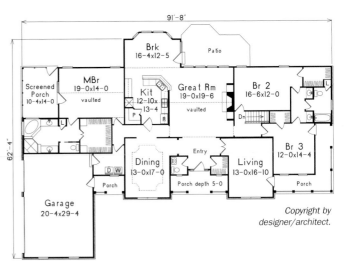

Copyright by
designer/architect.

*Images provided by
designer/architect.*

Plan #321004

Dimensions: 91'8" W x 62'4" D

Levels: 1

Square Footage: 2,808

Bedrooms: 3

Bathrooms: 2½

Foundation: Basement

Materials List Available: Yes

Price Category: F

*Images provided by
designer/architect.*

Copyright by designer/architect.

**Optional Basement Level
Floor Plan**

Plan #321036

Dimensions: 78'4" W x 68'6" D

Levels: 1, optional lower

Square Footage: 2,900

**Optional Basement Level
Sq. Ft.:** 1,018

Bedrooms: 4

Bathrooms: 2½

Foundation: Basement

Materials List Available: Yes

Price Category: F

Plan #261015

Dimensions: 79'4" W x 48' D

Levels: 2

Square Footage: 3,200

Main Level Sq. Ft.: 1,766

Upper Level Sq. Ft.: 1,434

Bedrooms: 4

Bathrooms: 3½

Foundation: Basement

Materials List Available: No

Price Category: G

Main Level Floor Plan

Images provided by designer/architect.

Upper Level Floor Plan

Copyright by designer/architect.

Plan #341039

Dimensions: 69'7" W x 61' D

Levels: 2

Square Footage: 3,740

Main Level Sq. Ft.: 2,047

Upper Level Sq. Ft.: 1,693

Bedrooms: 4

Bathrooms: 3½

Foundation: Crawl space, slab (basement option for fee)

Materials List Available: Yes

Price Category: H

Main Level Floor Plan

Images provided by designer/architect.

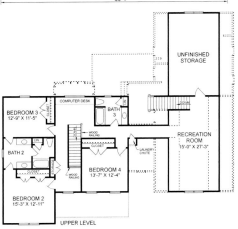

Copyright by designer/architect.

Images provided by designer/architect.

Plan #121081

Dimensions: 76'8" W x 68' D
Levels: 2
Square Footage: 3,623
Main Level Sq. Ft.: 2,603
Upper Level Sq. Ft.: 1,020
Bedrooms: 4
Bathrooms: 4½
Foundation: Basement
Materials List Available: Yes
Price Category: G

You'll love this impressive home if you're looking for perfect spot for entertaining as well as a home for comfortable family living.

Features:

• Entry: Walk into this grand two-story entryway through double doors, and be greeted by the sight of a graceful curved staircase.

• Great Room: This two-story room features stacked windows, a fireplace flanked by an entertainment center, a bookcase, and a wet bar.

• Dining Room: A corner column adds formality to this room, which is just off the entryway for the convenience of your guests.

• Hearth Room: Connected to the great room by a lovely set of French doors, this room features another fireplace as well as a convenient pantry.

Main Level Floor Plan

Upper Level Floor Plan

Copyright by designer/architect.

Plan #121019

Dimensions: 70' W x 60' D
Levels: 2
Square Footage: 3,775
Main Level Sq. Ft.: 1,923
Upper Level Sq. Ft.: 1,852
Bedrooms: 4
Bathrooms: 3
Foundation: Basement
Materials List Available: Yes
Price Category: H

Images provided by designer/architect.

The grand exterior presence is carried inside, beginning with the dramatic curved staircase.

Features:

- Ceiling Height: 8 ft.
- Den: French doors lead to the sophisticated den, with its bayed windows and wall of bookcases.
- Living Room: A curved wall and a series of arched windows highlight this large space.
- Formal Dining Room: The living room shares the curved wall and arched windows found in the living room.
- Screened Porch: This huge space features skylights and is accessible by another French door from the dining room.
- Family Room: Family and guests alike will be drawn to this room, with its trio of arched windows and fireplace flanked by bookcases.
- Kitchen: An island adds convenience and distinction to this large, functional kitchen.
- Garage: This spacious three-bay garage provides plenty of space for cars and storage.

Main Level Floor Plan

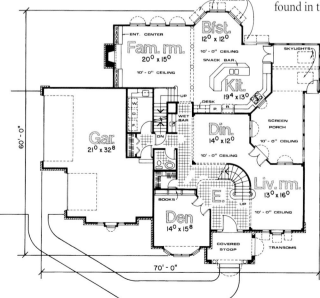

Upper Level Floor Plan

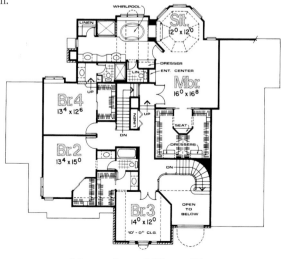

Copyright by designer/architect.

Images provided by designer/architect.

Plan #231030

Dimensions: 76' W x 81' D
Levels: 3
Square Footage: 4,200
Finished Basement Sq. Ft.: 377
Main Level Sq. Ft.: 2,120
Upper Level Sq. Ft.: 1,520
Third Floor Sq. Ft.: 183
Bedrooms: 5
Bathrooms: 4 full, 2 half
Foundation: Slab, crawl space, or basement
Materials List Available: No
Price Category: I

A busy family will delight in the many diverse spaces in this lovely home.

Features:

- **Reading Room:** Relax in this lovely room, which is defined by boxed columns.

- **Family Room:** Highlights here include a two-story vaulted ceiling, built-in media center, fireplace, and access to the rear deck.

- **Kitchen:** A dining nook, central island, desk, and adjacent mudroom combine for practicality.

- **Master Suite:** On the first floor for privacy, this suite runs the length of the house. The walk-in closet and bath with garden tub, double vanity, and separate shower add up to total luxury.

- **Special Spaces:** A balcony and loft make the second floor a treat. In the basement, you'll find a home theater and cellar for wine and food storage. The third floor includes a kid's retreat, and the room over the garage is ideal for a home office.

Main Level Floor Plan

Copyright by designer/architect.

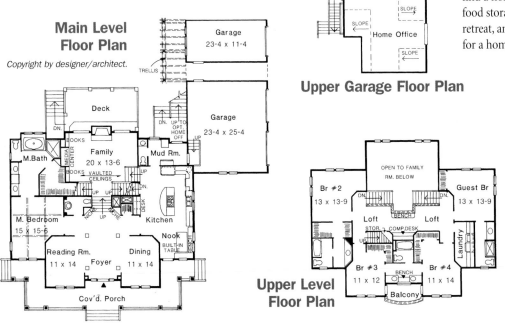

Upper Garage Floor Plan

Upper Level Floor Plan

Basement Floor Plan

Third Level Floor Plan

Plan #131050

Dimensions: 72'8" W x 47' D
Levels: 2
Square Footage: 2,874
Main Level Sq. Ft.: 2,146
Upper Level Sq. Ft.: 728
Bedrooms: 4
Bathrooms: 3
Foundation: Crawl space, slab, or basement
Materials List Available: Yes
Price Category: G

A gazebo and long covered porch at the entry let you know that this is a spectacular design.

Features:

- **Foyer:** This vaulted foyer divides the formal living room and dining room, setting the stage for guests to feel welcome in your home.

- **Great Room:** This large room is defined by several columns; a corner fireplace and vaulted ceiling add to its drama.

- **Kitchen:** An island work space separates this area from the bayed breakfast nook.

- **Master Suite:** You'll have privacy in this main-floor suite, which features two walk-in closets and a compartmented bath with a dual-sink vanity.

- **Upper Level:** The two large bedrooms share a bath and a dramatic balcony.

- **Bonus Room:** Walk down a few steps into this large bonus room over the 3-car garage.

Main Level Floor Plan

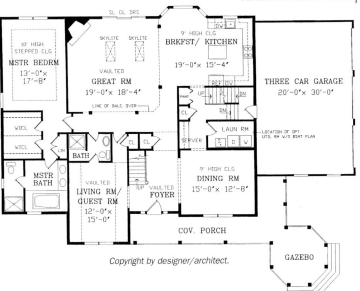

Copyright by designer/architect.

Upper Level Floor Plan

Rear Elevation

Plan #121023

Dimensions: 85'5" W x 74'8" D

Levels: 2

Square Footage: 3,904

Main Level Sq. Ft.: 2,813

Upper Level Sq. Ft.: 1,091

Bedrooms: 4

Bathrooms: 2½

Foundation: Basement

Materials List Available: Yes

Price Category: H

Images provided by designer/architect.

Spacious and gracious, here are all the amenities you expect in a fine home.

Features:

- Ceiling Height: 8 ft. except as noted.

- Foyer: This magnificent entry features a graceful curved staircase with balcony above.

- Sunken Living Room: This sunken room is filled with light from a row of bowed windows. It's the perfect place for social gatherings both large and small.

- Den: French doors open into this truly distinctive den with its 11-ft. ceiling and built-in bookcases.

- Formal Dining Room: Entertain guests with style and grace in this dining room with corner column.

- Master Suite: Another set of French doors leads to this suite that features two walk-in closets, a whirlpool flanked by vanities, and a private sitting room with built-in bookcases.

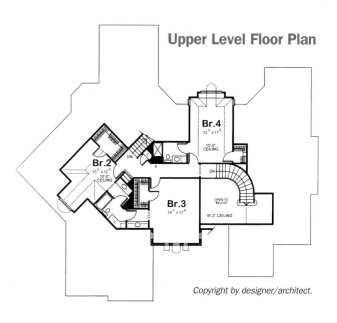

Copyright by designer/architect.

Plan #121018

Dimensions: 95'9" W x 70'2" D

Levels: 2

Square Footage: 3,950

Main Level Sq. Ft.: 2,839

Upper Level Square Footage: 1,111

Bedrooms: 4

Bathrooms: 2 full, 2 half

Foundation: Basement

Materials List Available: Yes

Price Category: H

Images provided by designer/architect.

A spectacular two-story entry with a floating curved staircase welcomes you home.

Features:

• Ceiling Height: 8 ft. except as noted.

• Den: To the left of the entry, French doors lead to a spacious and stylish den featuring a spider-beamed ceiling.

• Living Room: The volume ceiling, transom windows, and large fireplace evoke a gracious traditional style.

• Gathering Rooms: There is plenty of space for large-group entertaining in the gathering rooms that also feature fireplaces and transom windows.

• Master Suite: Here is the height of luxurious living. The suite features an oversized walk-in closet, tiered ceilings, and a sitting room with fireplace. The pampering bath has a corner whirlpool and shower.

• Garage: An angle minimizes the appearance of the four-car garage.

Main Level Floor Plan

Upper Level Floor Plan

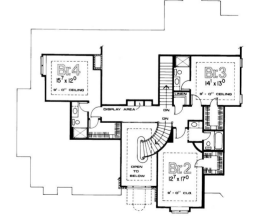

Copyright by designer/architect.

Images provided by designer/architect.

Plan #101019

Dimensions: 58'4" W x 55'2" D

Levels: 2

Square Footage: 2,954

Main Level Sq. Ft. 2093

Upper Level Sq. Ft. 861

Bedrooms: 4

Bathrooms: 3½

Foundation: Slab, crawl space, or basement

Materials List Available: No

Price Category: F

This luxurious home features a spectacular open floor plan and a brick exterior.

Features:

- Ceiling Height: 9 ft. unless otherwise noted.
- Foyer: This inviting two-story foyer, which vaults to 18 ft., will greet guests with an impressive "welcome."
- Dining Room: To the right of the foyer is this spacious dining room surrounded by decorative columns.
- Family Room: There's plenty of room for all kinds of family activities in this enormous room, with its soaring two-story ceiling.
- Master Suite: This sumptuous retreat boasts a tray ceiling. Optional pocket doors provide direct access to the study. The master bath features his and her vanities and a large walk-in closet.
- Breakfast Area: Perfect for informal family meals, this bayed breakfast area has real flair.
- Secondary Bedrooms: Upstairs are three large bedrooms with 8-ft. ceilings. One has a private bath.

Main Level Floor Plan

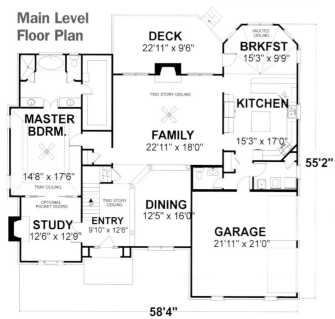

Upper Level Floor Plan

Copyright by designer/architect.

Plan #351004

Dimensions: 78' W x 49'6" D

Levels: 1

Square Footage: 1,852

Bedrooms: 3

Bathrooms: 2½

Foundation: Crawl space, slab, or basement

Materials List Available: Yes

Price Category: D

Images provided by designer/architect.

You'll love this design if you've been looking for a one-story home large enough for both a busy family life and lots of entertaining.

Features:

• Great Room: A vaulted ceiling, substantial corner fireplace, and door to the rear porch give character to this sizable, airy room.

• Dining Room: This well-positioned room, lit by a wall of windows, can comfortably hold a crowd.

• Kitchen: The center island and deep pantry add efficiency to this well-planned kitchen, which also features a raised snack bar.

• Master Suite: Two walk-in closets and a bath with jet tub and separate shower complement the spacious bedroom here.

• Garage Storage: Barn doors make it easy to store yard equipment and tools here. Finish the optional area at the rear of the garage or overhead for a home office or media room.

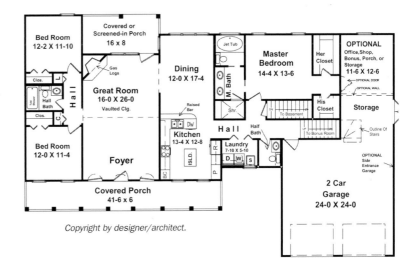

Copyright by designer/architect.

Rear
Elevation

Bonus Room

Plan #241018

Dimensions: 83'7" W x 64'10" D
Levels: 1½
Square Footage: 2,519
Main Level Sq. Ft.: 2,096
Upper Level Sq. Ft.: 423
Bedrooms: 4
Bathrooms: 4
Foundation: Slab
Materials List Available: No
Price Category: E

Images provided by designer/architect.

The wraparound veranda tells you how comfortable you'll be in this friendly home.

Features:

- Great Room: A fireplace, wet bar, and door to the rear porch make this room the heart of the home.

- Dining Room: A door to the veranda gives versatility to this lovely room.

- Kitchen: The cooks will love the U-shaped counter, center island, desk, and eating bar.

- Breakfast Room: The door to the porch makes it easy to enjoy dining outside in fine weather.

- Master Suite: The spacious bedroom is complemented by a walk-in closet and bath with vaulted ceiling and both tub and shower.

- Upper Floor: Both bedrooms have a dormer seat, large closet, and private bath. The balcony over the foyer is lovely, and the game room is a pleasure for the entire family.

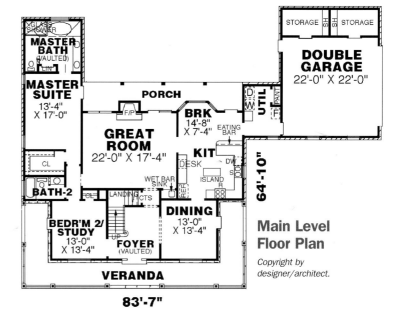

Main Level Floor Plan

Copyright by designer/architect.

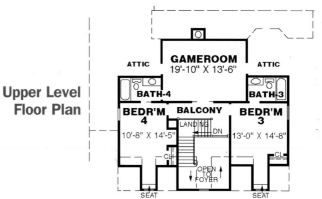

Upper Level Floor Plan

Images provided by designer/architect.

Plan #321002

Dimensions: 72' W x 28' D

Levels: 1

Square Footage: 1,400

Bedrooms: 3

Bathrooms: 2

Foundation: Basement, crawl space

Materials List Available: Yes

Price Category: B

If you're looking for a well-designed compact home with contemporary amenities, this could be the home of your dreams.

Features:

- **Porch:** Just the right size for some rockers and a swing, this porch could become your outdoor living area when the weather is fine.

- **Living Room:** A vaulted ceiling adds to the spacious feeling in this room, where friends and family are sure to gather.

- **Kitchen:** This space-saving design, in combination with the ample counter and cabinet space, makes cooking a pleasure.

- **Utility Room:** This large room is fitted with cabinets for extra storage space. You'll find storage space in the large garage, too.

- **Master Bedroom:** This room is somewhat secluded for privacy, making it an ideal place for some quiet time at the end of the day.

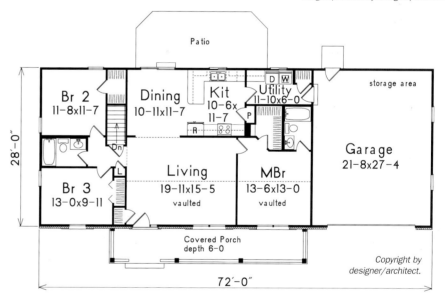

Copyright by designer/architect.

SMARTtip

Fabric Draping Ability

Test a fabric's draping ability by looking at a large piece in a fabric store. Gather at least two to three yards of material, holding one end in your hand. Check how it drapes. Does it fall into folds easily? Also look at the pattern when it is gathered. Does the design become lost in the folds? Ask a salesclerk or a friend to hold the fabric, and look at it from a few feet away.

Main Level Floor Plan

Images provided by designer/architect.

Plan #151181

Dimensions: 76'10" W x 59'2" D

Levels: 1½

Square Footage: 2,373

Main Level Sq. Ft.: 2,373

Bonus Sq. Ft.: 687

Bedrooms: 4

Bathrooms: 3

Foundation: Crawl space, slab (basement or walk-out basement option for fee)

Materials List Available: Yes

Price Category: E

Upper Level Floor Plan

Copyright by designer/architect.

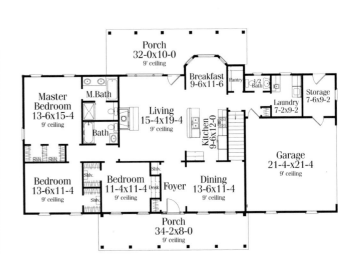

Plan #311026

Dimensions: 74' W x 49'8" D

Levels: 1

Square Footage: 1,916

Main Level Sq. Ft.: 1,916

Opt. Bonus Sq. Ft. 1,245

Bedrooms: 3

Bathrooms: 2½

Foundation: Basement, crawl space, or slab

Materials List Available: Yes

Price Category: D

Images provided by designer/architect.

Bonus Area

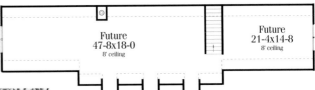

Copyright by designer/architect.

Rear View

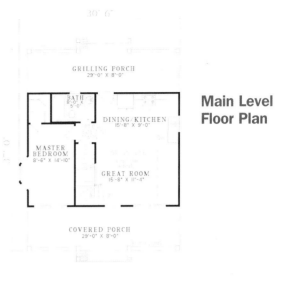

Main Level Floor Plan

GRILLING PORCH
29'-0" X 8'-0"

BATH
8'-0" X 5'-0"

DINING/KITCHEN
15'-8" X 9'-0"

MASTER BEDROOM
8'-6" X 14'-10"

GREAT ROOM
15'-8" X 11'-4"

COVERED PORCH
29'-0" X 8'-0"

Plan #151182

Dimensions: 30'6" W x 37' D
Levels: 1½
Square Footage: 975
Main Level Sq. Ft.: 616
Upper Level Sq. Ft.: 359
Bedrooms: 2
Bathrooms: 1
Foundation: Crawl space, slab (basement or walk-out basement option for fee)
Materials List Available: Yes
Price Category: A

Images provided by designer/architect.

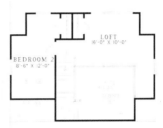

Upper Level Floor Plan

LOFT
16'-0" X 10'-0"

BEDROOM 2
8'-6" X 12'-0"

Copyright by designer/architect.

Garden Tub

M. Bath
13-8 x 9-4

Trayed Ceiling

Master Bedroom
13-6 x 15-2

Covered Porch
20-6 x 5

Bedroom #2
11 x 10-4

Clos.

C
7-2 x 5-6

C
6-2 x 4-0

CABINETS

RANGE   DW   BAR

Kitchen
9-10 x 10-4

Eating Area
10-10 x 10-4

Hall

Bath

Tub/Shr

STOR.
4-8 x 3-10

STAIRS TO OPTIONAL BASEMENT

ENTRY

C

P

Br

Clos.

DASHED LINES INDICATE WALLS IF BASEMENT OPTION IS CHOSEN.

GAS LOGS

Great Room
20-8 x 14-4

Cabs

Bedroom #3
11-2 x 10-4

Laund.
7-8x5-8

W
D

VAULT

Two Car Garage
19-4 x 25-10

Cabs

Covered Porch
21-8 x 5

Plan #351005

Dimensions: 61' W x 47'4" D
Levels: 1
Square Footage: 1,501
Bedrooms: 3
Bathrooms: 2
Foundation: Basement, crawl space, or slab
Materials List Available: Yes
Price Category: C

Images provided by designer/architect.

Copyright by designer/architect.

Flooring Options

Selecting a flooring material is one of the most important decisions you will make when decorating a room. The right material can enhance the color scheme and the overall look of the room, and flooring provides a unique tactile component to the design.

If you are are acting as your own designer, one of the first things you should do is learn about the various types of flooring—from wood to stone to vinyl—on today's market. The choices are myriad and innovations in technology have widened the range of finishes.

Choices in Wood

In bygone eras, a wood floor was simply one that was created by laying wide wood planks side by side. Later, as the milling of lumber improved, homeowners were able to choose narrower planks that look more refined than rustic. Parquet floors were created by woodcrafters with a flair for the dramatic and an appreciation of the artistic richness of wood grains set in nonlinear patterns.

Today's manufacturers have made it possible to have it all. The wood floor, factory- or custom-stained to suit a particular style or mood in a room, is still a traditional favorite. It's readily available in strips of 1 to 2¼ inches wide, or in country-style planks of 3 to 8 inches wide. The formal, sophisticated look of a parquet floor is unparalleled for richness of visual texture.

Types of Wood Flooring

Wood varieties available as a surface material are vast, and cost varies widely, depending on the type and grade of wood and on the choice of design.

Softwoods, like pine and fir, are often used to make simple tongue-and-groove floorboards. These floors are less expensive than hardwoods but also less durable. The hardwoods—maple, birch, oak, ash—are far less likely to mar with normal use. A hardwood floor is not indestructible; however, it will stand up to demanding use.

Both hardwoods and softwoods are graded according to their color, grain, and imperfections. The top of the line is known as clear, followed by select, No. 1 common, and No. 2 common. In addition to budget considerations, the decision whether to pay top dollar for clear wood or to economize with a lesser grade depends on use factors and on the design objectives. For example, if you plan to install a wood floor in a small room and then cover most of it with an area rug, the No. 2 common grade may be a good choice; lesser grades are also fine for informal rooms where a few defects just enhance a lived-in look. If your design calls for larger areas of rich wood grain that will be exposed, with scatter rugs used for color accents, a clear or select grade will make an attractive choice.

Finishing Options

Color stains—reds, blues, and greens—may work in settings where a casual or rustic feeling is desired. This, however, is a departure from the traditional use of

Wood flooring, below, fits well in both formal and informal spaces.

Laminate flooring, opposite, can mimic the look of real wood or natural stone.

Laminate Flooring

Laminate flooring is the great pretender among flooring materials. When your creative side tells you to install wood but your practical side knows it just won't hold up in the traffic-heavy location for which you're considering it, a wood floor look-alike might be just the thing. Faux wood and faux stone laminate floors provide you with the look you want, tempered with physical wear and care properties that you and your family can live with. Laminate is particularly suited to rooms where floors are likely to see heavy duty—kitchens, family rooms, hallways, and children's bedrooms and playrooms—anywhere stain and scratch resistance and easy cleanup count. Prolonged exposure to moisture will damage some laminate products, but many can now be used in wet areas. Manufacturers of laminate offer warranties against staining, scratching, cracking, and peeling for up to 25 years.

Laminate is made from paper impregnated with melamine, an organic resin, and bonded to a core of particleboard, fiberboard, or other wood by-products. It can be laid over virtually any subflooring surface, including wood and concrete. It can also be applied on top of an existing wood, ceramic, or vinyl tile, as well as vinyl or other sheet flooring. You can even install it over certain types of carpeting, but check the manufacturer's guidelines before doing so.

Installation and Care

The installation of laminate flooring is a reasonably quick and relatively easy do-it-yourself project. It requires sheets of a special foam underlayment followed by the careful placement, cutting, and gluing of the laminate.

Laminate is available in sheets that are ideal when your design calls for a uniform look, such as monotone stone, or a linear design that mimics strip or plank wood flooring. Laminate planks, squares, and blocks offer added design flexibility: with them, you can design your own tile patterns, lay strips of wood-look planks with alternating "stain" finishes, or border your floor with a contrasting color.

wood. Wood is not typically used to deliver color impact; instead it blends with and subtly enhances its surroundings. Natural wood stains range from light ash tones to deep, coffee-like colors. Generally, lighter stains make a room feel less formal, and darker, richer stains suggest a stately atmosphere. As with lighter colors, lighter stains create a feeling of openness; darker stains foster a more intimate feeling and can reduce the visual vastness of a large space.

Installation

If the design plan calls for the laying of unfinished wood strips, factor the cost of hiring a skilled professional into your budget. Many manufacturers offer products with installation kits that make wood flooring a do-it-yourself option for those whose skills are good but don't necessarily approach a professional carpenter's level. Some make strips or planks already finished and sealed. Most parquet tiles come finished and sealed as well.

Vinyl Sheet & Tile Flooring

Like laminate, resilient flooring is also available in design-friendly sheet or tile form. Resilient floors can be made from a variety of materials, including linoleum, asphalt, cork, or rubber. However, the most commonly used material in manufacturing today's resilient floors for homes is vinyl.

Price, durability, and easy maintenance make resilient flooring an attractive and popular choice. Do-it-yourself installation, an option even for those who are not particularly skilled, can mean further savings.

Sheet versus Tiles

Resilient flooring comes in an enormous array of colors and patterns, plus many of the flooring styles have a textured surface. With the tiles, you can combine color and pattern in limitless ways. Even the sheet form of resilient flooring can be customized with inlay strips.

Cushioned sheet vinyl offers the most resilience. It provides excellent stain resistance; it's comfortable and quiet underfoot and easy to maintain, with no-wax and never-wax finishes often available. These features make the floor especially attractive for areas with lots of kid traffic. Beware though: only the more expensive grades show an acceptable degree of resistance to nicking and denting. In rooms where furniture is often moved around, this could be a problem. Although the range of colors, patterns, and surface textures is wide, sheet floor-

Vinyl sheet flooring, left, is a good choice for high-traffic areas, such as kitchens, family rooms, and playrooms. Most products have a no-wax finish that is easy to maintain.

Vinyl flooring, above, comes in a variety of styles and colors. Tiles and sheet flooring can look like ceramic tiles and natural stone.

Ceramic tile, opposite, offers a number of possibilities—from simple patterns to more elaborate designs that feature borders and inlays.

ing is not as flexible as vinyl tile when it comes to customizing your look.

Regular sheet vinyl is less expensive than the cushioned types, but it carries the same disadvantages and is slightly less resilient. Except for the availability of no-wax finishes, a vinyl tile floor is as stain resistant and as easy to maintain as the sheet-vinyl products. Increased design possibilities are the trade-off.

Here, as with other flooring materials, one possible way out of the choice maze is to take the unconventional step of mixing flooring materials. For example, use a durable cushioned sheet vinyl in more trafficked areas, but frame it with a pretty vinyl tile or laminate border.

Ceramic Choices

Ceramic tile—actually fired clay—is an excellent choice for areas subject to a lot of traffic and in rooms where resistance to moisture and stains is needed. These features, combined with easy cleanup, have made ceramic tile a centuries-old tradition for flooring, walls, and ceilings in bathrooms and kitchens. Color, texture, and pattern choices available today make ceramic tile the most versatile flooring option in terms of design possibilities.

Tile Options

Some handcrafted ceramic tiles are very costly, but manufacturers have created a market full of design and style options.

Tiles come in a variety of sizes, beginning with 1-inch-square mosaic tiles up to large 16 x 16-inch squares. Other shapes, such as triangles, diamonds, and rectangles, are also available. Tile textures range from shiny to matte-finished and from glass-smooth to ripple-surfaced. Tiles are available either glazed or unglazed. Glazed tiles have a hard, often colored, surface that is applied during the firing process; the resulting finish can range from glossy to matte. Unglazed tiles, such as terra-cotta or quarry tiles, have a matte finish, are porous, and need to be sealed to prevent staining.

Consider using accent borders to create unique designs, such as a faux area rug, that visually separate sections of a room or separate one room from another. When added in a random pattern, embossed accent tiles add interest, variety, and elegance to an expanse of single-colored tiles.

Alas, no surfacing material is perfect. Ceramic tile offers long-lasting beauty, design versatility, and simplicity of maintenance, but it also has some hard-to-live-with features. Tile is cold underfoot, noisy when someone walks across it in hard-soled shoes, and not at all resilient—always expect the worst when something breakable falls on a tile floor. If you have infants and toddlers around, it may be best to wait a few years for your tiled floor.

Natural Stone

Like ceramic tile, stone and marble are classified as "non-resilients." Like tile, these materials offer richness of color, durability, moisture and stain resistance, and ease of maintenance. They also share with tile the drawbacks of being cold to the touch, noisy to walk on, and unforgivingly hard.

Stone and marble floors are clearly, unmistakably natural. As remarkably good as some faux surfaces look, no product manufactured today actually matches the rustic irregularity and random color variation of natural stone.

Picking a Flooring Material

Now that you've got the facts about each floor surface option, picking the right one for your design will be much less confusing. The following steps can make it downright simple.

Step 1: Make a "Use/Abuse" Analysis. Begin by asking yourself the most important question: How will this room used? Your answer should tell you just what kind of traffic the future floor surface will endure. With a relatively expensive investment like a floor, it's best not to guess. Instead, use this system to arrive at an accurate use/abuse analysis.

On a piece of paper, make columns headed "Who" and "Activities," and then list who in the family will use the room and what activities will occur there. Will the kids play with toys on the floor? Will they do arts and crafts projects with paint, glue, and glitter? Will the family gather on Saturday afternoons and snack while watching a football game on television? Is it a formal living room where you will entertain your friends and business clients? Is it a busy kitchen? Does the hallway extend from your front entrance or from a busier back door where the kids will drop off their hockey skates?

The answers to these questions will help you to determine how durable and resilient a flooring surface needs to be, whether warmth and softness are requirements, and how much maintenance will be necessary to keep the surface clean.

Step 2: Determine Your Design Objectives. Your choices are limited by the other elements in the room. Your color choices can enhance the color palette you are planning. Because you will be starting from scratch—including walls, furniture, and accessories—you have more flexibility, although your job is a bit more complex and involves more decisions.

Once you've determined your design objectives, compare your use/abuse analysis

High-traffic areas, below left, require flooring that can stand up to abuse.

Laminate flooring, below right, is a good choice for a variety of rooms.

to the types of flooring that meet both your style and use needs. From the list of options that are left, you can narrow down your choices even more.

Step 3: Draw and Use a Floor Plan.
After you have completed the use/abuse analysis and the list of design objectives, draw up a floor plan—a separate one for experimenting with your flooring ideas. Follow these guidelines: measure the length and width of the room, and plot it on graph paper, using a scale of 1 inch to 1 foot. If your room is larger than 8 x 10 feet, you can tape two pieces of 8½- x 11-inch graph paper together. Measure and mark the locations of entryways and any permanent features in the room, such as cabinets, fixtures, or appliances.

Make several photocopies of your floor plan. Reserve one copy as a template. Use the other copies for previewing pattern ideas for flooring that comes in tiles (ceramic, vinyl, or carpeting tiles). Buy multicolored pencils, and fill in your grid. You'll be able to determine not only how the pattern will look but also how many tiles of various colors you'll need to buy to complete the project. Don't forget to include such items as borders and inlays.

Step 4: Convert Your Overall Budget to Cost per Square Foot.
After you've completed the use/abuse analysis, determined your design objectives, and created a floor plan, the next step is determining cost.

Most flooring is priced in terms of square feet. To determine how many square feet are in your room, round the measurements up to the next foot. Then simply multiply the length by the width. For example, for a room measuring 10 feet 4 inches x 12 feet 6 inches, round the figures to 11 x 13 feet. Multiply 11 x 13 feet (that's 143 square feet). You will end up with extra flooring, but it is better to have more than less.

Some flooring—like carpeting—is priced in terms of square yards. To determine the number of square yards in your room, divide the number of square feet by nine. In our example, there are just under 16 square yards in 143 square feet.

Let's say you have a budget of $850 to purchase tile for your 10-foot-4-inch x 12-foot-6-inch room. For the sake of the illustration, let's assume your subflooring is adequate, you have the tools, and the cost of adhesive and grout for your room is about $75. That leaves you with $775. To determine how much you can spend per tile, divide the remainder by the number of square feet in the room. In our example, $775 divided by 143 square feet equals about $5.40 per square foot of tile.

Light colors, below left, make a room feel more open than darker colors.

Consider the rest of the room, below, when selecting flooring.

Plan #201084

Dimensions: 66'10" W x 54'5" D

Levels: 1

Square Footage: 2,056

Bedrooms: 3

Bathrooms: 2

Foundation: Crawl space, slab

Materials List Available: Yes

Price Category: D

Images provided by designer/architect.

This classic family home features beautiful country styling with lots of curb appeal.

Features:

- Ceiling Height: 8 ft.

- Open Plan: When guests arrive, they'll enter a foyer that is open to the dining room and den. This open area makes the home seem especially spacious and offers the flexibility for all kinds of entertaining and family activities.

- Kitchen: You'll love preparing meals in this large, well-designed kitchen. There's plenty of counter space, and the breakfast bar is perfect impromptu family meals.

- Master Suite: This spacious and elegant master suite is separated from the other bedroom for maximum privacy.

- Bonus Room: This unfinished bonus room awaits the time to add another bedroom or a home office.

- Garage: This attached garage offers parking for two cars, plus plenty of storage space.

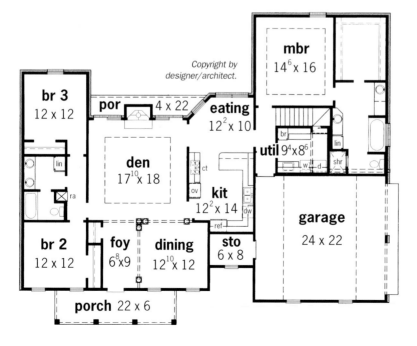

Copyright by designer/architect.

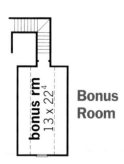

Bonus Room

Plan #201025

Dimensions: 62' W x 46' D
Levels: 1
Square Footage: 1,379
Bedrooms: 3
Bathrooms: 2
Foundation: Crawl space, slab
Materials List Available: Yes
Price Category: B

Images provided by designer/architect.

If you're looking for a mixture of practicality and luxury, you'll love the features of this house.

Features:

- Porch: In the right locale, this porch is ideal for sitting when the weather's warm.

- Den: A corner fireplace and door to the rear porch make this room a natural gathering spot, no matter the time of day or season.

- Kitchen: An angled bar makes a divider as well as a counter here. The U-shaped layout and good storage spaces will delight the family cook.

- Eating Nook: Tuck a table into the nook the windows create to complement the curve.

- Master Suite: The large bedroom is complemented by a walk-in closet and bath with double vanity.

- Storage Room: Off the garage, this room has lots of space for out of season tools and materials.

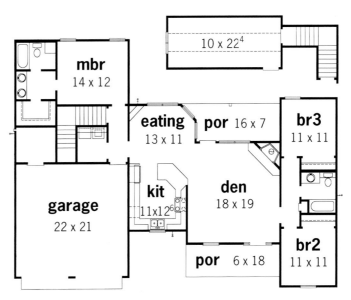

Copyright by designer/architect.

Plan #211111

Dimensions: 66' W x 74' D

Levels: 2

Square Footage: 3,035

Main Level Sq. Ft.: 2,008

Upper Level Sq. Ft.: 1,027

Bedrooms: 4

Bathrooms: 3½

Foundation: Crawl space

Materials List Available: Yes

Price Category: G

Kids can be kids without disturbing the adults, thanks to the rear stair in this large family house.

Features:

- Ceiling Height: 9 ft. unless otherwise noted.

- Formal Living Room: This large formal living room is connected to the formal dining room and to the family room by a pair of French doors, making this an ideal home for entertaining.

- Wet Bar: This wet bar is neatly placed between the kitchen and the family room, adding to the entertainment amenities.

- Deck: Step out of the family room onto a covered porch that leads to this spacious deck and a breezeway.

- Master Suite: This master suite is isolated for privacy. The master bath is flooded with natural light from sky windows in the sloped ceiling, and it has a dressing vanity with surrounding mirrors.

- Secondary Bedrooms: All secondary bedrooms have bath access and dual closets.

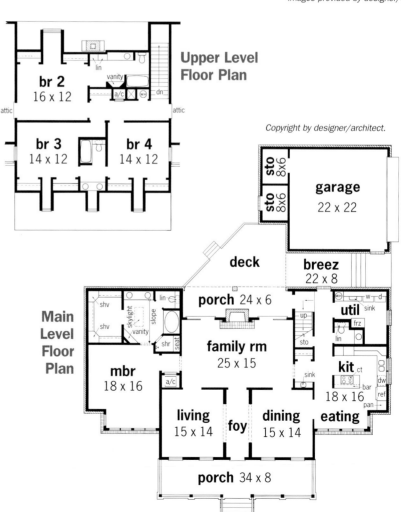

Plan #151089

Dimensions: 84' W x 55'6" D
Levels: 1
Square Footage: 1,921
Bedrooms: 3
Bathrooms: 3
Foundation: Crawl space, slab, or basement
Materials List Available: Yes
Price Category: D

Images provided by designer/architect.

If your family loves to combine indoor and outdoor living, this home's fabulous porches and deck space make it perfect.

Features:

- **Porches:** A huge wraparound front porch, sizable rear porch, and deck that joins them give you space for entertaining or simply lounging.

- **Living Room:** A fireplace and built-in media center could be the focal points in this large room.

- **Hearth Room:** Open to both the living room and kitchen, this hearth room also features a fireplace.

- **Kitchen:** This step-saving kitchen includes ample storage and work space, as well as an angled bar it shares with the hearth room. Atrium doors lead to the rear porch.

- **Bonus Upper Level:** A large game room and a full bath make this area a favorite with the children.

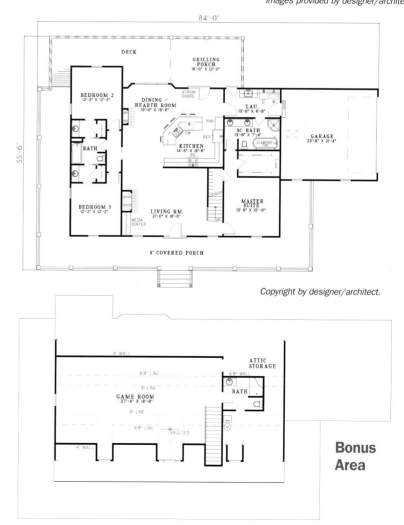

Copyright by designer/architect.

Bonus Area

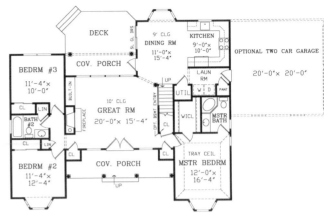

Copyright by designer/architect.

Images provided by designer/architect.

Plan #131014

Dimensions: 48' W x 43'4" D
Levels: 1
Square Footage: 1,380
Bedrooms: 3
Bathrooms: 2
Foundation: Basement, crawl space, or slab
Materials List Available: Yes
Price Category: B

Rear Elevation

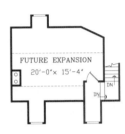

Bonus Room

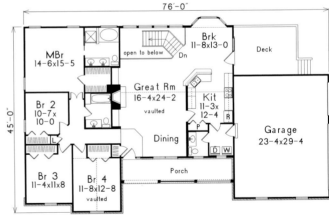

Images provided by designer/architect.

Plan #321006

Dimensions: 76' W x 45' D
Levels: 1, optional lower
Square Footage: 1,977
Optional Basement Level
Sq. Ft.: 1,416
Bedrooms: 4
Bathrooms: 2½
Foundation: Basement
Materials List Available: Yes
Price Category: D

Optional Basement Level Floor Plan

Copyright by designer/architect.

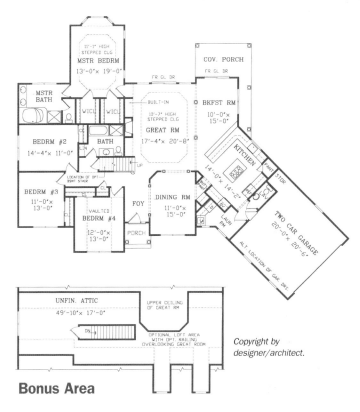

Bonus Area

Plan #131045

Dimensions: 81'4" W x 68'3" D

Levels: 1

Square Footage: 2,347

Bedrooms: 4

Bathrooms: 2½

Foundation: Basement, crawl space, or slab

Materials List Available: Yes

Price Category: E

Images provided by designer/architect.

Copyright by designer/architect.

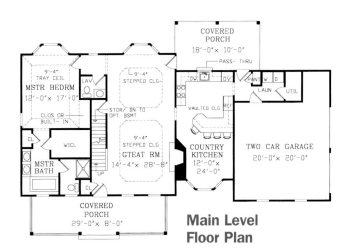

Main Level Floor Plan

Upper Level Floor Plan

Copyright by designer/architect.

Plan #131043

Dimensions: 65'8" W x 43'10" D

Levels: 2

Square Footage: 1,945

Main Level Sq. Ft.: 1,375

Upper Level Sq. Ft.: 570

Bedrooms: 3

Bathrooms: 2½

Foundation: Crawl space, slab, or basement

Materials List Available: Yes

Price Category: D

Images provided by designer/architect.

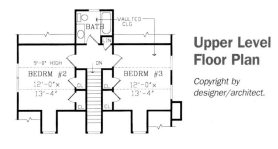

Plan #131027

Dimensions: 62'4" W x 53'6" D
Levels: 2
Square Footage: 2,567
Main Level Sq. Ft.: 2,017
Upper Level Sq. Ft.: 550
Bedrooms: 4
Bathrooms: 3
Foundation: Crawl space, slab, or basement
Materials List Available: Yes
Price Category: F

Images provided by designer/architect.

The features of this home are so good that you may have trouble imagining all of them at once.

Features:

- Great Room: Imagine a stepped ceiling, corner fireplace, built-media center, and wall of windows with a glass door to the backyard—in one room.

- Dining Room: A stepped ceiling and server with a sink add to the elegance of this formal room.

- Breakfast Room: Eat at the bar this room shares with the island kitchen, and admire the 12-ft. cathedral ceiling and bayed group of 8- and 9-ft. windows. Or go through the sliding glass door to the covered side porch.

- Master Suite: The bedroom has a tray ceiling and cozy sitting area, and a whirlpool tub, shower, and walk-in closet are in the skylighted bath.

- Optional Study: The private bath in bedroom 2 makes it ideal for a study or home office.

- Bonus Room: Enjoy the extra 300 sq. ft.

Breakfast Nook

Rear View

Great Room

Main Level Floor Plan

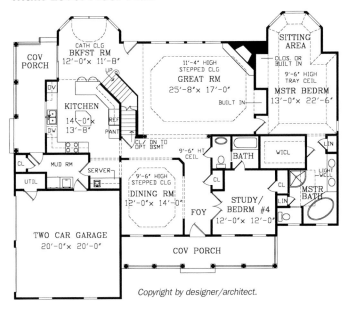

Copyright by designer/architect.

Upper Level Floor Plan

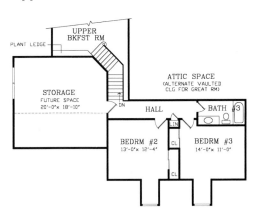

Painting Tips

As with any skill, there is a right and a wrong way to paint. There is a right way to hold a brush, a right way to maneuver a roller, a right way to spray a wall, etc. Follow these basic professional tips:

Brushing vs. Rolling. Some painters insist that only a brush-painted job looks right. However, most painters will "cut in" the edges with a brush, and then finish the main body of a wall or ceiling using a roller. Brushing alone can be time-consuming, and it is typically reserved for architectural woodwork.

Using the Right Brush. Use the largest brush with which you are comfortable. Professional painters seldom pick up anything smaller than a 4-inch brush. Most homeowners will achieve good results using a 4-inch brush for "cutting in" and for large surfaces, and an angled 2½- to 3-inch sash brush for trim around windows and doors. Be sure, also, to use brushes that are appropriate for the type of paint being applied. Oil-based paints require a natural bristle (also called "China bristles"), while water-based paints are applied with a synthetic bristle brush.

Handling a Brush. Many people grip a paintbrush as if they were shaking someone's hand. It is better to grip a brush more like a pencil, with the fingers and thumb wrapped around the metal ferrule. This grip provides the hand and wrist with a wider range of motion and therefore greater speed and precision. If your hand cramps, switch hands or switch temporarily to the handshake grip.

Wiping Rags. Before you begin painting, put a dust rag in your pocket. This is helpful for clearing away cobwebs and dust before painting. It is also handy for wiping off paint drips before they have a chance to dry.

Paint Hooks. When working on a ladder, use a good-quality paint hook to secure the paint bucket to your ladder. Avoid makeshift hooks made with wire or coat hangers. Paint hooks are inexpensive and available at virtually all paint and hardware stores.

Plan #151108

Dimensions: 84'6" W x 58'6" D
Levels: 1
Square Footage: 2,742
Bedrooms: 4
Bathrooms: 2½
Foundation: Crawl space, slab, or basement
Materials List Available: Yes
Price Category: F

The arched entry, with its elegant dual columns, sets the tone for this gracious home.

Features:

- Porches: The covered front porch and a screened rear porch add lounging space.

- Great Room: A fireplace, media center, and French doors to the sunroom are the focal points in this room with a 10-foot ceiling.

- Sunroom: Opening from the great room, one bedroom, and the screened porch, this room is a natural gathering spot.

- Dining Room: Columns define this spacious room with a 10-foot ceiling, where you'll dine in comfort.

- Kitchen: This well-planned work space features a snack bar open to the bayed breakfast nook.

- Master Suite: Atrium doors lead to the screened porch from this suite with two huge closets and a bath with two vanities and numerous amenities.

Optional Bonus Space Floor Plan

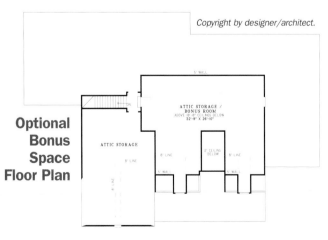

Images provided by designer/architect.

Plan #151105

Dimensions: 60'6" W x 91'4" D
Levels: 1
Square Footage: 2,039
Bedrooms: 4
Bathrooms: 2
Foundation: Crawl space, slab, or optional basement
Materials List Available: Yes
Price Category: D

If you've always wanted a wraparound porch with columns, this could be your dream home.

Features:

- **Great Room:** Just off the foyer, this spacious room features a handsome fireplace where friends and family are sure to gather.

- **Dining Room:** Columns set off this dining room, and the large window area allows natural lighting during the day.

- **Kitchen:** Open to the dining room, this well-planned kitchen features a large central island with a sink and a dishwasher on one side and an eating bar on the other.

- **Breakfast Room:** You'll love the unusual shape of this room and its windows overlooking the rear porch. Access to the porch is from a hallway here.

- **Master Suite:** Enjoy two walk-in closets, plus a bath with a corner whirlpool tub, glass shower, linen closet, vanity, and compartmentalized toilet.

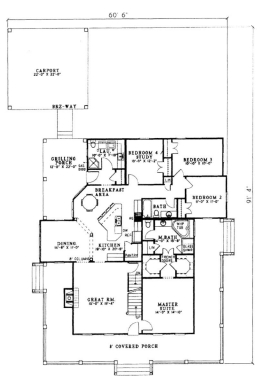

Bonus Area

Copyright by designer/architect.

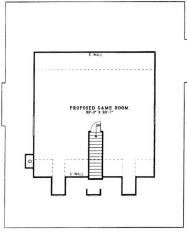

Plan #131034

Dimensions: 40' W x 32' D
Levels: 2 (Upper unfinished)
Square Footage: 1,040
Bedrooms: 5
Bathrooms: 2½
Foundation: Crawl space, slab, or basement
Materials List Available: Yes
Price Category: C

You'll love the versatility this expandable ranch-style home gives, with its unfinished, second story that you can transform into two bedrooms and a bath if you need the space.

Features:

- **Porch:** Decorate this country-style porch to accentuate the charm of this warm home.

- **Living Room:** This formal room features a wide, dramatic archway that opens to the kitchen and the dining room.

- **Kitchen:** The angled shape of this kitchen gives it character, while the convenient island and well-designed floor plan make cooking and cleaning tasks unusually efficient.

- **Bedrooms:** Use the design option in the blueprints of this home to substitute one of the bedrooms into an expansion of the master bedroom, which features an amenity-laden, private bathroom for total luxury.

Optional Main Level Floor Plan

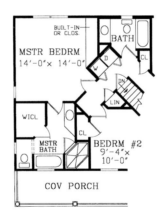

Main Level Floor Plan

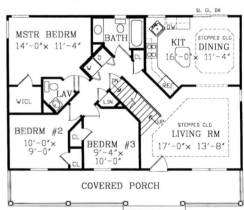

Kitchen

Upper Level Floor Plan

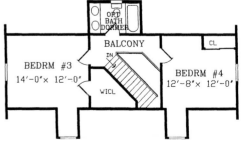

Copyright by designer/architect.

Plan #151014

Dimensions: 70'2" W x 51'4" D

Levels: 2

Square Footage: 2,698

Main Level Sq. Ft.: 1,813

Upper Level Sq. Ft.: 885

Bedrooms: 5

Bathrooms: 3

Foundation: Crawl space, slab, optional basement for fee

Price Category: D

Images provided by designer/architect.

A comfortable front porch welcomes you into this home that features a balcony over the great room, a study, and a kitchen designed for gourmet cooks.

Features:

- Ceiling Height: 9 ft.
- Front Porch: Stately 12-in.-wide pillars form the entryway.
- Foyer: Open to upper story.
- Great Room: A fireplace, vaulted 9-ft. ceiling, and balcony from the second floor add character to this lovely room.
- Dining Room: Open to the kitchen for convenience.
- Kitchen: A large walk-in pantry, well-designed work areas, and eat-in bar make this room a treasure.

- Breakfast Room: Enjoy this spot that opens to both the kitchen and a large covered porch at the rear of the house.
- Study: This quiet room has French doors leading to the yard.
- Master Suite: This spacious area has cozy window seats as well as his and her walk-in closets. The master bathroom is fitted with a whirlpool tub, a glass shower, and his and her sinks.

Upper Level Floor Plan

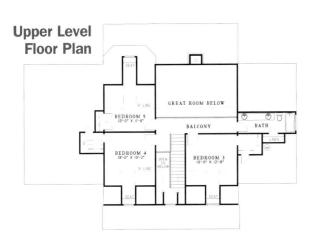

Main Level Floor Plan

Copyright by designer/architect.

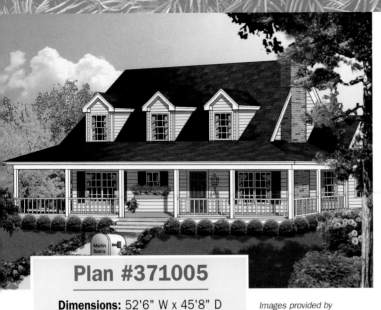

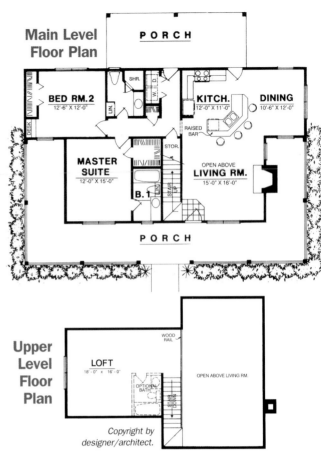

**Main Level
Floor Plan**

PORCH

BED RM. 2
12'-6" X 12'-0"

SHR.

KITCH.
12'-0" X 11'-0"

DINING
10'-6" X 12'-0"

RAISED BAR

MASTER SUITE
12'-0" X 15'-0"

STOR.

OPEN ABOVE
LIVING RM.
15'-0" X 16'-0"

B. 1

PORCH

*Images provided by
designer/architect.*

Plan #371005

Dimensions: 52'6" W x 45'8" D

Levels: 1

Square Footage: 1,250

Bedrooms: 2

Bathrooms: 2

Foundation: Slab
(crawl space option for fee)

Materials List Available: No

Price Category: B

**Upper
Level
Floor
Plan**

WOOD RAIL

LOFT
18'-0" x 16'-0"

OPEN ABOVE LIVING RM.

OPTIONAL BATH

STAIR DOWN

*Copyright by
designer/architect.*

**Main Level
Floor Plan**

DINING
13 x 12

KIT.
10 x 12

BRKFST.
8 x 14

LIVING
13 x 19

BEDROOM
16 x 12

PORCH

*Images provided by
designer/architect.*

Plan #381005

Dimensions: 43' W x 40' D

Levels: 2

Square Footage: 2,030

Main Level Sq. Ft.: 1,295

Upper Level Sq. Ft.: 735

Bedrooms: 3

Bathrooms: 2½

Foundation: Basement

Materials List Available: Yes

Price Category: D

**Upper Level
Floor Plan**

BEDROOM
16 x 22

BEDROOM
16 x 22

*Copyright by
designer/architect.*

Main Level Floor Plan

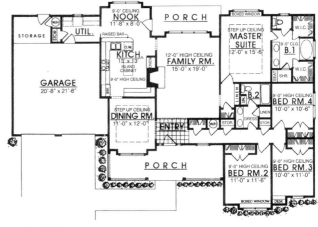

Plan #151172

Dimensions: 76'10" W x 53'4" D
Levels: 1½
Square Footage: 2,373
Upper Sq. Ft. (Bonus): 776
Bedrooms: 4
Bathrooms: 3
Foundation: Crawl space, slab (basement or daylight basement option for fee)
Materials List Available: Yes
Price Category: E

Images provided by designer/architect.

Upper Level Floor Plan

Copyright by designer/architect.

Plan #371007

Dimensions: 72'10" W x 48'4½" D
Levels: 1
Square Footage: 1,944
Bedrooms: 4
Bathrooms: 2
Foundation: Slab (crawl space option for fee)
Materials List Available: No
Price Category: D

Images provided by designer/architect.

Copyright by designer/architect.

Plan #131041

Dimensions: 42' W x 45' D
Levels: 2
Square Footage: 1,679
Main Level Sq. Ft.: 1,134
Upper Level Sq. Ft.: 545
Bedrooms: 3
Bathrooms: 2½
Foundation: Crawl space, slab, or basement
Materials List Available: Yes
Price Category: D

This rustic-looking two-story cottage includes contemporary amenities for your total comfort.

Features:

- Great Room: With a 9-ft.-4-in.-high ceiling, this large room makes everyone feel at home. A fireplace with raised hearth and built-in niche for a TV will encourage the whole family to gather here on cool evenings, and sliding glass doors leading to the rear covered porch make it an ideal entertaining area in mild weather.

- Kitchen: When people aren't in the great room, you're likely to find them here, because the convenient serving bar welcomes casual dining, and this room also opens to the p porch.

- Master Suite: Relax at the end of the day in this room, with its 9-ft.-4-in.-high ceiling and walk-in closet, or luxuriate in the private bath with whirlpool tub and dual-sink vanity.

- Optional Basement: This area can include a tuck-under two-car garage if you desire it.

Main Level Floor Plan

Upper Level Floor Plan

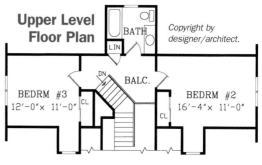

Great Room

Plan #131046

Dimensions: 68' W x 57'6" D
Levels: 2
Square Footage: 2,245
Main Level Sq. Ft.: 1,720
Upper Level Sq. Ft.: 525
Bedrooms: 3
Bathrooms: 2½
Foundation: Crawl space, slab, or basement
Materials List Available: Yes
Price Category: F

You'll love the mixture of country charm and contemporary amenities in this lovely home.

Features:

- Porch: The covered wraparound porch spells comfort, and the arched windows spell style.

- Great Room: Look up at the 18-ft. vaulted ceiling and the balcony that looks over this room from the upper level, and then notice the wall of windows and the fireplace that's set into a media wall for decorating ease.

- Kitchen: This roomy kitchen is also designed for convenience, thanks to its ample counter space and work island.

- Breakfast Room: The kitchen looks out to this lovely room, with its vaulted ceiling and sliding French doors that open to the rear covered porch.

- Master Bedroom: A 10-ft-ceiling and a dramatic bay window give character to this charming room.

Images provided by designer/architect.

Main Level Floor Plan

Copyright by designer/architect.

Upper Level Floor Plan

Plan #151171

Dimensions: 63'10" W x 72'2" D
Levels: 1
Square Footage: 2,131
Bedrooms: 3
Bathrooms: 2½
Foundation: Crawl space, slab (basement or daylight basement option for fee)
Materials List Available: Yes
Price Category: D

Images provided by designer/architect.

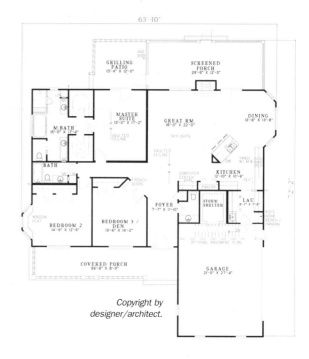

Copyright by designer/architect.

Plan #241029

Dimensions: 70' W x 53'5" D
Levels: 1
Square Footage: 2,074
Bedrooms: 3
Bathrooms: 2½
Foundation: Slab
Materials List Available: No
Price Category: D

Images provided by designer/architect.

Copyright by designer/architect.

Main Level Floor Plan

COVERED PORCH
44'-0" x 7'-6"
SL GL DRS

LAUN RM
UTIL

KITCHEN
8'-8" x 9'-8"

9'-4" CLG
GREAT RM
15'-0" x 23'-4"

9'-4" HIGH STEPPED CLG
MSTR BEDRM
12'-0" x 15'-0"

CL

BEDRM #2
10'-0" x 10'-0"

CL

VAULTED FOYER

MSTR BATH

CL

UP

COVERED PORCH
44'-0" x 7'-6"

44'-0" OVERALL

39'-0" OVERALL

Copyright by designer/architect.

Plan #131053

Dimensions: 44' W x 39' D
Levels: 1 (2)
Square Footage: 1,056 (1,673)
Main Level Sq. Ft.: 1,056
Opt. Upper Level Sq. Ft.: 617
Bedrooms: 2 (4)
Bathrooms: 2 (3)
Foundation: Basement, crawl space, or slab
Materials List Available: Yes
Price Category: B (C)

Images provided by designer/architect.

Rear Elevation

BATH
WICL   WICL
LIN

BEDRM #3
12'-4" x 13'-6"

BALCONY

BEDRM #4
12'-4" x 13'-6"

DN

UPPER FOYER CEILING

PLANT LEDGE

Optional Upper Level Floor Plan

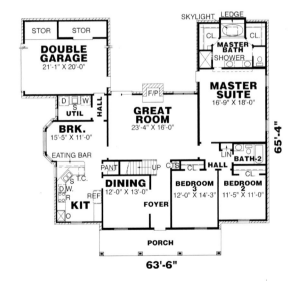

STOR   STOR

DOUBLE GARAGE
21'-1" X 20'-0"

SKYLIGHT LEDGE

CL   CL
MASTER BATH
SHOWER

D W
S
UTIL

HALL

F/P

GREAT ROOM
23'-4" X 16'-0"

MASTER SUITE
16'-9" X 18'-0"

BRK.
15'-5" X 11'-0"

EATING BAR

PANT

UP

CTS   CL

HALL

LIN
BATH-2
CL

65'-4"

S.T.C.
DW
R   REF

KIT

DINING
12'-0" X 13'-0"

FOYER

BEDROOM 3
12'-0" X 14'-3"

BEDROOM 2
11'-5" X 11'-0"

PORCH

63'-6"

Plan #241030

Dimensions: 63'6" W x 65'4" D
Levels: 1
Square Footage: 2,185
Bedrooms: 3
Bathrooms: 2
Foundation: Slab
Materials List Available: No
Price Category: D

Images provided by designer/architect.

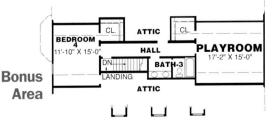

Bonus Area

BEDROOM 4
11'-10" X 15'-0"

CL

ATTIC

CL

HALL

DN

BATH-3

PLAYROOM
17'-2" X 15'-0"

LANDING

ATTIC

Copyright by designer/architect.

Plan #141014

Dimensions: 72' W x 38' D

Levels: 2

Square Footage: 2,091

Main Level Sq. Ft.: 1,362

Upper Level Sq. Ft.: 729

Bedrooms: 3

Bathrooms: 2½

Foundation: Basement

Materials List Available: Yes

Price Category: D

The wraparound front porch and front dormers evoke an old-fashioned country home.

Features:

- Ceiling Height: 8 ft. unless otherwise noted.

- Living Room: This spacious area has an open flow to the dining room, so you can graciously usher guests when it is time to eat.

- Dining Room: This elegant dining room has a bay that opens to the sun deck.

- Kitchen: This warm and inviting kitchen looks out to the front porch. Its bayed breakfast area is perfect for informal family meals.

- Master Suite: The bedroom enjoys a view through the front porch and features a master bath with all the amenities.

- Flexible Room: A room above the two-bay garage offers plenty of space that can be used for anything from a home office to a teen suite.

- Study Room: The two second-floor bedrooms share a study that is perfect for homework.

Images provided by designer/architect.

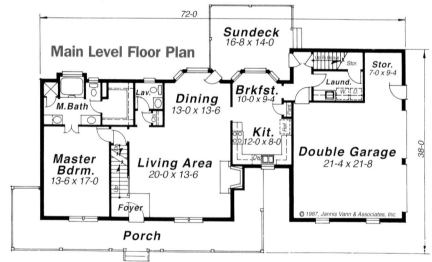

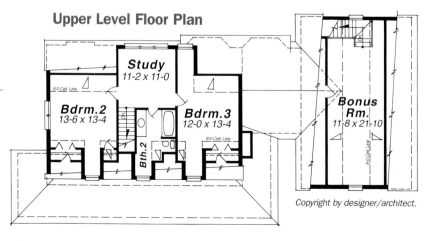

Copyright by designer/architect.

Plan #141010

Dimensions: 43'4" W x 37' D

Levels: 2

Square Footage: 1,765

Main Level Sq. Ft.: 1,210

Upper Level Sq. Ft.: 555

Bedrooms: 3

Bathrooms: 2½

Foundation: Basement

Materials List Available: No

Price Category: C

A Palladian window in a stone gable adds a new twist to a classical cottage design.

Features:

- Ceiling Height: 8 ft. unless otherwise noted.

- Living Area: Dormers open into this handsome living area, which is designed to accommodate gatherings of any size.

- Master Suite: This beautiful master bedroom opens off the foyer. It features a modified cathedral ceiling that makes the front Palladian window a focal point inside as well as out. The master bath offers a dramatic cathedral ceiling over the tub and vanity.

- Balcony: U-shaped stairs lead to this elegant balcony, which overlooks the foyer while providing access to two additional bedrooms.

- Garage: This garage is tucked under the house to improve the appearance from the street. It offers two bays for plenty of parking and storage space.

Images provided by designer/architect.

Copyright by designer/architect.

SMARTtip

Stone Tables

Marble- and stone-topped tables with plants are perfect for use in light-filled rooms. Warmed by the sun during the day, the tabletops catch leaf droppings and can stand up to the splatters of watering cans and plant sprayers.

Plan #101022

Dimensions: 66'2" W x 62' D

Levels: 1

Square Footage: 1,992

Bedrooms: 3

Bathrooms: 3

Foundation: Basement, crawl space, or slab

Materials List Available: Yes

Price Category: D

Images provided by designer/ architect.

Copyright by designer/architect.

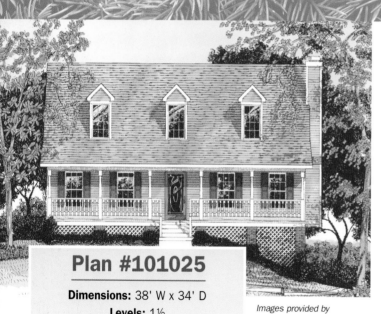

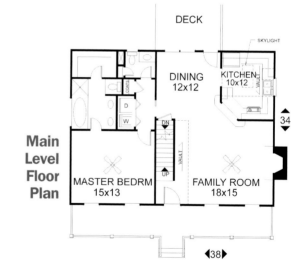

Plan #101025

Dimensions: 38' W x 34' D

Levels: 1½

Square Footage: 1,643

Main Level Sq. Ft.: 1,064

Upper Level Sq. Ft.: 579

Bedrooms: 3

Bathrooms: 2½

Foundation: Basement, crawl space

Materials List Available: No

Price Category: C

Images provided by designer/architect.

Copyright by designer/architect.

Today's Fireplace Technology

Handsome and romantic, but drafty. Thirty years ago, you might have described a traditional fireplace in this way. But that was before technological advancements finally made fireplaces more efficient. Now, not only can you expect your fireplace to provide ambiance and warmth, you can relax knowing that your energy dollars aren't going up in smoke. Over the centuries, people had tried to improve the efficiency of the fireplace so that it would generate the maximum heat possible from the wood consumed. But real strides didn't come until the energy crisis of the early 1970s. That's when designers of fireplaces and stoves introduced some significant innovations. Today, fireplaces are not only more efficient, but cleaner and easier to use.

The traditional fireplace is an all-masonry construction, consisting of only bricks and mortar. However, new constructions and reconstructions of masonry fireplaces often include either a metal or a ceramic firebox. This type of firebox has double walls. The space between these walls is where cool air heats up after being drawn in through openings near the floor of the room. The warm air exits through openings near the top of the firebox. Although a metal firebox is more efficient than an all-masonry firebox, it doesn't radiate heat very effectively, and the heat from the fireplace is distributed by convection—that is, the circulation of warmed air. This improvement in heating capacity comes from the warm air emitted by the upper openings. But that doesn't keep your feet toasty on a cold winter's night—remember, warm air rises.

A more recent development is the ceramic firebox, which is engineered from modern materials such as the type used in kilns. Fires in ceramic fireboxes burn hotter, cleaner, and more efficiently than in all-masonry or metal fireboxes. The main reason is that the back and the walls of a ceramic firebox absorb, retain, and reflect heat effectively. This means that during the time the fire is blazing, more heat radiates into the room than with the other fireboxes. Heat radiation is boosted by the fact that most ceramic units are made with

The warm glow of a realistic-looking modern zero-clearance gas fire, below, can make the hearth the heart of any room in the house.

Zero-Clearance Fireplace

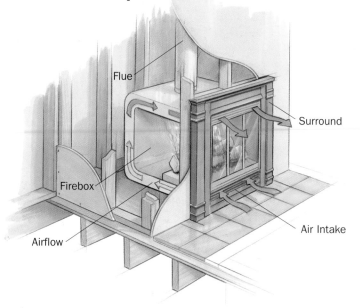

Flue
Surround
Firebox
Airflow
Air Intake

Traditional Masonry Fireplace

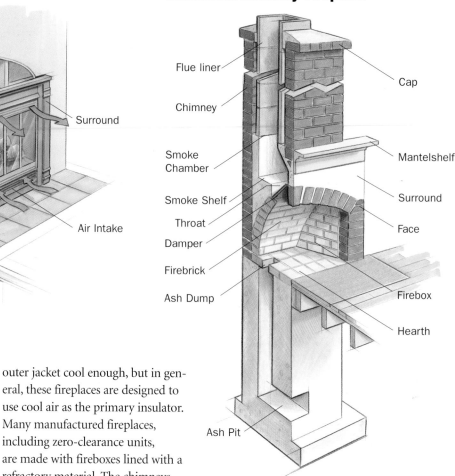

Flue liner
Chimney
Smoke Chamber
Smoke Shelf
Throat
Damper
Firebrick
Ash Dump
Ash Pit
Cap
Mantelshelf
Surround
Face
Firebox
Hearth

thick walls, and so the fire itself is not set as deeply into the hearth as it is with all-masonry or metal fireboxes. As a bonus, because heat is absorbed and retained by the material, the firebox actually radiates a significant amount of heat many hours after the fire has died down. By contrast, a metal firebox cools quickly once the heat source goes out.

In this type of efficient fireplace construction, a metal firebox is usually less expensive than a ceramic one, but the metal does break down over time, in a process professionals refer to as burnout. In addition, an air-circulating metal firebox can only be installed in masonry constructions that are built with ports for the intake of cool air and the discharge of warmed air, or in masonry fireplaces in which such ports can be added. On the other hand, ceramic fireboxes can be installed in any type of masonry fireplace and are not subject to burnout.

Manufactured Fireplaces

The metal fireplaces that are made today can be zero-clearance or freestanding. The zero-clearance units are so named because they can be installed safely against combustible surfaces such as wood. Any of a number of methods are used to keep the

outer jacket cool enough, but in general, these fireplaces are designed to use cool air as the primary insulator. Many manufactured fireplaces, including zero-clearance units, are made with fireboxes lined with a refractory material. The chimneys are also made of metal, and a variety of designs use noncombustible material or air as insulation to keep the outer surface at a safe temperature.

New-technology and traditional fireplaces are shown above. Woodstove-like inserts, below and opposite, make fireplaces more efficient.

The Advantages of a Manufactured Unit

There are some important pluses to choosing a zero-clearance manufactured fireplace. First is the price, which is relatively low, and second is the easy and quick installation. Also, these units are lightweight and can be installed over almost any type of flooring, including wood. This means they do not need elaborate foundations, which is another cost-saver. Manufactured fireplaces are also extremely efficient, and many are designed to provide both radiated heat from the firebox and convection heat from ducting.

Manufactured freestanding fireplaces are, in effect, stoves. They are available in an array of colors, finishes, shapes, and sizes. Like zero-clearance factory-built fireplaces, freestanding models are lightweight, offering the same advantages: no need for heavy masonry or additional reinforcement of flooring. And you have a choice of either a wood-burning or gas-powered unit. Heat efficiency is maximized because, in addition to the firebox, the chimney and all sides of the unit radiate heat into the room. Freestanding units may be the least expensive option because installation requires only a chimney hole and, depending on the type of flooring, a noncombustible pad. A major disadvantage is the space required for placement, because you cannot install most of these units near a combustible wall. Also, a freestanding fireplace is probably not the best choice for families with young children because so much heat is radiated from the exposed surfaces.

Hybrids

If you're looking for a way to get improved efficiency from a masonry fireplace, consider a gas insert (actually a prefabricated firebox equipped with gas logs). You can purchase either a venting insert or one that's nonventing. But be prepared to pay $1,500 to several thousand dollars for the unit in addition to the cost of installation. For a fraction of that amount you can simply replace real wood logs with ceramic logs powered by gas. Like inserts, these logs may or may not require venting. Consult an experienced plumber or heating contractor, and remember that once you convert to gas you cannot burn wood.

Improving a masonry fireplace on the inside by installing a metal firebox might also be an inspiration to think of the fireplace and mantel in a new design way. Pairing two or more finishing materials, such as metal and masonry, can make your fireplace a hybrid in more than one way. For example, combine a stone base with a metal hood and chimney to create a custom-designed fireplace that works as a room divider in a large space. The design options in terms of materials and technology are seemingly endless.

If you have plans for building an innovative custom design, carefully review them with an expert in fireplace construction and maintenance to make sure you're not doing something hazardous. Also, don't forget to check with your local building inspector so that you don't waste time and money on a project that may not comply with codes and regulations set forth where you live.

Enhancing the Basics

You can improve the efficiency of any manufactured fireplace, and of masonry and hybrid constructions as well, with a few extras. In a masonry fireplace, a device commonly referred to as a fresh-air intake accessory or an outside air kit may improve performance. A fresh-air accessory makes use of outside air instead of heated room air for combustion, thus improving the fireplace's efficiency. There is another way to make your fireplace more efficient that isn't high tech at all, however. Simply replace the traditional grate or firebasket with a superior design—one that provides greater air circulation and allows a better placement of logs. Another type, a heat-exchanger grate, works with a fan. The device draws in the room's air, reheats it quickly, and then forces it back into the room.

Capitalizing on Technology

Wood is the traditional fuel for a fireplace, and today's manufactured fireplaces offer designs that make the most of your cord of hardwood. However, wood is not the only fuel option. In fact, in some places, it's not an option at all. There are manufactured units that offer a choice of natural gas or propane as a fuel source, which heats ceramic logs designed to realistically simulate wood. The fire, complete with glowing embers, is often difficult to distinguish from one burning real wood.

In some areas of the country, fireplace emission regulations have become strict—in places such as much of Colorado and parts of Nevada and California so strict that new construction of wood-burning fireplaces has been outlawed. In these areas, manufactured units using alternative fuels allow homeowners all the benefits of a wood-burning fireplace without the adverse impact on air quality.

Most of the units available today also offer a variety of amenities, including built-in thermostatic control and remote-control devices for turning the fire on and off and regulating heat output.

The Importance of a Clean Sweep

Finally, one of the most important factors in the use of a fireplace or stove is the regular inspection and cleaning of the stovepipe, flue, and chimney. To understand why, remember that the burning of wood results in the combustion of solids as well as combustible gases. However, not everything that goes into the firebox is burned, no matter how efficient the appliance. One of the by-products of wood burning is the dark brown or black tar called creosote, a flammable substance that sticks to the linings of chimney flues.

Although the burning temperature of creosote is high, it can ignite and cause a chimney fire. It may be brief and without apparent damage, but a chimney fire may also be prolonged or intense and result in significant fire and smoke damage or, at worst, the loss of your home if the creosote buildup is great enough. Creosote causes other problems, too. It decreases the inside diameter of stovepipes and flues, causing slower burning. This makes burning less efficient and contributes to further deposits of creosote. In addition, because creosote is acidic, it corrodes mortar, metal, and eventually even stainless-steel and ceramic chimney liners.

To prevent costly and dangerous creosote buildup, have your chimney professionally cleaned by a qualified chimney sweep. How often depends on the amount of creosote deposited during the burning season, and this, in turn, depends largely on how and what kind of wood you burn. Professional sweeps usually recommend at least annual cleaning. Depending on where you live, you'll spend about $150, perhaps less, for a cleaning.

You'll enjoy a warm glow at the highest efficiency if you use a glass-front wood-burning or gas-fueled, right, fireplace insert.

Fireside Arrangements

Creating an attractive, comfortable setting around a fireplace should be easy. Who doesn't like the cozy ambiance of relaxing in front of a fire? But there are times when the presence of a fireplace in a room poses problems with the layout. A fireplace can take up considerable floor and wall space, and like any other permanent feature or built-in piece of furniture, its size or position can limit the design possibilities.

The Fireplace and the Space

What is the room's size and shape—large, small, square, long and narrow, L-shaped?

Where is the fireplace located—in the center of a wall, to the side, or in a corner? What other permanent features, such as windows, doors, bookcases, or media units, will you have to work with in your arrangement? How much clearance can you allow around the furniture for easy passage? How close do you want to be to the fire? Think of these questions as you consider the design basics presented below.

Scale and Proportion. Remember the importance of spatial relationships. For example, a fireplace may seem large in a room with a low ceiling; conversely, it may appear small in a room with a vaulted ceil-

ing. Size is relative. Applied to objects on the mantel or the wall above the fireplace, correct scale and proportion happen when the objects are the appropriate size for the wall or the fireplace.

Balance. Sometimes the architectural features of a mantel or surround are so strong, you'll have to match them with furnishings of equal visual weight. Or they may be so ornate or plain that you'll have to play them up or tone them down to make them work with the rest of the decor. That's balance. But balance also refers to arrangements: symmetrical, asymmetrical, and radial.

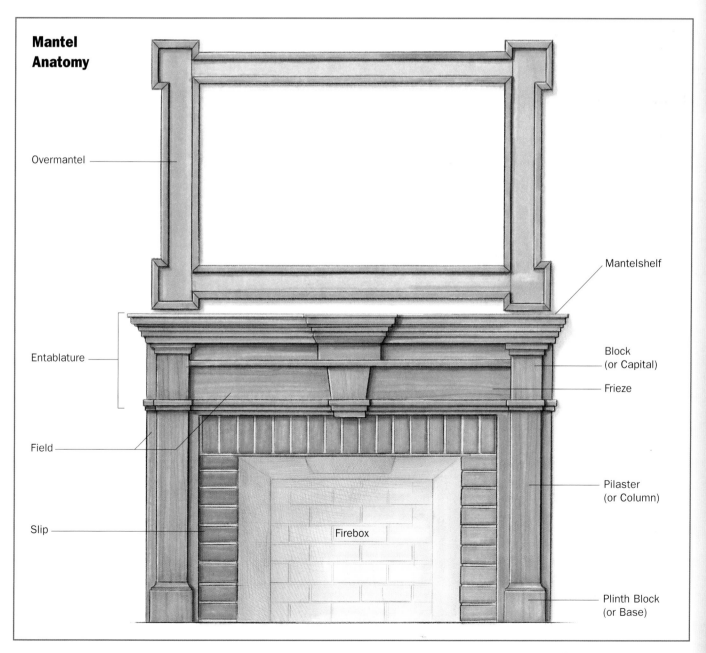

Mantel Anatomy

Overmantel

Mantelshelf

Entablature

Block (or Capital)

Frieze

Field

Slip

Pilaster (or Column)

Firebox

Plinth Block (or Base)

Line. Shape depends on line. Different types of lines suggest various qualities. Pay attention to the lines when you're creating arrangements and relationships among objects. Some lines are inherent in a room or an architectural feature, but you can modify them. For example: vertical lines are stately and dignified, which is just the look you want for your fireplace, but unfortunately, it's rather wide and squat instead. Solution? Create an arrangement above the fireplace that extends high on the wall, or hang a tall mirror or frame over than mantel.

What if the fireplace is too tall? Does it overwhelm the rest of the furniture? Add horizontal lines by moving seating pieces farther apart to the right and left of the hearth. Install wall art on the sides of the fireplace.

If the room is boxy, avoid grouping pieces at right angles to the fireplace and each other. Instead, de-emphasize the boxy shape by placing them on the diagonal to open the square. Use upholstered pieces with rounded arms or curvaceous cushions, legs, or frames. Create a radial arrangement. With the hearth as the central point, create a semicircular hub of furnishings that include seating and a small table or two.

Rhythm. Keep the eye moving at a measured pace by repeating motifs, colors, or shapes. For example, you might pick up the color from a tiled surround to use as an accent color in fabrics on upholstered pieces, curtains, pillows, throws, or other decorative accessories. Or repeat architectural features of the fireplace with other similar elements in the room, such as molding or other woodwork details.

Variety. Don't go overboard trying to match everything exactly. The most interesting rooms and arrangements mix objects of different sizes, shapes, lines, and sometimes even styles (as long as they are compatible).

Harmony. Create harmony among all of the parts of your design by connecting all of the elements either by color or motif. For example, in a display of family photos the frames may all be different shapes, styles, and heights, but because each one is made of brass, the overall appearance looks harmonious. Or you could assemble a wall vignette of frames over the fireplace, all different in finish but tied together by the subject matter of each one—all landscapes, for example, or all pink cabbage roses. Unifying diverse items in this way creates a finished-looking scheme.

How to Make a Hinged Fireboard

You'll need a hinged three-panel wooden fireplace screen, which you can buy or make. If you buy one, you'll have to sand and prime it thoroughly before applying the new finish over the existing one. Ideally, it's best to work on unfinished wood.

The screen used for this project features two 9 x 36-inch side panels and one 26 x 36-inch center panel that were cut from a ¾-inch-thick sheet of plywood. If you aren't handy with a circular saw or table saw, ask your local lumber supplier to cut the panels to your desired dimensions. Attach the side and center panels with two-way (piano) hinges, which are easy to install. Simply mark their location along the inside edges of the panel pieces, drill pilot holes, and then screw the hinges into place. To finish, prime the boards; then paint or stencil a design onto each panel. For Victorian authenticity, decoupage the panels with a motif cut out of a piece of fabric, wallpaper, old greeting cards, or postcards.

Symmetrical versus Asymmetrical Arrangements

If you like the symmetry of classic design, balance your arranged pieces accordingly. For example, position two sofas or love seats of the same size perpendicular to the fireplace and exactly opposite each other. Or place a single sofa parallel with the fireplace, with two chairs opposite one another and equidistant from both the sofa and the hearth. Try out a low coffee table or an oversize ottoman in the center of the arrangement. Leave the peripheral areas outside the main grouping for creating small impromptu conversation areas during parties and gatherings or to accommodate a modest dining area or home-office station.

If your design sense is less formal or contemporary, try an asymmetrical grouping in front of the fire. Turn seating pieces at a 45-degree angle from the hearth.

In a large open space, locate seating not directly in front of the hearth but slightly off to the side. Counterbalance the arrangement with a large table and chairs, a hutch, bookcases, or any element of relatively equal weight. This layout works especially well when the ceiling is vaulted (as most great rooms are) or when the hearth is massive. In many contemporary homes, especially where there is a zero-clearance unit, the fireplace is not on an outside wall, nor is it necessarily in a central location. This means you can put the fireplace almost anywhere.

Comfortable Arrangements

You may want an intimate environment in front of the fire, but the room is so large that it feels and looks impersonal. Large rooms afford lots of leeway for arranging, but people often make the mistake of pushing all of the furniture against the walls. If that's what you're doing, pull the major seating pieces closer together and near the fire, keeping a distance of only 4 to 10 feet between sofas and chairs. For the most comfortable result, create one or more small groupings that can accommodate up to four to six people in different areas of the room.

Modular Seating. Instead of a standard sofa and chairs, consider the convenience of modular seating, too, which comes in any number of armless and single-arm end pieces. The advantage of these separate upholstered units is that you can easily add, take away, or rearrange the modules to suit any of your layout or seating needs. Create an L or a U arrangement in front of the fire; subtract pieces, moving one or two outside of the area for an intimate

A raised hearth, above, reinforces the idea of a fireplace as a focal point, and it provides seating near the fire. Place other furniture to the sides of the hearth.

grouping. Use an area rug to further define the space. Or put the pieces together to make one large arrangement in any configuration. Versatile furnishings such as an ottoman with a hinged top or an antique trunk can double as seating, a low table, or storage.

A Quick Guide to Buying Firewood

How much wood you need to buy in a season depends on a number of factors, but there are three major variables: how often and how long you burn fires; the efficiency of your fireplace or stove; and the type of wood you burn. In general, hard, dense woods are ideal for fuel. As a rule of thumb, the wood from deciduous trees is best. (Deciduous trees are those that shed their leaves annually.) These include oak, maple, walnut, birch, beech, ash, and the wood from fruit trees such as cherry and apple.

Avoid burning wood from evergreens—those cone-bearing (coniferous) trees with needles instead of leaves. The wood of coniferous trees is soft and it will burn faster, so a greater volume of wood will be consumed per hour compared with hardwood. A greater problem with softwoods, however, is the resin content. Resin is the gummy substance that's used in the manufacture of some wood stains and shellacs, and when resin is burned it gives off a byproduct called creosote. Creosote, which is flammable, accumulates in flues and chimneys, and this buildup represents a potential fire hazard.

The wood you purchase should also be seasoned, which means that the tree should have been cut down at least six months or, preferably, a year prior to the burning of the wood. Ideally, the wood should be cut and split soon after the tree is felled, allowing for more effective drying. The moisture in unseasoned (or green) wood tends to have a cooling effect, preventing complete combustion and making it harder to keep a fire blazing. A low-burning fire also increases creosote. (It's okay to burn green wood occasionally, but make sure to use small logs or split sticks and add them to an already hot fire.)

Mantel Vignettes

A grouping of objects on your mantel can be as simple or complex as you like. To make your display lively, choose a variety of shapes and sizes. For dramatic impact, group related objects that you can link in theme or color.

Remember that a symmetrical arrangement has classical overtones and will reinforce the formality of traditional designs. Stick with similar objects: a pair of Chinese ginger jars or antique silver candlesticks arranged in mirror fashion on either side of the mantel equidistant from the center, for example. Or keep the look simple by placing a single but important object in the center; it could be a mantel clock, a floral arrangement, or some other objet d'art.

Asymmetry, on the other hand, brings a different dynamic to a mantel vignette with mismatched pieces. Try placing a large object to one side of the mantel, and then balance that piece by massing several small objects or a different type of object of similar scale on the opposite side. An example might be an arrangement of books of varying heights and sizes at one end of the mantel and a simple large vase at the other end. Or you might oppose tall thin candlesticks with one fat candle.

A simple brick wall, left, serves as a backdrop for a gleaming fireplace insert.

Plan #241027

Dimensions: 54' W x 32' D
Levels: 2
Square Footage: 1,754
Main Level Sq. Ft.: 937
Upper Level Sq. Ft.: 817
Bedrooms: 3
Bathrooms: 2½
Foundation: Slab
Materials List Available: No
Price Category: C

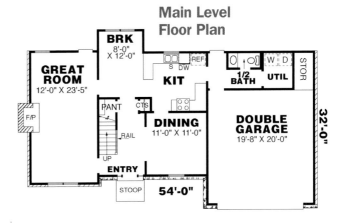

Images provided by designer/architect.

Main Level Floor Plan

BRK 8'-0" X 12'-0"
GREAT ROOM 12'-0" X 23'-5"
KIT
1/2 BATH
UTIL
STOR
REF
S / DW
W / D
F/P
PANT
CTS
DINING 11'-0" X 11'-0"
DOUBLE GARAGE 19'-8" X 20'-0"
RAIL
UP
ENTRY
STOOP
54'-0"
32'-0"

Upper Level Floor Plan

Copyright by designer/architect.

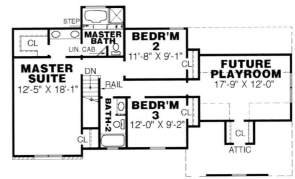

STEP
MASTER BATH
LIN. CAB.
CL
BEDR'M 2 11'-8" X 9'-1"
CL
FUTURE PLAYROOM 17'-9" X 12'-0"
MASTER SUITE 12'-5" X 18'-1"
DN
RAIL
BATH-2
BEDR'M 3 12'-0" X 9'-2"
CL
CL
CL
ATTIC

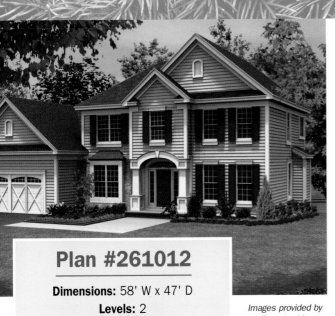

Plan #261012

Dimensions: 58' W x 47' D
Levels: 2
Square Footage: 2,648
Main Level Sq. Ft.: 1,452
Upper Level Sq. Ft.: 1,196
Bedrooms: 4
Bathrooms: 2½
Foundation: Basement
Materials List Available: No
Price Category: F

Images provided by designer/architect.

Rear Elevation

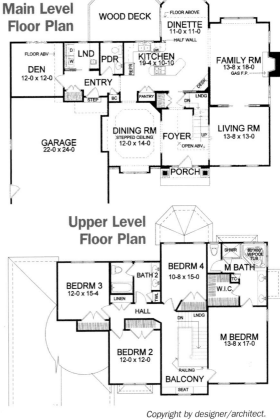

Main Level Floor Plan

WOOD DECK
FLOOR ABOVE
DINETTE 11-0 x 11-0
HALF WALL
FAMILY RM 13-8 x 18-0
GAS F.P.
FLOOR ABV
LND
PDR
KITCHEN 19-4 x 10-10
DEN 12-0 x 12-0
D / W
REFR
ENTRY
STEP
BC
PANTRY
DESK
DN
LNDG
DINING RM STEPPED CEILING 12-0 x 14-0
FOYER
OPEN ABV
LIVING RM 13-8 x 13-0
GARAGE 22-0 x 24-0
UP
PORCH

Upper Level Floor Plan

SHWR
80"X60" W/POOL TUB
BEDRM 4 10-8 x 15-0
M BATH
BEDRM 3 12-0 x 15-4
BATH 2
W.I.C.
TC
LINEN
TWL
HALL
DN
LNDG
M BEDRM 13-8 x 17-0
BEDRM 2 12-0 x 12-0
RAILING
BALCONY
SEAT

Copyright by designer/architect.

Plan #221022

Dimensions: 79' W x 55' D

Levels: 2

Square Footage: 3,382

Main Level Sq. Ft.: 2,376

Upper Level Sq. Ft.: 1,006

Bedrooms: 4

Bathrooms: 3½

Foundation: Basement

Materials List Available: No

Price Category: G

Images provided by designer/architect.

The traditional-looking facade of stone, brick, and siding opens into a home you'll love for its spaciousness, comfort, and great natural lighting.

Features:

- Ceiling Height: 9 ft.

- Great Room: The two-story ceiling here emphasizes the dimensions of this large room, and the huge windows make it bright and cheery.

- Sunroom: Use this area as a den or an indoor conservatory where you can relax in the midst of health-promoting and beautiful plants.

- Kitchen: This well-planned kitchen features a snacking island and opens into a generous dining nook where everyone will gather.

- Master Suite: Located on the main floor for privacy, this area includes a walk-in closet and a deluxe full bathroom.

- Upper Level: Look into the great room and entryway as you climb the stairs to the three large bedrooms and full bath on this floor.

Main Level Floor Plan

Upper Level Floor Plan

Plan #121063

Dimensions: 84' W x 52' D

Levels: 2

Square Footage: 3,473

Main Level Sq. Ft.: 2,500

Upper Level Sq. Ft.: 973

Bedrooms: 4

Bathrooms: 3½

Foundation: Basement

Materials List Available: Yes

Price Category: G

Enjoy the many amenities in this well-designed and gracious home.

Features:

- **Entry:** A large sparkling window and a tapering split staircase distinguish this lovely entryway.

- **Great Room:** This spacious great room will be the heart of your new home. It has a 14-ft. spider-beamed window that serves to highlight its built-in bookcase, built-in entertainment center, raised hearth fireplace, wet bar, and lovely arched windows topped with transoms.

- **Kitchen:** Anyone who walks into this kitchen will realize that it's designed for both convenience and efficiency.

- **Master Suite:** The tiered ceiling in the bedroom gives an elegant touch, and the bay window adds to it. The two large walk-in closets and the spacious bath, with columns setting off the whirlpool tub and two vanities, complete this dream of a suite.

Main Level Floor Plan

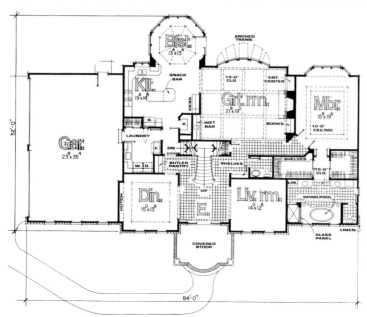

Upper Level Floor Plan

Copyright by designer/architect.

Plan #361028

Dimensions: 62' W x 38' D
Levels: 2
Square Footage: 2,086
Main Level Sq. Ft.: 1,128
Upper Level Sq. Ft.: 958
Bedrooms: 3
Bathrooms: 2½
Foundation: Crawl space
Materials List Available: No
Price Category: D

Images provided by designer/architect.

The clean, elegant lines on the interior of this lovely home suit its classic exterior appearance.

Features:

- Family Room: A fireplace flanked by windows and windows with a door to the rear patio highlight this spacious room.

- Living Room: The bay window here imparts elegance to this slightly formal room.

- Dining Room/Den: Double doors open to this room with a lovely bay window and convenient sets of built-ins you can use for a china closet.

- Kitchen: The family cook will love the U-shaped counters, large pantry, and snack bar shared with the dining nook.

- Dining Nook: A bay window graces this area, allowing sunlight pour into this cheerful space.

- Master Suite: The spacious bedroom connects to a walk-in closet and bath with a double vanity.

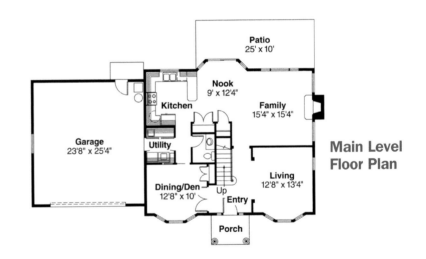

Main Level Floor Plan

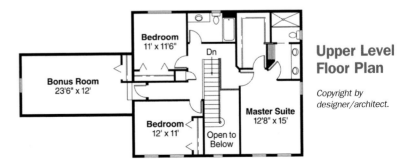

Upper Level Floor Plan

Copyright by designer/architect.

Plan #361023

Dimensions: 64' W x 54' D

Levels: 2

Square Footage: 2,304

Main Level Sq. Ft.: 1,172

Upper Level Sq. Ft.: 1,132

Bedrooms: 4

Bathrooms: 2½

Foundation: Basement, crawl space

Materials List Available: No

Price Category: E

You'll love the convenient layout inside this substantial home, which is designed to suit a busy, active family life.

Features:

- **Family Room:** This spacious room has a cozy fireplace and a door to the rear covered porch.

- **Living Room:** Pocket doors between this room and the family room allow for versatility.

- **Dining Room:** You'll find two built-in storage spaces in this room that's just off the foyer.

- **Kitchen:** A central island adds convenience to the L-shaped layout of this room. The laundry room is an added bonus that you're sure to appreciate.

- **Dining Nook:** Just right for a table and chairs, this nook makes serving breakfast and lunch a treat.

- **Master Suite:** Two large walk-in closets and a bath with split vanities and a built-in cabinet add luxury to the generous bedroom.

Images provided by designer/architect.

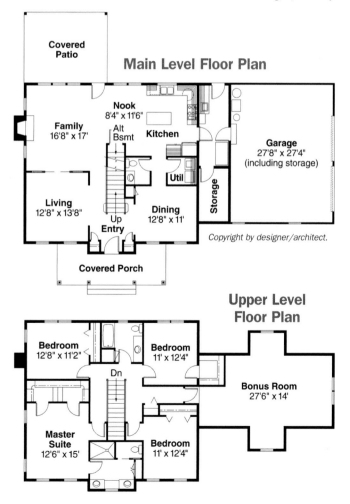

Main Level Floor Plan

Covered Patio

Family 16'8" x 17'

Nook 8'4" x 11'6"

Kitchen

Alt Bsmt

Living 12'8" x 13'8"

Dining 12'8" x 11'

Util

Storage

Garage 27'8" x 27'4" (including storage)

Up Entry

Covered Porch

Copyright by designer/architect.

Upper Level Floor Plan

Bedroom 12'8" x 11'2"

Bedroom 11' x 12'4"

Dn

Bonus Room 27'6" x 14'

Master Suite 12'6" x 15'

Bedroom 11' x 12'4"

Plan #261003

Dimensions: 61'8" W x 58'4" D
Levels: 2
Square Footage: 2,974
Main Level Sq. Ft.: 1,569
Upper Level Sq. Ft.: 1,405
Bedrooms: 4
Bathrooms: 2½
Foundation: Basement
Materials List Available: No
Price Category: F

Images provided by designer/architect.

The formal good looks of the exterior of this home are complemented by an interior that's filled with welcoming comfort.

Features:

- **Family Room:** A bank of windows, fireplace, and built-in shelves make this room ideal for the whole family.

- **Living Room:** Across the foyer from the dining room, this can be a formal space for entertaining.

- **Dinette:** The bay makes an ideal frame for a table, and you'll love the door to the backyard.

- **Kitchen:** The kitchen has a central work island, ample counter and pantry space, and angled bar.

- **Den:** Set off from the other rooms for privacy, the den makes a place to relax at the end of the day.

- **Master Suite:** A bay window, private balcony, walk-in closet, and bath with a corner tub and separate shower make a luxurious hideaway.

Main Level Floor Plan

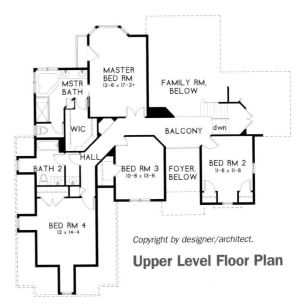

Copyright by designer/architect.

Upper Level Floor Plan

Plan #261006

Dimensions: 73'10" W x 60' D
Levels: 2
Square Footage: 4,583
Main Level Sq. Ft.: 2,575
Upper Level Sq. Ft.: 2,008
Bedrooms: 4
Bathrooms: 3 full, 2 half
Foundation: Basement
Materials List Available: No
Price Category: I

Images provided by designer/architect.

The imposing exterior hides a home that's as thoroughly comfortable as it is beautiful.

Features:

- Family Room: This room has a two-story ceiling, built-in cabinets, and a wood box, fireplace, wet bar, fish tank, and three doors to the deck.

- Dining Room: This room features a decorative ceiling and convenient access to the kitchen.

- Living Room: A fireplace makes this sunken room feel extra cozy in cool weather.

- Kitchen: The central work island and angled snack bar are practical features here.

- Dinette: Windows in this rounded turret room provide natural light, and the gas fireplace warms it in the evening.

- Master Suited: You'll love the tray ceiling, two walk-in closets, cedar closet, and bath with a whirlpool tub in the rounded turret area.

Main Level Floor Plan

Copyright by designer/architect.

Upper Level Floor Plan

Plan #261002

Dimensions: 83'8" W x 43' D
Levels: 2
Square Footage: 2,976
Main Level Sq. Ft.: 1,845
Upper Level Sq. Ft.: 1,131
Bedrooms: 4
Bathrooms: 2½
Foundation: Basement
Materials List Available: No
Price Category: F

Images provided by designer/architect.

You'll love the contemporary elements inside this traditional-looking home.

Features:

- Family Room: At the back of the house, this room has a vaulted two-story ceiling, windows on three walls, and handsome masonry fireplace.

- Living Room: This spacious room features a windowed alcove you can use as a focal point.

- Dining Room: A stepped ceiling and bay window give interest to this slightly formal room.

- Den: A window seat makes this room a treat.

- Kitchen: You'll love the angled work island, desk, and pantry in this room.

- Dinette: This large room features sliding glass doors that lead into the backyard.

- Master Suite: You'll love the spaciousness, large walk-in closet, and whirlpool tub in the bay.

Main Level Floor Plan

Upper Level Floor Plan

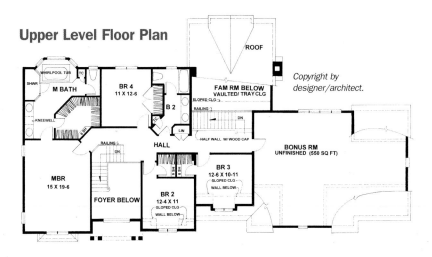

Copyright by designer/architect.

Plan #261005

Dimensions: 64' W x 31' D

Levels: 2

Square Footage: 2,419

Main Level Sq. Ft.: 1,228

Upper Level Sq. Ft.: 1,191

Bedrooms: 4

Bathrooms: 2½

Foundation: Basement

Materials List Available: No

Price Category: E

Images provided by designer/architect.

You'll love the spacious rooms and convenient layout of this lovely Colonial-style home.

Features:

- Ceilings: Ceilings are 9 ft. tall or higher, adding to the airy feeling inside this home.

- Foyer: This two-story foyer gives a warm welcome.

- Family Room: Everyone will gather in this well-positioned room, with its handsome fireplace and generous dimensions.

- Living Room: Both this room and the dining room are ideal for formal entertaining.

- Kitchen: A cook's dream, this kitchen has ample counter space, a large island, and a pantry.

- Master Suite: Enjoy the luxury of the walk-in closet, dual vanities, whirlpool tub, and shower here.

- Additional Bedrooms: Extensive closet space makes it easy to live in each of the bedrooms.

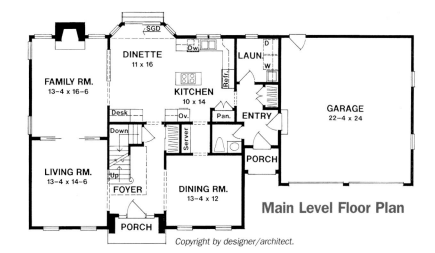

Main Level Floor Plan

Copyright by designer/architect.

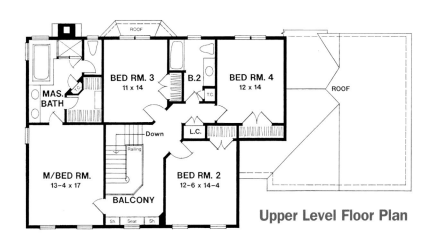

Upper Level Floor Plan

Plan #231026

Dimensions: 72' W x 78'6" D
Levels: 2
Square Footage: 3,215
Main Level Sq. Ft.: 2,311
Upper Level Sq. Ft.: 904
Bedrooms: 3
Bathrooms: 2½
Foundation: Crawl space
Materials List Available: No
Price Category: G

Images provided by designer/architect.

This sumptuous home is so well designed that every element adds to its gracious feeling.

Features:

- First Floor: An open floor plan unites all the rooms on this floor, but clever design elements give each room an individual character.

- Great Room: A fireplace and sliding doors opening to the rear terrace invite everyone into this spacious area that's ideal for entertaining.

- Kitchen: You'll love the central work and dining island, pantry, and windowed breakfast nook in this kitchen.

- Studio: A private entrance adds to the quiet this somewhat isolated space can offer you.

- Master Suite: The balcony, masonry fireplace, walk-in closet, and bath with garden tub and double vanities are sure to charm you.

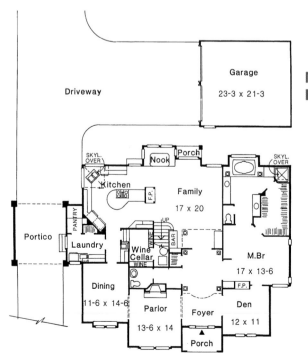

Main Level Floor Plan

Upper Level Floor Plan

Copyright by designer/architect.

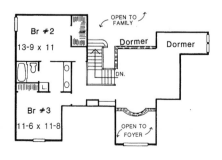

Plan #201126

Dimensions: 82'10" W x 54' D

Levels: 2

Square Footage: 3,813

Main Level Sq. Ft.: 2,553

Upper Level Sq. Ft.: 1,260

Bedrooms: 4

Bathrooms: 3½

Foundation: Crawl space, slab

Materials List Available: Yes

Price Category: H

The impressive exterior of this traditional Southern home is matched by a spacious interior filled with elegant yet comfortable rooms.

Features:

- **Den:** A fireplace flanked by built-ins for media and books, a wet bar, and a door to the rear covered porch make this room a natural gathering spot.

- **Living Room:** This room is separated by the foyer from the equally formal dining room and is lit by graceful windows that set a formal tone.

- **Kitchen:** The family cook will love the spacious area in this well-designed work space.

- **Eating Nook:** Built-in storage space and a large bay window make this room lovely yet practical.

- **Master Suite:** Raised ceilings, a private porch, and two walk-in closets add up to luxury here.

- **Upper Level:** The children are sure to love their private den, walk-in closets, and handy baths.

Images provided by designer/architect.

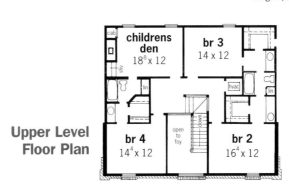

Upper Level Floor Plan

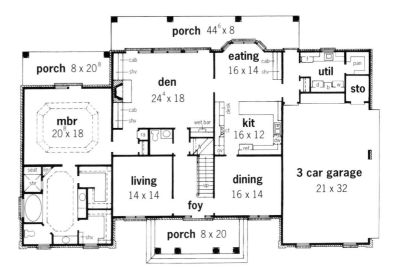

Main Level Floor Plan

Copyright by designer/architect.

Plan #201061

Dimensions: 64'10" W x 54'10" D
Levels: 1
Square Footage: 2,387
Bedrooms: 4
Bathrooms: 2½
Foundation: Crawl space, slab
Materials List Available: Yes
Price Category: E

Images provided by designer/architect.

The classic good looks of the exterior hint at the clean lines you'll find on the interior of this home.

Features:

- Den: You're sure to love the decorative ceiling, fireplace flanked by cabinets and shelves, and windowed wall with doors that open to the porch.

- Porch: Running the length of the den, the rear porch is an ideal place for summer entertaining.

- Dining Room: Arched windows let light pour into this room, with its boxed column entryway.

- Eating Nook: You'll love the large windows, which let light pour into this sizable family eating nook.

- Kitchen: A long, U-shaped counter helps to make this kitchen layout an efficient place to work. Use one side of the counter as a snack bar, too.

- Master Suite: The large bedroom features a decorative ceiling, and the bath includes a walk-in closet, two vanities, tub, and separate shower.

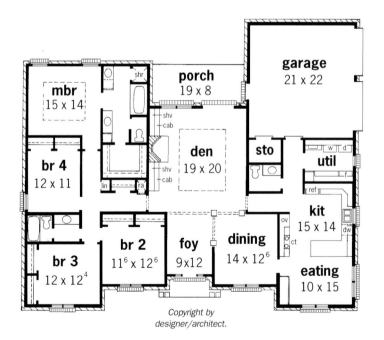

Copyright by designer/architect.

Plan #321008

Dimensions: 57' W x 52'2" D
Levels: 1
Square Footage: 1,761
Bedrooms: 4
Bathrooms: 2
Foundation: Basement
Materials List Available: Yes
Price Category: C

One look at the roof dormers and planter boxes that grace the outside of this ranch, and you'll know that the interior is planned for comfortable family living.

Features:

- Great Room: A vaulted ceiling in this room points up its generous dimensions. Put a grouping of chairs near the fireplace to take advantage of the cozy spot it creates in chilly weather.

- Kitchen: Open to the great room, this kitchen has been planned for convenience. It features a pass-through to the dining area for easy serving when you've got a crowd to feed.

- Master Bedroom: A vaulted ceiling here makes you feel especially pampered, and the walk-in closet and amenity-filled bath add to that feeling.

- Additional Bedrooms: Great closet space characterizes all the rooms in this home, making it easy for children of any age to keep it organized and tidy.

Images provided by designer/architect.

Copyright by designer/architect.

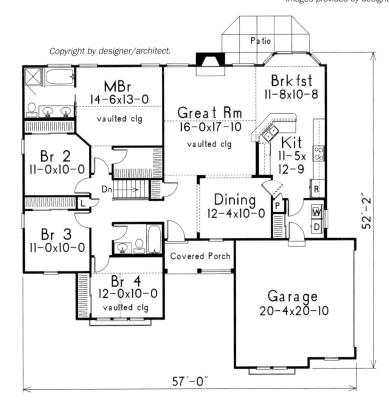

SMARTtip

Hanging Wallpaper

Use liner paper to smooth out a damaged wall and to provide uniform support for expensive paper.

Plan #271027

Dimensions: 61' W x 44' D
Levels: 2
Square Footage: 2,463
Main Level Sq. Ft.: 1,380
Upper Level Sq. Ft.: 1,083
Bedrooms: 4
Bathrooms: 2½
Foundation: Basement
Materials List Available: Yes
Price Category: D

Images provided by designer/architect.

This post-modern design uses half-round transom windows and a barrel-vaulted porch to lend elegance to its facade.

Features:

- **Living Room:** A vaulted ceiling and a striking fireplace enhance this formal gathering space.
- **Dining Room:** Introduced from the living room by square columns, this formal dining room is just steps from the kitchen.

- **Kitchen:** Thoroughly modern in its design, this walk-through kitchen includes an island cooktop and a large pantry. Nearby, a sunny, bayed breakfast area offers sliding-glass-door access to an angled backyard deck.
- **Family Room:** Columns provide an elegant preface to this fun gathering spot, which sports a vaulted ceiling and easy access to the deck.
- **Master suite:** A vaulted ceiling crowns this luxurious space, which includes a private bath and bright windows.

Main Level Floor Plan

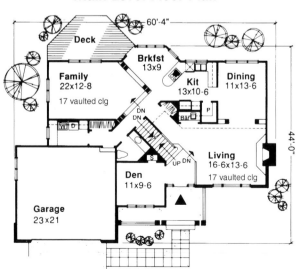

Upper Level Floor Plan

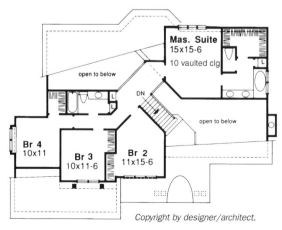

Copyright by designer/architect.

Plan #121077

Dimensions: 64' W x 46' D
Levels: 2
Square Footage: 2,480
Main Level Sq. Ft.: 1,369
Upper Level Sq. Ft.: 1,111
Bedrooms: 4
Bathrooms: 2½
Foundation: Basement
Materials List Available: Yes
Price Category: E

Images provided by designer/architect.

You'll love this design if you've been looking for a home that mixes formal and informal living spaces.

Features:

- **Entry:** An angled staircase is the focal point in this lovely two-story entry.
- **Living Room:** To the left of the entry, a boxed ceiling, transom-topped windows, and corner columns highlight this formal living room and the dining room.
- **Den:** On the right side of the entry, French doors open to this cozy den with its boxed window and built-in bookcase.
- **Family Room:** Sunken to set it off, the family room has a beamed ceiling and a fireplace flanked by windows.

Main Level Floor Plan

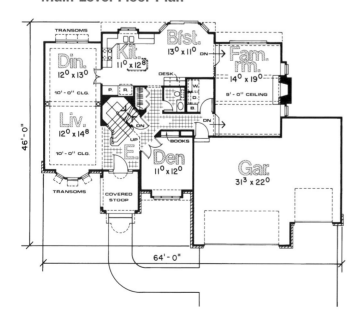

Upper Level Floor Plan

Copyright by designer/architect.

Plan #121034

Dimensions: 92'8" W x 59'4" D
Levels: 1
Square Footage: 2,223
Bedrooms: 2
Bathrooms: 2
Foundation: Basement
Materials List Available: Yes
Price Category: E

Images provided by designer/architect.

This home features a flowing, open floor plan coupled with an abundance of amenities.

Features:

- Ceiling Height: 8 ft. unless otherwise noted.

- Foyer: This elegant entry features a curved staircase and a view of the formal dining room.

- Formal Dining Room: Magnificent arched openings lead from the foyer into this dining room. The boxed ceiling adds to the architectural interest.

- Great Room: A wall of windows, a see-through fireplace, and built-in entertainment center make this the perfect gathering place.

- Covered Deck: The view of this deck, through the wall of windows in the great room, will lure guests out to this large deck.

- Hearth Room: This room shares a panoramic view with the eating area.

- Kitchen: This kitchen features a corner pantry, a built-in desk, and a curved island.

Main Level Floor Plan

Optional Basement Level Floor Plan

Copyright by designer/architect.

Plan #121031

Dimensions: 52' W x 51'4" D
Levels: 2
Square Footage: 1,772
Main Level Sq. Ft.: 1,314
Upper Level Sq. Ft.: 458
Bedrooms: 3
Bathrooms: 2½
Foundation: Basement
Materials List Available: Yes
Price Category: C

This home features architectural details reminiscence of earlier fine homes.

Features:

• Ceiling Height: 8 ft. unless otherwise noted.

• Foyer: This grand entry soars two-stories high. The U-shaped staircase with window leads to a second-story balcony.

• Great Room: You'll be drawn to the impressive views through the triple-arch windows at the front and rear of this room.

• Kitchen: Designed for maximum efficiency, this kitchen is a pleasure to be in. It features a center island, a full pantry, and a desk for added convenience.

• Breakfast Area: This area adjoins the kitchen. Both rooms are flooded with sunlight streaming from a shared bay window.

• Master Suite: The stylish bedroom includes a walk-in closet. Luxuriate in the whirlpool tub at the end of a long day .

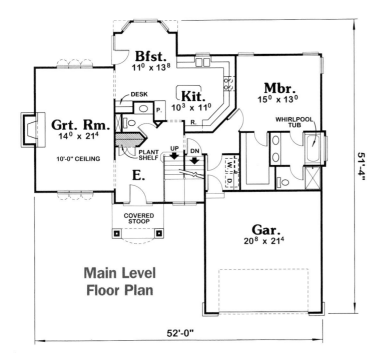

Main Level Floor Plan

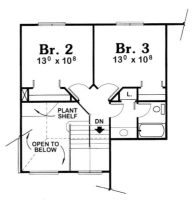

Copyright by designer/architect.

Upper Level Floor Plan

Creating a Media Room

A successor to the low-tech TV rooms of the 1950s and '60s, today's media room can offer a multimedia experience. It can be outfitted with everything from DVD and VHS players to sophisticated home-theater setups complete with speakers inconspicuously mounted into walls and ceilings.

However, creating a media room means more than hooking up electronics. You'll need proper housing for all of the components, such as a big-screen TV, as well as comfortable, attractive furnishings. You can go the custom route, or check out what's on the market. Cabinetry that's designed specifically for the equipment is readily available. So is movie-house-style row seating complete with cup holders and reclining chaises. You can also find floor-to-ceiling soundproofing systems that help hold and enhance the rich sound from digital equipment. It's your choice. It all depends on how much you want to spend.

A freestanding media cabinet, opposite, can be decorative and practical.

Semicustom kitchen cabinetry, above, can be outfitted and installed to suit your media-room needs.

Media-Wise Moves

No matter the size of your budget or the physical dimensions of your space, there are a full range of options that will make a media room look as good as it sounds.

Furniture

The focus here should be on functionality—enhancing your comfort and the entertainment experience. You can achieve both by furnishing the room with chairs, sectionals, and sofas that are upholstered in soft fabrics. Upholstery absorbs sound and can provide the comfort level you need when watching a two-hour movie. Add plush pillows to create an even cozier, more sound-friendly environment.

Leather furniture is always a fallback option. Although it does absorb sound better than hard materials, it can't compete with soft fabrics such as cotton, wool, and blended fabrics in terms of comfort or sound retention.

One smart option is a large upholstered storage ottoman, which can serve many purposes. It adds extra seating, serves as a coffee table, and provides a place for remote controls, DVDs, the television listings, and other media-room paraphernalia.

Cabinetry and Storage. Factor a lot of storage into your media-room plans. First, you need space for various components, such as a DVD player, VCR, receiver, CD player, and so forth. Next there's what will indeed be a growing collection of DVDs, videotapes, CDs, and remote controls. If you plan to order custom cabinetry for the space, buy your sound system and home-theater components first. Then have the cabinetmaker design the unit based on their specifications.

In terms of design, the cabinetry should accommodate components at eye level for easy operation. The topmost and lowest shelves can be reserved for lesser-used items. If you'll build the cabinet yourself, remember that there should be enough space around the components to "breathe;" built-in electronics need ventilation. Plus, you have to leave openings in the back to pull through any wires that have to be plugged into wall outlets.

In addition, be sure to include plenty of rollout drawers in the design to hold your library of favorite disks and tapes. Leave room for future purchases, too. Another option is to store tapes in a closet, a handsome trunk, or even a basket. Stockpiling tapes, CDs, and other clutter around the television screen can detract from the viewing experience.

When not in use, large TV monitors can look like big, ugly boxes. Hide smaller televisions—27- or 32-inch—behind the handsome doors of a semicustom TV cabinet. Very large screens should probably be housed behind pocket, tambour, or concealed doors. Large cabinet doors that swing out into the room can obstruct traffic or even your view of the screen.

Walls, Floors, Ceilings, and Doors

Light-colored walls will reflect sunlight and artificial light and increase glare. Both can wash out the TV screen. For the same reason, mirrors and other shiny materials or glossy finishes in a media room don't make sense. Choose deep neutrals for walls, or even try a darker tone. Walls lined with corkboard, upholstered in fabric, or outfitted with high-tech sound-absorbing glass-fiber panels covered in fashionable fabrics are all good options.

Acoustical ceiling tiles are a simple and effective solution to prevent sound from leaking into other areas. They come in a range of styles, one of which is bound to fit in with your decor.

Carpeting is not only easy on the feet

One homeowner created a comfortable corner, above, for enjoying his collection of old recordings.

Stock cabinets, opposite, can be outfitted with optional features, such as drawers that neatly store CDs, DVDs, and VHS cassettes.

but also on the ear, preventing harsh echoes from bouncing around the room. Hard floor surfaces such as tile, stone, and marble can reflect and distort the sound coming from even the most expensive home-theater receiver and speakers. Cover the floor in a low-pile, low-maintenance Berber, sisal, or industrial carpet to keep sound true and pure.

Lighting

Indirect illumination that provides ambient light without on-screen glare is best for a media room. Lamps in a media room should have black or dark opaque lampshades that direct light up and down. Translucent shades radiate light in all directions. Rather than one or two bright-light sources, install several low-level lights. Dimmers will allow you to adjust lights for comfort. As a general rule, no light should be brighter than the TV screen. To avoid eyestrain and distraction, position light sources behind you and not between you and the screen.

If you want to create movie-house ambiance, install wall sconces like ones reminiscent of grand old theaters. Because you'll probably want to watch movies in a darkened room, make sure your plan includes aisle lighting, which you can plug into outlets. Wire them to one remote so you can dim them simultaneously.

Don't forget that you'll have to control natural light unless you plan to limit your home theater use to evenings. There are creative ways to reduce natural light as well. Shutters and blinds are easily adjustable window treatments. You can also check out the possibility of certain curtains that are made especially for home theaters.

Plugging into Your TV Options

Technology has clearly taken television to the next level. Even if you have an older standard model, you can improve the picture quality of broadcast viewing simply by adding cable, and even more by adding digital cable or digital satellite. But nothing beats DVDs for watching movies.

HDTV, or high-definition television, has twice the picture clarity of standard TV, whether you're watching network or cable TV broadcasts or viewing a DVD. Ironically, most HDTVs don't contain high-definition tuners. So, although the picture may be better, you're not getting true HDTV unless you buy the tuning box, which is sold separately and costs around $700. Still, it's an improvement over the old versions.

Plasma and LCD TV Screens.

Thin TV is also a trend that is here to stay. Slimmed down flat-screen plasma TVs and LCD screens provide brilliant colors, better contrast and resolution, and a greater viewing angle. Because the screen is flat, there is no problem with glare. Having the lights on or off does not affect the picture. LCDs are smaller; screens range from 15 to 30 inches diagonally. Plasma TVs start at 32

Plump upholstered seating, opposite, arranged at the proper distance from the screen, lets you view TV and movies comfortably.

Ready-to-assemble furniture, above, is an affordable alternative to custom or semicustom cabinets.

inches and go up to big-screen size from there. Most of them accept HDTV signals, but they are usually not powerful enough to display all of the high resolution.

Rear Projection. The screen size of a rear-projection TV is large—40 to 82 inches—and can be viewed in natural light without sacrificing picture quality. In general, the picture is often inferior, unless it is an HDTV format. Another drawback: rear projection TVs must be watched at eye-level and straight-on for optimal viewing.

Front Projection. This system has a separate screen, which can either drop down from the ceiling or remain fixed on the wall, and a projector that is mounted at ceiling height across the room from the screen. It's akin to a movie-theater system. Front projection is expensive and requires a professional to install it. Although even minor light can wash out the picture, the image quality is unbeatable when the room is dark.

More Tips

If you're thinking of creating a home theater in your new house, here are a few pointers.

- Most home-theater designers recommend televisions screens that are at least 27 inches wide.
- Seating distance can add or subtract from the viewing quality. For optimal viewing,

there should be a distance between you and the TV that is 2 to 2½ times the width of the screen. That means placing sofa and chairs 54 to 68 inches from a 27-inch screen, for example. If your TV is a wide-screen high-definition model, place it a distance that is 1½ times the screen's diagonal width from your seating area.

- Five speakers will create a full-home theater sound. Place one speaker on each side of the TV screen, level with your ears when you are seated, and about 3 feet from the sidewalls. Place two speakers behind the sofa about 6 to 8 feet off the floor and at least as wide apart as the front speakers. Put the fifth speaker on top of the TV.
- Replace a collection of remote controls with a single universal model that can control everything from the DVD player to the lights (with a special receiver).

Plan #271053

Dimensions: 70' W x 34' D
Levels: 2
Square Footage: 2,458
Main Level Sq. Ft.: 1,067
Upper Level Sq. Ft.: 346
Bedrooms: 3
Bathrooms: 2½
Foundation: Daylight basement or crawl space
Materials List Available: No
Price Category: E

The octagonal shape and window-filled walls of this home create a powerful interior packed with panoramic views.

Features:

- Great Room: Straight back from the angled entry, this room is brightened by sunlight through windows and sliding glass doors. Beyond the doors, a huge wraparound deck offers plenty of space for tanning or relaxing. A spiral staircase adds visual interest.

- Kitchen: This efficient space includes a convenient pantry.

- Master Suite: On the upper level, this romantic master suite overlooks the great room below. Several windows provide scenic outdoor views. A walk-in closet and a private bath round out this secluded haven.

- Basement: The optional basement includes a recreation room, as well as an extra bedroom and bath.

Images provided by designer/architect.

Main Level Floor Plan

Upper Level Floor Plan

Optional Basement Level Floor Plan

Plan #111021

Dimensions: 34' W x 44' D

Levels: 2

Square Footage: 2,221

Main Level Sq. Ft.: 1,307

Upper Level Sq. Ft.: 914

Bedrooms: 4

Bathrooms: 3

Foundation: Pier

Materials List Available: No

Price Category: E

If you've got a view you want to admire, choose this well-designed home, with its comfortable front porch and spacious second-floor balcony.

Features:

- **Porch:** Double doors open to both the living and dining rooms for complete practicality.

- **Living Room:** The spacious living room anchors the open floor plan in this lovely home.

- **Dining Room:** Natural light pours into this room from the large front windows.

- **Kitchen:** An angled snack bar that's shared with the dining room doubles as a large counter.

- **Master Suite:** Double doors lead from the bedroom to the balcony. The bath includes a tub, separate shower, and double vanity.

- **Sitting Area:** This quiet area is nestled into a windowed alcove between the study and the master suite.

Main Level Floor Plan

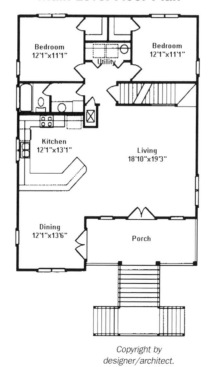

Copyright by designer/architect.

Upper Level Floor Plan

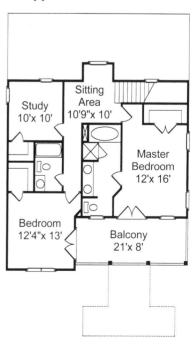

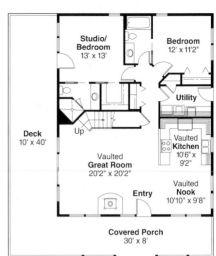

Main Level Floor Plan

Studio/Bedroom 13' x 13'

Bedroom 12' x 11'2"

Utility

Deck 10' x 40'

Vaulted Kitchen 10'6" x 9'2"

Up

Vaulted Great Room 20'2" x 20'2"

Entry

Vaulted Nook 10'10" x 9'8"

Covered Porch 30' x 8'

Images provided by designer/architect.

Plan #361008

Dimensions: 42' W x 48' D
Levels: 2
Square Footage: 1,749
Main Level Sq. Ft.: 1,280
Upper Level Sq. Ft.: 469
Bedrooms: 3
Bathrooms: 3
Foundation: Crawl space, basement, or slab
Materials List Available: No
Price Category: C

Upper Level Floor Plan

Vaulted Loft 18'10" x 22'2"

Dn

Open to Great Room Below

Copyright by designer/architect.

Plan #361020

Dimensions: 38' W x 44' D
Levels: 2½
Square Footage: 1,434
Main Level Sq. Ft.: 1,318
Upper Level Sq. Ft.: 116
Bedrooms: 1
Bathrooms: 2
Foundation: Crawl space
Materials List Available: No
Price Category: B

Images provided by designer/architect.

Upper Level Floor Plan

Dn

Observatory 7' x 12'

Up

Garage 15' x 28'6"

Up

Garage Level Floor Plan

Copyright by designer/architect.

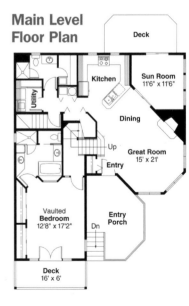

Main Level Floor Plan

Deck

Kitchen

Sun Room 11'6" x 11'6"

Utility

Dining

Up

Great Room 15' x 21'

Entry

Vaulted Bedroom 12'8" x 17'2"

Entry Porch

Dn

Deck 16' x 6'

**Main Level
Floor Plan**

*Images provided by
designer/architect.*

Plan #341045

Dimensions: 38' W x 44' D

Levels: 2

Square Footage: 1,440

Main Level Sq. Ft.: 720

Upper Level Sq. Ft.: 720

Bedrooms: 3

Bathrooms: 2

Foundation: Crawl space, slab
(basement option for fee)

Materials List Available: Yes

Price Category: B

**Upper Level
Floor Plan**

Copyright by designer/architect.

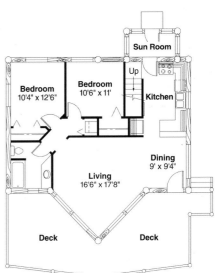

**Main Level
Floor Plan**

Plan #361026

Dimensions: 34' W x 38' D

Levels: 2

Square Footage: 1,401

Main Level Sq. Ft.: 948

Upper Level Sq. Ft.: 453

Bedrooms: 3

Bathrooms: 2

Foundation: Crawl space

Materials List Available: No

Price Category: B

*Images provided by
designer/architect.*

Upper Level Floor Plan

Copyright by designer/architect.

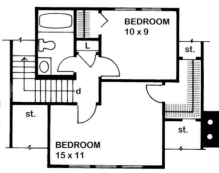

Main Level Floor Plan

DINING
11 x 10

KIT.
15 x 10

P

d

LIVING
14 x 13

PORCH

Plan #381012

Dimensions: 29' W x 26' D
Levels: 2
Square Footage: 1,035
Main Level Sq. Ft.: 605
Upper Level Sq. Ft.: 430
Bedrooms: 2
Bathrooms: 1½
Foundation: Basement
Materials List Available: Yes
Price Category: B

Images provided by designer/architect.

BEDROOM
10 x 9

L

st.

st.

d

Upper Level Floor Plan

Copyright by designer/architect.

st.

BEDROOM
15 x 11

st.

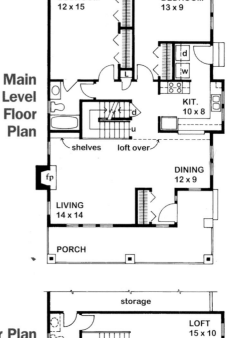

Main Level Floor Plan

BEDROOM
12 x 15

BEDROOM
13 x 9

d

w

L

KIT.
10 x 8

shelves   loft over

fp

DINING
12 x 9

LIVING
14 x 14

PORCH

Plan #381014

Dimensions: 30' W x 46' D
Levels: 2
Square Footage: 1,315
Main Level Sq. Ft.: 1,100
Upper Level Sq. Ft.: 215
Bedrooms: 2
Bathrooms: 2
Foundation: Basement
Materials List Available: Yes
Price Category: B

Images provided by designer/architect.

storage

LOFT
15 x 10

Upper Level Floor Plan

Copyright by designer/architect.

shelf

OPEN

**Main Level
Floor Plan**

*Images provided by
designer/architect.*

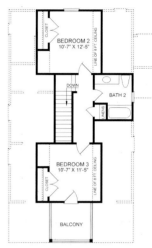

Upper Level Floor Plan

Copyright by designer/architect.

Plan #341038

Dimensions: 26' W x 39' D

Levels: 2

Square Footage: 1,560

Main Level Sq. Ft.: 1,014

Upper Level Sq. Ft.: 546

Bedrooms: 3

Bathrooms: 2½

Foundation: Crawl space, slab
(basement option for fee)

Materials List Available: Yes

Price Category: C

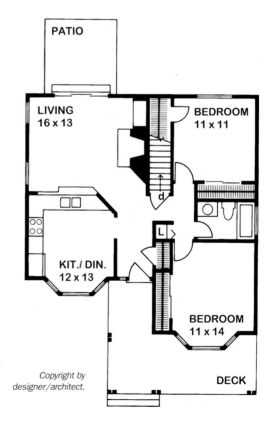

*Images provided by
designer/architect.*

Plan #381016

Dimensions: 32' W x 39'8" D

Levels: 1

Square Footage: 910

Bedrooms: 2

Bathrooms: 1

Foundation: Basement

Materials List Available: Yes

Price Category: A

*Copyright by
designer/architect.*

Main Level Floor Plan

Upper Level Floor Plan

Copyright by designer/architect.

Images provided by designer/architect.

Covered Porch

Bedroom 10'8" x 15'2"

Bedroom 11'4" x 11'8"

Utility

Kitchen

Entry

Up

Vaulted Great Room 24'8" x 25'4"

Deck

Master Suite 16'2" x 17'2"

Study 8'6" x 9'2"

Vaulted Loft 8' x 13'

Dn

Open to Great Room Below

Plan #361022

Dimensions: 34' W x 54' D

Levels: 2

Square Footage: 1,844

Main Level Sq. Ft.: 1,159

Upper Level Sq. Ft.: 685

Bedrooms: 3

Bathrooms: 2

Foundation: Crawl space

Materials List Available: No

Price Category: D

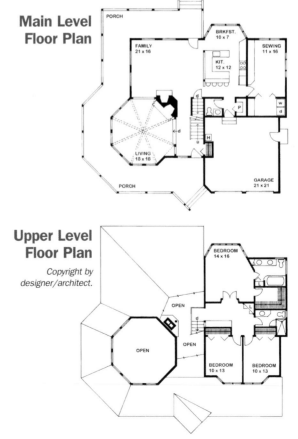

Main Level Floor Plan

PORCH

FAMILY 21 x 16

BRKFST. 10 x 7

SEWING 11 x 16

KIT. 12 x 12

LIVING 18 x 18

PORCH

GARAGE 21 x 21

Upper Level Floor Plan

Copyright by designer/architect.

Images provided by designer/architect.

BEDROOM 14 x 16

OPEN

OPEN

OPEN

BEDROOM 10 x 13

BEDROOM 10 x 13

Plan #381006

Dimensions: 59'10" W x 52' D

Levels: 2

Square Footage: 2,230

Main Level Sq. Ft.: 1,370

Upper Level Sq. Ft.: 860

Bedrooms: 3

Bathrooms: 2½

Foundation: Basement, crawl space

Materials List Available: Yes

Price Category: E

Images provided by designer/architect.

Plan #321064

Dimensions: 34' W x 47' D
Levels: 2
Square Footage: 1,769
Main Level Sq. Ft.: 1,306
Upper Level Sq. Ft.: 463
Bedrooms: 3
Bathrooms: 2
Foundation: Basement
Materials List Available: Yes
Price Category: C

You'll love the way that this spacious A-frame home, with its distinctive interior design, complements any site.

Features:

- Living Room: With an elegant cathedral ceiling and a handsome fireplace, this room makes an ideal spot for entertaining in every season.

- Kitchen: The "U-shape" of this kitchen and adjoining dining area create a warm welcome for friends and family. This an ideal work spot, thanks to the thoughtful layout and ample counter and cabinet space.

- Master Suite: A sloped ceiling gives drama to this secluded suite. A walk-in closet adds practicality, and the amenities in the private bath provide the luxury that will make this area a true retreat.

- Secondary Bedrooms: The secondary bedrooms have large double closets for convenient storage space as well as access to natural lighting from their well-positioned windows.

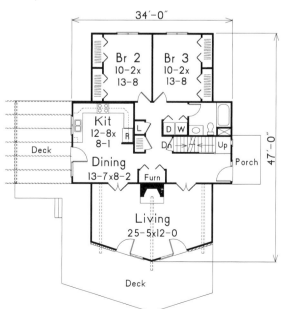

Main Level Floor Plan

Copyright by designer/architect.

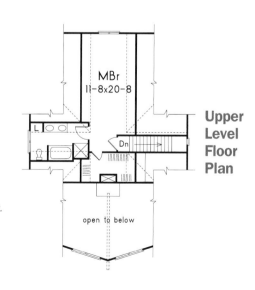

Upper Level Floor Plan

Plan #321009

Dimensions: 55'8" W x 46'4" D

Levels: 1

Square Footage: 2,295

Bedrooms: 3

Bathrooms: 2

Foundation: Basement

Materials List Available: Yes

Price Category: E

Images provided by designer/architect.

If you've got a site with great views, you'll love this home, which is designed to make the most of them.

Features:

- **Porch:** This wraparound porch is an ideal spot to watch the sun come up or go down. Add potted plants to create a lush atmosphere or grow some culinary herbs.

- **Great Room:** You couldn't ask for more luxury than this room provides, with its vaulted ceiling, large bay window, fireplace, dining balcony, and atrium window wall.

- **Kitchen:** No matter whether you're an avid cook or not, you'll relish the thoughtful design of this room.

- **Master Suite:** This suite is truly a retreat you'll treasure. It has two large walk-in closets for good storage space, and sliding doors that open to an exterior balcony where you can sit out to enjoy the stars. The amenity-filled bath adds to your enjoyment of this suite.

Rear View

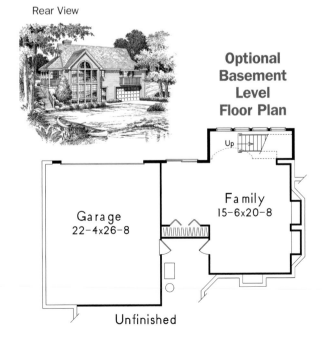

Optional Basement Level Floor Plan

Copyright by designer/architect.

Plan #231001

Dimensions: 67'6" W x 58' D

Levels: 1

Square Footage: 2,177

Bedrooms: 3

Bathrooms: 2½

Foundation: Crawl space

Materials List Available: No

Price Category: D

This home is ideal for a family with many interests and activities because no matter what you want to do, there's a room for it.

Features:

- Parlor: Between the raised ceiling and the location, this room is made for entertaining.

- Dining Room: A butler's pantry and raised ceiling give a tone of formality here.

- Den: Use the den as a quiet space when the house is filled with noisy children having fun.

- Family Room: A fireplace, door to the rear covered porch, and proximity to the kitchen make this a natural gathering spot.

- Kitchen: A central island doubles as a snack bar when the bayed eating nook is full.

- Master Suite: You'll love the angled wall, walk-in closet, and luxurious bath with a garden tub, separate shower, and double vanity.

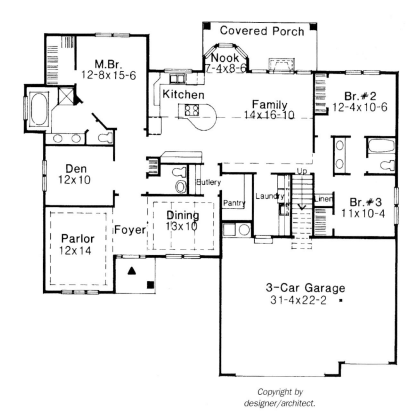

Copyright by designer/architect.

Let Us Help You
Plan Your
Dream Home

Whether you've always dreamed of building your own home or you can't find the right house from among the dozens you've toured, our collection of Northeastern-inspired home plans can help you achieve the home of your dreams. You could have an architect create a one-of-a-kind home for you, but the design services alone could end up costing up to 15 percent of the cost of construction—a hefty premium for any building project. Isn't it a better idea to select from among the hundreds of unique designs shown in our collection for a fraction of the cost?

What does Creative Homeowner Offer?

In this book, Creative Homeowner provides hundreds of home plans from the country's best architects and designers. Our designs are among the most popular available. Whether your taste runs from traditional to contemporary, Victorian to early American, you are sure to find the best house design for you and your family. Our plans packages include detailed drawings to help you or your builder construct your dream house. **(See page 281.)**

Can I Make Changes to the Plans?

Creative Homeowner offers three ways to help you achieve a truly unique home design. Our customizing service allows for extensive changes to our designs. **(See page 282.)** We also provide reverse images of our plans, or we can give you and your builder the tools for making minor changes on your own. **(See page 283.)**

Can You Help Me Stay on Budget?

Building a house is a large financial investment. To help you stay within your budget, Creative Homeowner can provide you with general construction costs based on your zip code. **(See page 283.)** Also, many of our plans come with the option of buying detailed materials lists to help you price out construction costs.

Is There Anything I Missed?

A typical construction crew consists of a number of skilled professionals. If you plan on doing all or part of the work yourself, or you want to keep tabs on your builder, we offer best-selling building and design books at attractive prices. (See our company Web site at www.creativehomeowner.com.) Our home-building books cover all phases of home construction. For more home plans, Creative Homeowner offers a library of plans books. **(See page 288.)**

Our Plans Packages Offer:

All of our home plans are the result of many hours of work by leading architects and professional designers. Most of our home plans include each of the following.

Frontal Sheet
This artist's rendering of the front of the house gives you an idea of how the house will look once it is completed and the property landscaped.

Detailed Floor Plans
These plans show the size and layout of the rooms. They also provide the locations of doors, windows, fireplaces, closets, stairs, and electrical outlets and switches.

Foundation Plan
A foundation plan gives the dimensions of basements, walk-out basements, crawl spaces, pier foundations, and slab construction. Each house design lists the type of foundation included. If the plan you choose does not have the foundation type you require, our customer service department can help you customize the plan to meet your needs.

Roof Plan
In addition to providing the pitch of the roof, these plans also show the locations of dormers, skylights, and other elements.

Exterior Elevations
These drawings show the front, rear, and sides of the house as if you were looking at it head on. Elevations also provide information about architectural features and finish materials.

Interior Elevations and Details
Interior elevations show specific details of such elements as fireplaces, kitchen and bathroom cabinets, built-ins, and other unique features of the design.

Cross Sections
These show the structure as if it were sliced to reveal construction requirements, such as insulation, flooring, and roofing details.

Frontal Sheet

Floor Plan

Foundation Plan

Roof Plan

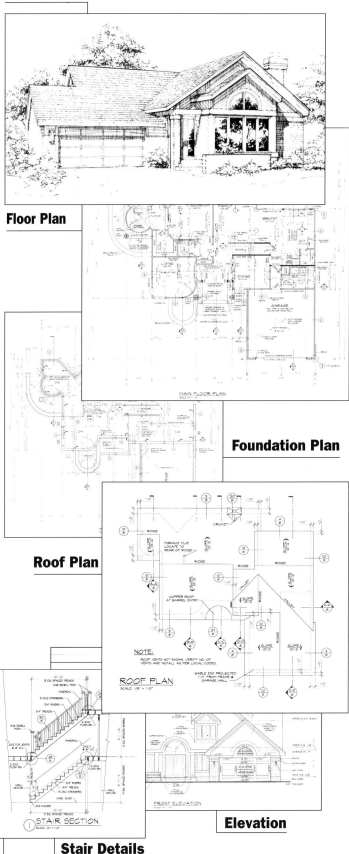

Cross Sections

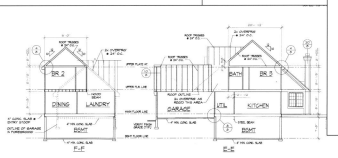

Stair Details

Elevation

Customize Your Plans in 4 Easy Steps

1 **Select the home plan** that most closely meets your needs. Purchase of a reproducible master is necessary in order to make changes to a plan.

2 **Call 1-800-523-6789 to place your order.** Tell our sales representative you are interested in customizing your plan. To receive your customization cost estimate, we will send you a checklist (via fax or email) for you to complete indicating the changes you would like to make to your plan. There is a $50 nonrefundable consultation fee for this service. If you decide to continue with the custom changes, the $50 fee is credited to the total amount charged.

3 **Fax the completed checklist** to 1-201-760-2431 or email it to us at customize@creativehomeowner.com. Within three business days of receipt of your checklist, a detailed cost estimate will be provided to you.

4 **Once you approve the estimate,** a 75% retainer fee is collected and customization work begins. Preliminary drawings typically take 10 to 15 business days. After approval, we will collect the balance of your customization order cost before shipping the completed plans. You will receive five sets of blueprints or a reproducible master, plus a customized materials list if desired.

Modification Pricing Guide

Categories	Average Cost For Modification
Add or remove living space	Quote required
Bathroom layout redesign	Starting at $120
Kitchen layout redesign	Starting at $120
Garage: add or remove	Starting at $400
Garage: front entry to side load or vice versa	Starting at $300
Foundation changes	Starting at $220
Exterior building materials change	Starting at $200
Exterior openings: add, move, or remove	$65 per opening
Roof line changes	Starting at $360
Ceiling height adjustments	Starting at $280
Fireplace: add or remove	Starting at $90
Screened porch: add	Starting at $280
Wall framing change from 2x4 to 2x6	Starting at $200
Bearing and/or exterior walls changes	Quote required
Non-bearing wall or room changes	$65 per room
Metric conversion of home plan	Starting at $400
Adjust plan for handicapped accessibility	Quote required
Adapt plans for local building code requirements	Quote required
Engineering stamping only	Quote required
Any other engineering services	Quote required
Interactive illustrations (choices of exterior materials)	Quote required

Note: *Any home plan can be customized to accommodate your desired changes. The average prices above are provided only as examples of the most commonly requested changes, and are subject to change without notice. Prices for changes will vary according to the number of modifications requested, plan size, style, and method of design used by the original designer. To obtain a detailed cost estimate, please contact us.*

Before Customization

After

Decide What Type of Plan Package You Need

How Many Plans Should You Order?

Standard 8-Set Package. We've found that our 8-set package is the best value for someone who is ready to start building. Once the process begins, a number of people will require their own set of blueprints. The 8-set package provides plans for you, your builder, the subcontractors, mortgage lender, and the building department.
Minimum 4-Set Package. If you are in the bidding process, you may want to order only four sets for the bidding round and reorder additional sets as needed.
1-Set Study Package. The 1-set package allows you to review your home plan in detail. The plan will be marked as a study print, and it is illegal to build a house from a study print alone. It is a violation of copyright law to reproduce a blueprint without permission.

Buying Additional Sets

If you require additional copies of blueprints for your home construction, you can order additional sets within 60 days of the original order date at a reduced price. The cost is $45.00 for each additional set. For more information, contact customer service.

Reproducible Masters

If you plan to make minor changes to one of our home plans, you can purchase reproducible masters. Printed on vellum paper, an erasable paper that you can reproduce in a copying machine, reproducible masters allow an architect, designer, or builder to alter our plans to give you a customized home design. This package also allows you to print as many copies of the modified plans as you need for construction.

Mirror-Reverse Sets

Plans can be printed in mirror-reverse—we can "flip" plans to create a mirror image of the design. This is useful when the house would fit your site or personal preferences if all the rooms were on the opposite side than shown. As the image is reversed, the lettering and dimensions will also be reversed, meaning they will read backwards. Therefore, when ordering mirror-reverse drawings, you must order at least one set of right-reading plans. A $50.00 fee per order will be charged for mirror-reverse (regardless of the number of mirror-reverse sets ordered).

EZ Quote: Home Cost Estimator

EZ Quote is our response to one of the most frequently asked questions we hear from customers: "How much will the house cost me to build?" EZ Quote: Home Cost Estimator will enable you to obtain a calculated building cost to construct your new home, based on labor rates and building material costs within your zip code area. This summary is useful for those who want to know the total construction costs before purchasing sets of home plans. It will also provide a level of comfort when you begin soliciting bids from builders. The cost is $29.95 for the first EZ Quote and $14.95 for each additional one. Available only in the U.S. and Canada.

CompleteCost Estimator

CompleteCost Estimator is a valuable tool for use in planning and constructing your new home. It combines the detail of a materials list with line-by-line cost estimating. The result is a complete, detailed estimate—similar to a bid—that will act as a checklist for all the items you will need to select or coordinate during our building process. CompleteCost Estimator is only available for certain plans (please see Plan Index) and may only be ordered with the purchase of a set of home plans. The cost is $125 for CompleteCost Estimator.

Materials List

Available for most of our plans, the Materials List provides you an invaluable resource in planning and estimating the cost of your home. Each Materials List outlines the quantity, dimensions, and type of materials needed to build your home (with the exception of mechanical systems). You will get faster, more-accurate bids from your contractors and building suppliers—and avoid paying for unused materials. A Materials List may only be ordered with the purchase of a set of home plans.

Order Toll Free by Phone
1-800-523-6789
By Fax: 201-760-2431

Regular office hours are
8:30AM–7:00PM ET, Mon–Fri

Orders received 3PM ET, will be
processed and shipped within two
business days.

Order Online
www.ultimateplans.com

Mail Your Order
Creative Homeowner
Attn: Home Plans
24 Park Way
Upper Saddle River, NJ 07458

Canadian Customers
Order Toll Free 1-800-393-1883

Mail Your Order (Canada)
Creative Homeowner Canada
Attn: Home Plans
113-437 Martin St., Ste. 215
Penticton, BC V2A 5L1

Before You Order

Our Exchange Policy

Blueprints are nonrefundable. However, should you find that the plan you have purchased does not fit your needs, you may exchange that plan for another plan in our collection within 60 days from the date of your original order. The entire content of your original order must be returned before an exchange will be processed. You will be charged a processing fee of 20% of the amount of the original plan set, the cost difference between the new plan set and the original plan set (if applicable), and shipping costs for the new plans. Contact our customer service department for more information. Please note: reproducible masters may only be exchanged if the package is unopened.

Building Codes and Requirements

At the time of creation, our plans meet the building code requirements published by the Building Officials and Code Administrators International, the Southern Building Code Congress International, the International Conference of Building Officials, or the Council of American Building Officials. Because building codes vary from area to area, some drawing modifications and/or the assistance of a professional designer or architect may be necessary to comply with your local codes or to accommodate specific building site conditions. We strongly advise you to consult with your local building official for information regarding codes governing your area.

Blueprint Price Schedule

Price Code	1 Set	4 Sets	8 Sets	Reproducible Masters	Materials List
A	$290	$330	$380	$510	$60
B	$360	$410	$460	$580	$60
C	$420	$460	$510	$610	$60
D	$470	$510	$560	$660	$70
E	$520	$560	$610	$700	$70
F	$570	$610	$670	$750	$70
G	$620	$670	$720	$850	$70
H	$700	$740	$800	$900	$70
I	$810	$850	$900	$940	$80

Shipping & Handling

	1-4 Sets	5-7 Sets	8+ Sets or Reproducibles
US Regular (7–10 business days)	$15	$20	$25
US Priority (3–5 business days)	$25	$30	$35
US Express (1–2 business days)	$40	$45	$50
Canada Regular (8–12 business days)	$35	$40	$45
Canada Expedited (3–5 business days)	$50	$55	$65
Canada Express (1–2 business days)	$60	$70	$80
Worldwide Express (2–5 business days)	$80	$80	$80

Note: All delivery times are from date the blueprint and package is shipped.

Order Form

Please send me the following:

Plan Number: _____

Price Code: _____ (see Plan Index)

Indicate Foundation Type: (see plan page for availability)

☐ Slab ☐ Crawl space ☐ Basement ☐ Walk-out basement

Basic Blueprint Package	Cost
☐ Reproducible Masters	$_____
☐ 8-Set Plan Package	$_____
☐ 4-Set Plan Package	$_____
☐ 1-Set Study Package	$_____
☐ Additional plan sets: __ sets at $45.00 per set	$_____
☐ Print in mirror-reverse: $50.00 per order __ sets printed in mirror-reverse	$_____

Important Extras

☐ Materials List	$_____
☐ EZ Quote for Plan #_____ at $29.95	$_____
☐ Additional EZ Quotes for Plan #s_____ at $14.95 each	$_____

Shipping (see chart above)	$_____
SUBTOTAL	$_____
Sales Tax (NJ residents only add 6%)	$_____
TOTAL	$_____

Order Toll Free: 1-800-523-6789   By Fax: 201-760-2431
Creative Homeowner
24 Park Way
Upper Saddle River, NJ 07458

Name _____
(Please print or type)

Street _____
(Please do not use a P.O. Box)

City _____ State _____

Country _____ Zip _____

Daytime telephone (____)_____

Fax (____)_____
(Required for reproducible orders)

E-Mail _____

Payment ☐ Check/money order *Make checks payable to Creative Homeowner*

☐ VISA   ☐ MasterCard   ☐ American Express Cards   ☐ DISCOVER

Credit card number _____

Expiration date (mm/yy) _____

Signature _____

Please check the appropriate box:
☐ Licensed builder/contractor   ☐ Homeowner   ☐ Renter

Copyright Notice

All home plans sold through this publication are protected by copyright. Reproduction of these home plans, either in whole or in part, including any form and/or preparation of derivative works thereof, for any reason without prior written permission is strictly prohibited. The purchase of a set of home plans in no way transfers any copyright or other ownership interest in it to the buyer except for a limited license to use that set of home plans for the construction of one, and only one, dwelling unit. The purchase of additional sets of the home plans at a reduced price from the original set or as a part of a multiple-set package does not convey to the buyer a license to construct more than one dwelling.

Similarly, the purchase of reproducible home plans (sepias, mylars) carries the same copyright protection as mentioned above. It is generally allowed to make up to a maximum of 10 copies for the construction of a single dwelling only. To use any plans more than once, and to avoid any copyright license infringement, it is necessary to contact the plan designer to receive a release and license for any extended use. Whereas a purchaser of reproducible plans is granted a license to make copies, it should be noted that because blueprints are copyrighted, making photocopies from them is illegal.

Copyright and licensing of home plans for construction exist to protect all parties. Copyright respects and supports the intellectual property of the original architect or designer. Copyright law has been reinforced over the past few years. Willful infringement could cause settlements for statutory damages to $150,000.00 plus attorney fees, damages, and loss of profits.

Plan #	Price Code	Page	Total Finished Area Square Feet	Materials List	CompleteCost
101003	C	67	1593	Yes	No
101004	C	155	1787	No	No
101005	D	155	1992	Yes	No
101008	D	66	2008	Yes	No
101009	D	66	2097	No	No
101011	D	51	2184	No	No
101014	C	53	1598	No	No
101016	D	11	1985	No	No
101019	F	206	2954	No	No
101022	D	238	1992	Yes	No
101023	B	102	1197	No	No
101025	C	238	1643	No	No
111004	F	28	2698	No	No
111021	E	271	2221	No	No
121001	D	156	1911	Yes	No
121009	B	58	1422	Yes	No
121018	H	205	3950	Yes	No
121019	H	201	3775	Yes	No
121020	E	55	2480	Yes	No
121023	H	204	3904	Yes	No
121031	C	263	1772	Yes	No
121034	E	262	2223	Yes	No
121037	E	54	2292	Yes	No
121050	D	27	1996	Yes	No
121051	D	26	1808	Yes	No
121052	D	15	2093	Yes	No
121061	G	189	3025	Yes	No
121062	G	188	3448	Yes	No
121063	G	249	3473	Yes	No
121064	D	20	1846	Yes	No
121065	G	197	3407	Yes	No
121067	F	46	2708	Yes	No
121068	E	45	2391	Yes	No
121073	E	153	2579	Yes	No
121074	E	47	2486	Yes	No
121076	G	144	3067	Yes	No
121077	E	261	2480	Yes	No
121081	G	200	3623	Yes	No
121082	F	196	2932	Yes	No
121083	F	41	2695	Yes	No
121084	C	59	1728	Yes	No
121086	D	22	1998	Yes	No
121088	E	22	2340	Yes	No
121090	F	12	2645	Yes	No
121092	D	23	1887	Yes	No
131002	D	98	1709	Yes	No
131003	C	19	1466	Yes	No
131007	D	68	1595	Yes	No
131009	E	51	2018	Yes	No
131013	C	42	1489	Yes	No
131014	C	222	1380	Yes	No
131027	F	224	2567	Yes	No
131030	F	112	2470	Yes	No
131034	C	228	1040	Yes	No
131036	F	81	2585	Yes	No
131041	D	232	1679	Yes	No
131043	E	223	1945	Yes	No
131045	F	223	2347	Yes	No
131046	F	233	2245	Yes	No
131050	G	203	2874	Yes	No
131051	F	40	2431	Yes	No
131052	D	97	2171	Yes	No
131053	B	235	1056	Yes	No
141009	C	11	1683	No	No
141010	C	237	1765	No	No
141013	D	57	1936	No	No
141014	D	236	2091	Yes	No
141015	E	56	2364	Yes	No
141017	E	10	2480	No	No
141030	E	158	2323	Yes	No
141031	E	147	2367	No	No
141034	H	180	3656	Yes	No
141038	C	87	1668	No	No
151002	E	23	2444	No	Yes
151004	D	131	2107	No	Yes
151010	B	130	1379	No	Yes
151014	F	229	2698	No	Yes
151037	C	50	1538	No	Yes
151057	F	191	2951	No	Yes
151089	D	221	1921	No	Yes
151100	E	18	2247	No	Yes
151105	D	227	2039	No	Yes
151108	F	226	2742	No	Yes
151117	D	25	1957	No	Yes
151118	F	24	2784	No	Yes
151169	C	97	1525	No	Yes
151171	D	234	2131	No	Yes
151172	E	231	2373	No	Yes
151174	F	191	2815	No	Yes
151177	E	100	2470	No	Yes
151180	G	183	3167	No	Yes
151181	E	210	2373	No	Yes
151182	A	211	975	No	Yes
151183	F	182	2952	No	Yes
151184	F	94	2755	No	Yes
151185	F	179	2955	No	Yes
151186	F	185	2975	No	Yes
151187	E	94	2405	No	Yes
161001	C	162	1782	Yes	No
161003	C	65	1508	Yes	No
161007	C	67	1611	Yes	No
161009	C	64	1651	Yes	No
161016	D	16	2101	Yes	No
161020	D	21	2082	Yes	No
161024	C	44	1698	No	No
161029	I	194	4589	Yes	No
161030	I	181	4562	Yes	No
161033	I	172	5125	Yes	No
161038	E	38	2209	No	No
161039	E	39	2320	Yes	No
161040	E	80	2403	Yes	No
161052	E	61	2484	Yes	No
161067	D	96	2160	Yes	No
181080	D	9	2042	Yes	No
181085	D	13	2183	Yes	No
201025	B	219	1379	Yes	No
201034	C	132	1660	Yes	No
201061	E	258	2387	Yes	No
201062	E	43	2551	Yes	No
201067	F	157	2735	Yes	No
201084	D	218	2056	Yes	No
201103	E	134	2490	Yes	No
201126	H	257	3813	Yes	No
211002	C	146	1792	Yes	No
211030	C	37	1600	Yes	No
211047	D	36	2009	Yes	No
211062	F	17	2682	Yes	No
211075	H	8	3568	Yes	No
211111	G	220	3035	Yes	No
211144	E	93	2542	Yes	No